BERLIN 1936

Also by Oliver Hilmes

Franz Liszt: Musician, Celebrity, Superstar
Malevolent Muse: The Life of Alma Mahler
Cosima Wagner: The Lady of Bayreuth

Berlin 1936

Fascism, Fear, and Triumph
Set Against
Hitler's Olympic Games

OLIVER HILMES

TRANSLATED FROM THE GERMAN BY
JEFFERSON CHASE

Other Press
New York

First softcover edition 2020
ISBN 978-1-63542-041-8

Originally published in German as *Berlin 1936: Sechzehn Tage im August*
By Oliver Hilmes

Copyright © 2016 Siedler Verlag,
a division of Verlagsgruppe Random House GmbH, München, Germany

English-language translation copyright © Jefferson Chase 2018

Published in the United Kingdom in 2018 by Bodley Head, an imprint of Vintage.
Vintage is part of the Penguin Random House group of companies.

Production editor: Yvonne E. Cárdenas

This book was set in India by Integra Software Services Pvt. Ltd, Pondicherry, India.

10 9 8 7 6 5 4 3 2 1

Library of Congress Cataloging-in-Publication Data

Names: Hilmes, Oliver, author. | Chase, Jefferson S., translator.
Title: Berlin 1936 : sixteen days in August / Oliver Hilmes ; translated from the
German by Jefferson Chase.
Other titles: Berlin 1936. English
Description: New York : Other Press, 2018.
Identifiers: LCCN 2017031868 | ISBN 9781590519295 (hardcover) |
ISBN 9781590519301 (ebook)
Subjects: LCSH: Olympic Games (11th : 1936 : Berlin, Germany) | Berlin (Germany)—
History—1918-1945. | Olympics—Political aspects—Germany. | National socialism
and sports.
Classification: LCC GV722 1936 .H5413 2018 | DDC 796.48—dc23
LC record available at https://lccn.loc.gov/2017031868

For my family

Contents

Berlin in the summer of 1936. Hundreds of thousands of onlookers crowd the streets every day and wait for Adolf Hitler to drive by.

Saturday, 1 August 1936

REICH WEATHER SERVICE FORECAST FOR BERLIN: Heavy clouds and occasional rain showers. Moderate wind from the west/southwest. Somewhat cooler with highs of 19°C.

The telephone is ringing softly in Henri de Baillet-Latour's hotel suite. "It's 7:30 a.m., Your Excellency," the porter says. "*Bon*," the count replies. "I'm already awake." The employees at the Hotel Adlon where Baillet-Latour is residing treat their guest with irreproachable deference. He is something like a head of state, although he doesn't lead a nation, preside over a republic or rule a monarchy. Henri de Baillet-Latour is the president of the International Olympic Committee, the IOC. Today, at precisely 5:14 p.m., the Olympic flag will be raised at Berlin's Olympic Stadium, and the 60-year-old Belgian will assume a kind of sovereignty over Berlin's sporting venues for the next sixteen days.

In the meantime, Baillet-Latour has a busy schedule. He has to attend a religious service with his colleagues from the Olympic Committee, review a Wehrmacht guard of honor and place a wreath at Berlin's Memorial to the Fallen in the Great War.

After the military ceremony, Hermann Göring—in his capacity as the state premier of Prussia—will officially welcome the IOC members.

It's now 8 a.m., and the sound of marches, wake-up calls and the song *"Freut euch des Lebens"* (Rejoice in Life) are sounding on Pariser Platz in front of the hotel. The "Great Wakening," as this ritual is known, is one of many ways the National Socialists are seeking to honor the IOC. As Henri de Baillet-Latour stands at the window of his suite, watching the action, he no doubt feels like a head of state, with the Adlon as his seat of government. The IOC has taken up quarters in one of Berlin's best neighborhoods. The hotel is located directly across from the French embassy; on the left is the Brandenburg Gate, and directly adjacent to Berlin's most famous landmark is Palais Blücher, property of the United States of America. That spacious building is normally the home of the American embassy, but it is still being rebuilt after a fire in 1931. To the right of the Adlon on Pariser Platz is Berlin's venerable Academy of Fine Arts, while next to it on Wilhelmstrasse is Palais Strousberg, which contains the British embassy.

Baillet-Latour has now finished breakfast and is preparing to leave the hotel. To celebrate this special day, the count has dressed formally in gray trousers, a dark cutaway jacket, gaiters, a top hat and a magnificent chain of office. When Joseph Goebbels sees him, the German propaganda minister can only shake his head, later noting in his diary: "The Olympians look like the directors of a flea circus."

*

Pauline Strauss is someone who speaks her mind. The wife of the famous composer Richard Strauss is not chary about telling total strangers precisely what she thinks of them. Even friends and acquaintances aren't exempt from her legendary tactlessness. "Mrs. Strauss, who contrary to her usual self had been quite charming over tea, now had another of her semi-hysterical fits of impoliteness," Count Harry Kessler would later recall of their encounter in a Berlin gourmet restaurant. The tables are covered with expensive china, luxurious silver cutlery and hand-ground glasses. Liveried waiters move about almost noiselessly, and the diners are all conversing in hushed tones. Everyone except Pauline Strauss, that is. As Kessler relates an apparently not very interesting anecdote about a famous Parisian restaurateur, Mrs. Strauss loudly interjects: "He'll be long dead by the time you finish this story! How can someone tell something so bland so slowly! You should feast your eyes on that fattened pig over there instead." The diners look around in bewilderment. "The fat pig, that overweight officer over there." Mrs. Strauss points at a rather corpulent lieutenant sitting at the next table. "What's the problem? I'm just flirting with that pig," says Mrs. Strauss, continuing to stare before adding triumphantly, "You see, the fattened pig is looking at me as though he's in love. I think he'll come over and sit with us." The rest of the group is mortified. The writer Hugo von Hofmannsthal stares down at his plate, at a loss for words, while Richard Strauss turns first white, then red. But Strauss doesn't comment on his wife's scandalous behavior, no doubt in order to avoid exacerbating the situation. It is rumored that once, when he had chastised her for making a similar scene, she had said loudly enough for everyone present to hear: "One more word from you, Richard, and I'll take to Friedrichstrasse and go off with the first man who crosses my path."

It's no wonder that Pauline Strauss is the nightmare of all hotel porters, waiters and servant girls. The Strausses, accompanied by their housekeeper Anna, arrived in the Hotel Bristol yesterday. The Bristol is only a stone's throw away from the Adlon on Berlin's splendid boulevard Unter den Linden. As goes without saying, the hotel offers all the most modern conveniences. The spacious rooms and suites are appointed with exquisite furniture, and all have their own bath. Moreover, the hotel's public rooms are particularly splendid. The library, for instance, is done out in the Gothic style, while the tea salon is full of heavy English leather furniture.

Richard Strauss has had little opportunity to enjoy the amenities of his hotel. Yesterday he was busy with rehearsals, this afternoon he has the world premiere of a new composition, and tomorrow morning he'll leave Berlin and return to Bavaria. As one of the most important contemporary composers, Richard Strauss is always a busy man. The previous March he went on a concert tour of Italy and France. In April he conducted orchestras in Paris and Cologne, and in June in Zurich and once again in Cologne. In between performances, the 72-year-old Strauss somehow finds the time to compose new works. The piece that he'll debut in a few hours is called "Olympic Hymn" and was commissioned by the IOC for the opening ceremony today. Strauss has boasted about being capable to put anything to music. "If you want to be a true musician, you have to be able to set a restaurant menu to music," he once mockingly remarked. For Strauss, writing music is a matter of hard work and discipline. With stoic calm, he sits at his desk creating work after work. Years later Theodor W. Adorno will disparagingly call him a "composing machine." Strauss, Adorno will write, betrayed modernism and sold out to a mass audience, becoming a master of superficiality who only composed what he could sell for hard currency.

The "Olympic Hymn" for choir and large symphony orchestra definitely falls into that category. Strauss couldn't care less about sport. Skiing, he once opined, is an activity for rural postmen in Norway. In February 1933, upon learning that the town where he lived in Bavaria, Garmisch, was planning a special levy to finance the Winter Olympics, Strauss protested vehemently. In a letter to the district council, he wrote: "On the assumption that it will go to covering the costs of this sports foolishness and totally unnecessary Olympics propaganda, I object to this new tax on citizens. Since I don't use any sporting facilities— bobsleigh runs, ski jumps and the like—and can do without a triumphal arch at the train station, I ask to be freed from this tax, which should be passed on to all those who have an interest in the Olympic Games and similar sorts of swindles. My wallet has been burdened enough by government taxes to support layabouts in the name of so-called social security and all the doorto-door beggars rampant in Garmisch."

Such objections didn't deter Strauss from demanding 10,000 reichsmarks for composing a hymn to "sports foolishness." That fee, however, was well beyond the Olympic Committee's budget, and in the end, after some negotiations, Strauss agreed to forgo his honorarium. So it's hardly surprising that he was less than enthusiastic about the job. "I'm keeping the Christmas boredom at bay by composing an Olympic hymn for the proletarians," Strauss wrote to the writer Stefan Zweig in December 1934. "I am a dedicated enemy of sport. I despise it. It's true: the devil makes work for idle hands."

The lyrics were chosen in a public competition, won by the unemployed actor and occasional poet Robert Lubahn. Some of the lines were changed after Goebbels complained that Lubahn's poem didn't reflect the spirit of the Third Reich. "Peace shall be the battle cry," for instance, became "Honor shall be the battle cry." "The rule of law is the highest thing" was altered to "Loyalty to one's oath is the highest thing." However much he may have disliked the changes, Lubahn had to accept them, and the IOC, as the body that had commissioned the hymn, voiced no objections. Richard Strauss presumably didn't care one way or the other.

In December 1934, immediately after finishing the four-minute composition, Strauss contacted Hans Heinrich Lammers, the director of the Reich Chancellery, and asked if he could play the piece for Hitler. "As the Führer and the patron of the Olympic Games, it's especially important that he like it," Strauss wrote. After a bit of back and forth—Hitler was less eager for a meeting than the composer—a date was set for late March 1935. After the private performance in Hitler's Munich flat, Strauss presented "his Führer" with an autographed copy of the sheet music, which the dictator gratefully accepted.

There were concrete, practical reasons why Strauss cozied up to the regime. His new opera, *The Silent Woman*, was set to premiere in Dresden in June 1935. Goebbels opposed this work because the libretto was written by the Jewish author Zweig, a persona non grata in the Third Reich, but Hitler gave special permission for the opera to be performed. The "Olympic Hymn" was Strauss's way of saying thank you. Nonetheless, a short time later, the world-famous composer got himself into trouble after the Gestapo intercepted a letter in which he made fun of his position as the president of the Reich Music Chamber. In mid-July 1935, Strauss was forced to step down, and *The Silent Women* was performed only three times. The incident would have spelled the end for a lesser-known artist. But Strauss is too high profile for the Nazis to do without him. Now, one year later, in the summer of 1936, the whole affair has been forgotten, and Strauss is being allowed to direct the first ever public performance of the "Olympic Hymn." As the composer and his wife take breakfast in the Hotel Bristol's terrace salon, and Pauline bullies the staff as usual, Strauss imagines what it will be like to conduct in front of more than 100,000 proletarians this afternoon.

*

"Where exactly are we?" Max von Hoyos asks his companion Hannes Trautloft. Max has just woken up and has no idea how long he's slept. He yawns, rubs his eyes and stretches out his arms. "Still on the River Elbe," Hannes answers. Max doesn't seem particularly surprised. "I'm starving!" he exclaims, swinging himself out of his bunk. The two young men are sharing a berth aboard the steamship *Usaramo* on its way from Hamburg to Spain. They and more than eighty others are part of a group called the Travel Club Union. This exclusively male party behaves somewhat oddly, keeping its distance from the other passengers. When asked about the purpose of their journey, they say nothing. They don't seem stylish enough to be affluent tourists on a cruise. They could almost be mistaken for soldiers, if they weren't wearing civilian clothing. They have a conspicuous amount of luggage. What do all the large crates loaded onto the ship in Hamburg contain? Again, no answers are forthcoming. One thing is for sure: something isn't right about the Travel Club Union.

*

At noon, the Hitler Youth holds a rally in Berlin's Lustgarten. Some 29,000 boys and girls stand at attention. The roof of the City Palace affords a good view of the broad stretch of land between the Old Museum, Berlin Cathedral and the palace itself. It's impossible to make out individuals. All you can see is a mass of people. Like so many things these days, the rally is a powerful demonstration aimed at foreign visitors. Adolf Hitler can rely on Germany's youth—that's the message. It can also be understood as a warning.

The various items on today's agenda interlock like a well-oiled mechanism. The ceremony welcoming the members of the IOC ends on time, and the guests of honor only need to walk a few yards from the domed hall of the Old Museum to get to the Lustgarten. A speaker's podium has been installed on the steps outside the building. One after another, Reich Youth Leader Baldur von Schirach, Reich Sports Leader Hans von Tschammer und Osten, Education Minister Bernhard Rust and Joseph Goebbels address the Hitler Youth. "An imposing spectacle," the propaganda minister records in his diary. "How can you say something original about it? Then the Olympic flame arrives. A moving moment. It's raining slightly."

The journey of the Olympic torch, of which the Lustgarten is the penultimate stop, is not the Ancient Greek tradition it is often taken to be. It's the brainchild of a sports official from the southern German city of Würzburg. The 52-year-old secretary general of the Olympic Organizing Committee, Carl Diem, is one of the central figures behind the Berlin Games. In his inventive eyes, the 1,800-mile-long trip the torch has made from Athens to Delphi, Thessaloníki, Sofia, Belgrade, Budapest, Vienna, Prague, Dresden and Berlin connects antiquity with the present day. It doesn't matter that there were no torch processions at the original Olympic Games. Diem is only interested in depicting the Berlin event as a particularly solemn occasion. At the Propaganda Ministry, which has been responsible for organizing the Hitler Youth rally, Goebbels was immediately enthusiastic about the idea. At Goebbels's behest, the athlete carrying the torch runs through the ranks of the Hitler Youth up to the Old Museum, where he lights an altar of fire. Then the young man continues to the City Palace and ignites a second flame at what is called the "Banner Altar of Nations."

A fleet of limousines is now ready to chauffeur the IOC representatives and other guests of honor to the Reich Chancellery on Wilhelmstrasse. There, Henri de Baillet-Latour thanks Hitler for Germany's hospitality. The dictator keeps his reply short, stressing the ability of the Olympic Games to bring various peoples together. Under 2 p.m., the itinerary for the day simply reads: "Snack."

*

Between 3:00 and 3:07 p.m., Hitler's guests leave the Chancellery and head to the Olympic Stadium. The lines of limousines turn from Wilhelmstrasse onto the "Via Trumphalis." That's what the organizers of the Games call the 7-mile-long, extremely wide thoroughfare from the Lustgarten in the east of the city to the Olympic Stadium in the west. The original Via Triumphalis in Rome was where victorious generals could ceremoniously re-enter the city. In Berlin, Hitler glides along it in an open Mercedes on his way to the Games, which will take place in an arena modeled on a Roman amphitheater. Bread and circuses.

The entire route is lined with gigantic swastikas and Olympic flags and is guarded by 40,000 SA men. Behind the paramilitaries are hundreds of thousands of curious onlookers hoping to get a glimpse of the event planned on the itinerary for 3:18 p.m.: "Führer departs for the Olympic Stadium."

Somewhere in the crowd is a 35-year-old American named Thomas Clayton Wolfe. Tom, as friends call him, is from Asheville, North Carolina, and has only just arrived in Berlin. At 6' 6" tall and weighing 265 pounds, he is hard to overlook. He might be taken for a shot-putter. But Wolfe is a writer, and a fairly famous one at that, whose first novel, *Look Homeward, Angel*, appeared in German translation in 1932. The book was a major success for his publisher Ernst Rowohlt. The critics were enthusiastic about the young author from the New World, and within the space of a few years the book sold 10,000 copies.

Wolfe first traveled to Germany in late 1926, spending two weeks in Stuttgart and Munich. Since then, he's returned nearly every year. In 1935 he visited Berlin for the first time, confiding to his notebooks: "I had an experience that cannot happen to me often now. It was my experience again to enter for the first time one of the great capital cities of the world. This time the city was—Berlin." The following weeks in the capital of the Third Reich were ones of total intoxication: "A wild, fantastic, incredible whirl of parties, teas, dinners, all-night drinking bouts, newspaper interviews, radio proposals, photographers, etc...." With Wolfe and Berlin it was love at first sight. The writer initially seemed to care little that Berlin was the epicenter of a brutal dictatorship that persecuted, imprisoned and murdered its political enemies. Although his views would later change, the American author praised the Germans as the "cleanest, kindest, warmest-hearted, and most honorable people I've met in Europe."

Wolfe left Berlin in mid-June 1935, determined to return as soon as possible. Now he's back. Rowohlt has just published the German translation of his novel *Of Time and the River*, and publicity needs to be done. The fact that the Olympic Games are taking place in Berlin was another good reason for the American author and sports fan to make the boat trip across the Atlantic.

As he did the year before, Tom takes a room in the Hotel am Zoo. It's not considered one of Berlin's best addresses, but it does have its advantages. Wolfe prefers its easygoing comfort to the fussiness of the Adlon, the Bristol or the Eden. He especially likes the fact that Hotel am Zoo is on Kurfürstendamm. What is there to do at the Brandenburg Gate? Kurfürstendamm is where the real Berlin is. Tom always feels that it's a magical moment when he leaves his hotel, looks left and sees the golden tower clock of the Kaiser Wilhelm Memorial Church. Every time he's seized by Berlin's special magic, and he realizes that he's fallen under the city's spell. Kurfürstendamm is crammed with cafés, restaurants and bars, and for Tom, the boulevard is one great coffeehouse: "The crowds sauntered underneath the trees on the Kurfürstendamm, the terraces of the cafés were jammed with people, and always, through the golden sparkle of the days, there was a sound of music in the air." Wolfe wouldn't want to be anywhere else in Berlin.

Right now, though, he's standing like many others along the Via Triumphalis, waiting. "The Leader came by slowly in a shining car," Wolfe will remember, "a little dark man with a comic-opera mustache, erect and standing, moveless and unsmiling, with his hand upraised, palm outward, not in Nazi-wise salute, but straight up, in a gesture of blessing such as the Buddha or Messiahs use."

*

At precisely 1 p.m. the gates of the Olympic Stadium open. The roughly 100,000 spectators from all over the world have been instructed to get to their seats by 3:30. An 804-foot-long Zeppelin, the *Hindenburg*, one of the biggest airships ever built, is circling above the stadium. Down below, inside the arena, the Olympic Symphony Orchestra is entertaining people with a concert. Along with Franz Lizst's magnificent *Les Préludes*, the program features the prelude to Wagner's *Meistersinger*—there's no avoiding Hitler's favorite composer in the Third Reich. The great clock on the tower of the stadium's Marathon Gate reads 3:53. Trumpets and trombones positioned high up in the arena suddenly break out into a fanfare. Seven minutes later, at exactly 4 p.m., Adolf Hitler enters the stadium and descends the Marathon Gate's massive steps. He is accompanied by members of the International and German National Olympic Committees. The fanfares die down, and the orchestra strikes up Wagner's "Homage March." The event's organizers grit their teeth and put up with this piece of music, one of Wagner's most vapid, written in honor of the Bavarian king Ludwig II. The title of the piece is more important than the music. The point is to show reverence for Hitler, who is striding through the arena to his box seat like a Roman emperor. The Führer has to pause briefly when Carl

Diem's five-year-old daughter steps in front of him, proffering a bouquet of flowers. "*Heil*, my Führer," the girl is reported to have said. Both her father and Hitler himself act pleasantly surprised, as if they were caught off guard by this hardly spontaneous little interruption.

Once Hitler has reached his box seat, the orchestra begins to play the "double anthem" introduced by the Nazis, consisting of the first verses of both the German national anthem and the "Horst Wessel Song," the hymn to a street brawler who was considered one of the Nazi movement's first martyrs. The flags of the nations competing at the Olympics are raised, and the Olympic bell rings out from across the Maifeld, the large sports field next to the stadium. With that, the Olympic nations march into the stadium, led by Greece and concluding with Germany. The British athletes are given a rather cool reception—"very embarrassing," Goebbels will note in his diary—but the French, who extend their right arms in salute, are greeted with veritable ovations. French representatives will later claim that their athletes were performing the Olympic salute, and not the Nazi greeting, but the two are scarcely distinguishable. The people in the stadium, at any rate, think the French are executing a *Hitlergruss*.

Henri de Baillet-Latour has taken his seat to Hitler's right. On the Führer's left is an older gentleman whom Goebbels would probably consider a typical flea-circus director: Theodor Lewald, president of the German Olympic Organizing Committee. Together with the secretary general Diem, the 75-year-old lawyer and sports official is the driving force behind the eleventh

Olympic Games. Without Lewald and Diem, there would be no event in Berlin. His Excellency, as Lewald is respectfully referred to, is allowing himself to be used by the Nazis. Lewald is what the anti-Semites call a "half Jew." In these Olympic Games, he serves as a token, a symbolic figure intended to demonstrate to the global public that the regime is not meddling with the sporting competition. In truth, Lewald's days are numbered. But before he resigns his post, as he has already agreed to do under duress, His Excellency will be allowed to fulfill his duties.

Shortly after 5 p.m. Lewald steps up to the microphone to begin a speech that lasts fifteen minutes. He has chosen his opening words with great care. He could have started with "My dear Reich Chancellor," which would have been in line with protocol. He could have welcomed Henri de Baillet-Latour and the other major Olympic officials and greeted the ambassadors in attendance. Such an opening would have conformed to diplomatic niceties. But Lewald has decided to go for a briefer salutation. "My Führer" is all he says.

Hitler speaks next. Baillet-Latour has instructed him carefully on how to inaugurate the event. According to Olympic protocol, the head of state of the host nation is to say: "I declare open the Games in Berlin to celebrate the eleventh Olympiad of the modern era." The Führer is said to have replied: "Count, I will try to learn this sentence by heart." But Hitler's Austrian grammar gets in the way. What he says is "I declare the Games in Berlin to celebrate the eleventh Olympiad of the modern era as being opened." These are the only words he will publicly utter during the event.

The Olympic flag is raised, artillery guns fire a salute and some 20,000 white doves are released into the heavens above Berlin. Richard Strauss is sitting on a chair next to the orchestra, his legs crossed, looking bored. Someone whispers in his ear, telling him the time has come. At 5:16 p.m., Strauss gets up, climbs onto his conductor's platform and signals to the brass players up on the Marathon Gate. A brief fanfare echoes through the arena before the entire orchestra joins in. The Olympic Symphony Orchestra consists of the Berlin Philharmonic and the Berlin State Orchestra. The choir has been put together from various ensembles and numbers 3,000 male and female singers. Joseph Goebbels is a great admirer of Strauss's "Olympic Hymn." "It is truly wonderful," he gushed after one of the rehearsals. "That fellow really can compose." Hitler, too, is satisfied with Strauss, telling one of his assistants to summon the composer to be congratulated after the ceremony. "Handshake with Hitler," Pauline Strauss will note in her diary.

Spectators get no respite. As Strauss is still climbing down from his platform, the torch bearer charged with taking the Olympic flame the final miles from the Lustgarten to the stadium arrives through the Eastern Gate, runs across the oval track to the Marathon Gate and ignites a giant bowl of fire. Then Spyridon Louis, the gold medalist in the marathon at the first modern-day Games in Athens in 1896, presents Hitler with a symbolic olive branch from Olympia in Greece. At the end of the ceremony, the athletes—represented by the German weight-lifter Rudolf Ismayr—take the Olympic oath. After reciting the vow, he waves a swastika flag instead of the Olympic one.

Baillet-Latour is appalled at this violation of protocol. But what can he do?

The opening ceremony is almost over. Before Hitler leaves the stadium at 6:16 p.m., the musicians perform the "Hallelujah Chorus" from Georg Friedrich Händel's *Messiah*—the final item on the program. As the choir sings "And he shall reign for ever and ever, king of kings and lord of lords for ever, hallelujah, hallelujah," the Polish ambassador to Germany, Józef Lipski, discreetly taps Baillet-Latour on the shoulder. "We have to be on our guard against a people with such a talent for organization," Lipski whispers in the count's ear. "They could mobilize their entire nation just as smoothly for war."

*

Austria's ambassador to Germany, Stephan Tauschitz, also files an unsettling report about the Olympic opening ceremony to the state secretary for foreign affairs in Vienna, writing: "A former Austrian officer residing in Berlin, who came to be seated amidst spectators from Austria in the Olympic Stadium, told me that in Germany he had rarely seen people as fanatical as these Austrians. The calls of '*Heil Hitler!*' and '*Sieg heil!*' from the Austrians, particularly the female ones, were a series of hoarse cries that could not have been any more fervent...An elderly visitor from Vienna who was seated not far from our source said that he had been unable to see Hitler because when the Führer entered the stadium his eyes were filled with tears."

DAILY REPORT OF THE STATE POLICE OFFICE, BERLIN: "The tailor Walter Harf, born 1 December 1890, of Lützow-strasse 45, is accused of remarking to his wife on the occasion of the Olympic opening ceremony: 'Now they'll have to assassinate the Führer like the king of England.' Harf's arrest has been ordered if reliable witnesses can be found for this accusation."

The Quartier Latin is a meeting place for the beautiful and the wealthy. Leon Henri Dajou is always on hand to welcome his elegant guests.

Sunday, 2 August 1936

REICH WEATHER SERVICE FORECAST FOR BERLIN: Mostly cloudy, with occasional light rain. No change in temperature, with slight breezes. Highs of 19°C.

Toni Kellner is a suspicious woman. When she comes home to her one-room flat at Tegeler Weg 9 in Berlin's Charlottenburg district, she immediately locks the door behind her and fastens the chain. Since April, Johanna Christen has lived in the flat across from Kellner, but in all those months she's hardly ever seen her neighbor. Once she heard noises in the building stairwell and looked through the peephole in her door. She saw an amply proportioned woman in a long coat who wore an old-fashioned hat. After a few seconds the woman disappeared again behind her locked door.

Toni Kellner seldom has visitors. Every once in a while, her 30-year-old daughter Käthe comes by. She will later describe her mother as a warmhearted but pedantic person. Käthe will testify that Toni was a person of small daily rituals. When she got up in the morning, the first thing she did was tear yesterday's page from the calendar on her washstand. Another occasional visitor is Anna Schmidt, the widow of a man Kellner used to work with. Schmidt will later say that Kellner agreed on a special signal with her few personal acquaintances. She only opens her flat door if a visitor knocks three times with the brass lid of the letter box. Why is Toni Kellner so secretive? What is she afraid of?

Toni Kellner is a transvestite. Born in June 1873 as Emil Kellner, she felt early on that she was trapped in the wrong body. Emil became a policeman, married out of sheer desperation and wore his wife's clothing when she was out of the house. The marriage fell apart, and Emil quit the police force. Relieved of a great burden, he applied for a so-called transvestite certificate allowing him to put on women's clothing, and the Prussian Ministry of Justice gave him a new, gender-neutral first name. Emil became Toni Kellner, and the former police officer was now a woman with a secret. From then on she had her outfits tailored and worked as a private detective. In the transvestite scene, Toni was known as "Big Polly." Presumably these were Toni's happiest years. Weimar Berlin was home to a flourishing subculture of bars, clubs and meeting places for those who lived outside the prevailing sexual norms. All that changed when Hitler came to power. In the Third Reich, transvestites are generally suspected of being homosexuals. In 1935 the Nazis strengthened the notorious, antigay paragraph 175 of the Reich legal code and established a Reich Center for the Prevention of Homosexuality and Abortion. In the eyes of the National Socialist guardians of German morals, transvestites are perverts. Only those who can prove their heterosexuality are given extensions of the transvestite certificates issued in the Weimar Republic. It's no wonder that Toni Kellner is afraid—afraid of her neighbors, the Hitler Youths playing in the street and the SA men who regularly march down Tegeler Weg.

For a while now, Kellner has felt unwell. It's her heart. And the asthma. At least that's what she surmises. She doesn't dare consult a doctor. On the last day of her life, Toni is wearing a blouse, panties and knee-high laced boots. Suddenly she feels nauseous and collapses backward on her bed. Blood drips from her mouth: an artery has burst.

No one misses her. It takes fourteen days for a neighbor to complain about the stink coming from Kellner's flat. At first the police are unable to open the door since, as was her wont, she locked it in several places. They call the fire brigade. When the firemen enter Toni's flat via the kitchen window, the calendar on her washstand reads 2 August 1936.

DAILY REPORT OF THE STATE POLICE OFFICE, BERLIN: "By order of SS Group Leader Heydrich, the Olympic Police Command Staff is to make four copies of their daily reports as an ongoing service to the Gestapo, which will distribute them. It was determined that Captain Göres from the uniformed police corps will collect the daily reports in question. Captain Göres refused to submit four copies of the daily reports, saying that this was technically impossible. For this reason, there can be no distribution of the daily reports as ordered."

*

It is from his archenemy Alfred Rosenberg, of all people, that Joseph Goebbels learns about his wife's affair. "During the night, Magda admitted that the thing with Lüdecke was true," Goebbels notes in his diary. "I'm very depressed about this. She lied to me constantly. Huge loss of trust. It's all so terrible. You can't get through life without compromises. That's the terrible thing!" Magda Goebbels's affair happened three years ago, but for political reasons the matter is very unpleasant for her husband. In Kurt Georg Lüdecke, his wife could have hardly chosen a more embarrassing partner for her amorous adventure. Lüdecke was a windbag from the early days of the Nazi Party, a dandy, gigolo and swindler, whom Hitler repeatedly used for delicate special missions. In the United States, where Lüdecke lived for several years, he tried to get Henry Ford to donate money to the perpetually cash-strapped party. In Rome he wooed Benito Mussolini. Lüdecke constantly ran foul of the law by seducing rich women and trying to blackmail them afterward. When Hitler came to power, Lüdecke sought to get what he saw as his piece of the pie, but he was arrested instead. A man like him makes a lot of enemies. In 1934, Lüdecke emigrated permanently to the United States and began to write a tell-all book about Hitler. Now Goebbels is nervous. He can't bear to think of what will happen if this swindler also makes his affair with Magda known to the public.

*

Erna and Willi Rakel are simple people. She earns her money as a factory worker, while her husband is a glassblower. The Rakels live at Wendenschlossstrasse 212 in the Köpenick district. It's a simple residential building with sixteen tenants. Quarters are cramped; the back courtyard is narrow and dark. The toilets are on the staircase between floors. Erna and Willi share theirs with the Mehls (he a pipe-layer, she a housewife), a seamstress named Rabe and the widow Lehmann. Wendenschlossstrasse is Berlin at its most unspectacular, worlds away from the chic cafés, bars and shops of Kurfürstendamm. Indeed, all of Köpernick is salt of the earth. At Wendenschlossstrasse 202, Luise Burtchen runs a small laundrette, the neighboring house contains a warehouse for a linoleum factory, and at number 218 is a nitrite plant. After work, the men meet up for a beer at Bernhard Woicke's pub.

People in Wendenschlossstrasse noticed little of the opening of the Olympic Games the day before. Tourists never find their way here. Erna isn't interested in sport anyway. She has other problems. For a long time, she's felt unwell. There's nothing wrong with the 25-year-old physically; the problems are psychological. She, too, carries a secret around with her. It must be a dark one since she doesn't share it with anybody. She can't talk to Willi. Perhaps Willi is part of the problem—we simply don't know.

What we do know is that around noon Erna enters the Neukölln station of the *S-Bahn*, Berlin's overground public transport system. The station is part of a circle line that goes all the way around the city. Unsurprisingly, on the second day of the Olympics, it's very busy—many of the passengers are on their way to the Games. People laugh and are in a jolly mood. Erna makes her way through the mass of travelers waiting for the next train until she's right there in the front, around two feet from the tracks. She hears garbled words come over the loudspeakers. "Attention...circle train arriving...please stand clear." When the approaching 12:34 train is only a few yards away from her, Erna Rakel takes a step forward.

*

At 3 p.m. in the Olympic Stadium, the women's javelin event begins. Fourteen athletes are competing, including three Germans: Ottilie "Tilly" Fleischer, Luise Krüger and Lydia Eberhardt. Together with Austria's Herma Bauma, Krüger is the favorite. But, on only her second attempt, Fleischer records a throw of 44.69 meters, breaking the previous Olympic record from Los Angeles by exactly one centimeter. After three further attempts, Fleischer reaches 45.18 meters, smashing her own Olympic record. With that, the butcher's daughter from Frankfurt am Main wins the first gold for Germany at the 1936 Olympic Games. Krüger takes the silver medal; bronze goes to Poland's Maria Kwaśniewska.

After the awards ceremony, Hitler invites the three athletes to have their photo taken with him at his box, much to the irritation of the Olympic Committee, which considers itself to be the host of the Games. But the German dictator knows how powerful photographs can be. "I almost burst into tears in front of the Führer," Tilly Fleischer is quoted as saying in a newspaper. The German press makes a meal of Hitler's congratulations. Several photos are taken of the Führer, Göring and Reich Sports

Leader Hans von Tschammer und Osten next to the 24-year-old Fleischer. No tears can be made out on the images. But the photo shows a small, roughly 20-inch-tall oak sapling given to all gold medalists. In her photo album, Fleischer drily notes: "Adolf + I with oak."

*

Hubertus Georg Werner Harald von Meyerinck comes from a venerable family of Prussian officers and high-level civil servants. He was supposed to go into the military or at least become a clergyman, but from early on he felt drawn to theater and film. In any case, it's hard to imagine someone nicknamed "Hupsi" having much success in the military or religion. By 1936, Hupsi the actor has already become something of a household name. With his slicked-back hair, monocle and pencil-thin mustache, he usually portrays oleaginous villains, upper-class oddballs, scatterbrained aristocrats and gallant eccentrics. Hupsi can snarl like a Prussian corporal or talk through his nose like an arrogant snob. That's made him very popular. Meyerinck appears in around ten films a year. At the end of May, his latest one premiered in the Primus Palast cinema on Potsdamer Strasse in downtown Berlin. In the comedy *Orders Are Orders*, Hupsi played a cavalry captain and swindler out to make some easy money.

Meyerinck is a staple of Berlin's famous nightlife, frequenting restaurants like Schlichter or, on fancy occasions, Horcher. He can also be found in trendy watering holes like Aenne Maenz, Mampe, the Taverne, the Ciro Bar and Sherbini. But his favorite place to party is the Quartier Latin. You could almost call it his local, were that not too profane a word for this sort of luxurious *établissement*. The Quartier Latin on the corner of Nürnberger Strasse and Kurfürstendamm is the most elegant and expensive club in the German capital. Tuxedos are required for men, evening gowns for women, and money for patrons of both sexes. The dress code is strictly enforced—no exceptions are made, no matter how famous someone is. You won't see any Brownshirts or people in uniform at the Quartier Latin. At first glance you might think that time has stood still since 1926 or perhaps 1928, but appearances are deceiving. The club is by no means a holdover from the Roaring Twenties. It first opened in 1931, and its short heyday comes during the Third Reich.

The Quartier Latin consists of a tiny entrance hall with a cloakroom and two connected rooms. In the first is the bar with a few cocktail tables and bar stools; in the second is the restaurant, which has a dance floor and a stage for the band. It goes without saying that only live music is played in the Quartier Latin.

As soon as Hubert von Meyerinck or another famous customer enters the bar, Leon Henri Dajou is immediately at his service. Dajou is a one-man welcoming committee, helping film divas out of their fur coats, showing groups of industrialists to their tables and taking initial orders. Dajou is the Quartier Latin's owner, and he's everywhere, directing his team of employees this way and that with a keen eye and concise instructions.

Hupsi calls Dajou a friend, but in reality he doesn't know much about him. Dajou comes from Romania, so one story goes, but other versions have him immigrating to Germany from

Algeria or Morocco and beginning his career as a professional dance partner in the Hotel Adlon. Rumor has it that Hedda Adlon, the wife of the hotelier, fell for this gigolo and kept him as her lover, providing him with the money to open his own establishment. But no one knows for sure.

Dajou's origins may be shrouded in darkness, but there's no question that he's doing fantastic business. He's able to afford a flat on Kurfürstendamm and a luxury Cadillac, which he loves to drive through the streets and always parks directly in front of the Quartier Latin. Dajou also has a girlfriend, Charlotte Schmidtke. In her late 20s, good-looking and blond, she could be a model. In fact, Miss Schmidtke doesn't work for a living, but she still resides in a luxuriously decorated five-room flat just off Kurfürstendamm. It is said that Dajou gives her the necessary pocket money for this sort of lifestyle. But again, nothing is certain. Whenever Hubert von Meyerinck asks his friend Dajou something personal, he just laughs. He's not laughing at or about Hupsi—he's laughing away the question. "Well, you know, Hupsi..." he'll say, and then top up the actor's glass of champagne.

The patrons of the Quartier Latin are as glamorous as their host is mysterious. Sitting at one of the tables is the great Pola Negri, who has just finished shooting her latest film, *Moscow–Shanghai*. Negri is wearing an ermine coat with long black gloves. Her face is powdered white, and her lips glow blood-red, making her look like a latter-day Lucretia Borgia. But instead of a glass of poison, her hand holds her favorite drink, whisky, which is available in the Quartier Latin for the small fortune of 2.25

marks (6 dollars). At another table, the film producer Willi Forst is chewing the fat with the actress Elsa Wagner; in the corner, the writer Lally Horstmann, the daughter of a Jewish banking family, is talking to her husband, the filthy-rich art collector Alfred Horstmann. At the bar is Berlin's police president, Count Wolf-Heinrich von Helldorff. He's known as a brutal Machiavellian with blood on his hands, but you wouldn't think that to see him drinking champagne in his tuxedo in the Quartier Latin. Another one of the regulars is Ernst Udet, a highly decorated fighter pilot and Luftwaffe colonel who only ever sips from his glass but shows himself to be a passionate lover of swing music. Every time the 24-year-old publisher's son Axel Springer—later the conservative publisher of West Germany's most popular tabloid—visits Berlin, he always stops by the Quartier Latin. The young Springer is a bon vivant and a snob, and the club is right up his street. Just to be safe, he leaves his wife, Martha, in Hamburg every time he decides to partake of Berlin's nightlife. In August 1936 Springer is often seen in the company of a stunning-looking woman from Chile. It's whispered that she's the singer and actress Rosita Serrano, who has recently moved to Berlin and is scheduled to appear shortly in the Wintergarten cabaret theater. On numerous occasions Horst Winter, whose small jazz band has been booked by the Quartier Latin during the Olympic Games, observes Springer and his female companion dancing the night away, locked in deep embraces. "One evening they both turned up with bandaged wrists," Winter will later remember. "People speculated about a heartache-inspired suicide pact, but the two of them seemed to have got over it somehow."

Leon Henri Dajou knows all the secrets, big and small, of his customers—but his lips are sealed. Discretion is his first and foremost principle. Only rarely does he lose control and join the ranks of the gleeful revelers, but when he does, the results are scenes scarcely imaginable in such an elegant establishment in the capital of the Third Reich. In early 1935 a group of regulars visited the club, and Dajou treated them to a round of cognac on the house. One round led to another until everyone was more or less inebriated. Suddenly a lady sprang to her feet, went to the dance floor and began to gyrate around ecstatically. In order to dance more freely she lifted her skirt but it kept on riding down again. Dajou, seeing the problem, stepped onto the dance floor and simply helped her out of her skirt. "Miss, we're going to have to call the police," joked the actor Ernst Dumke. "You're not showing enough skin." The young lady didn't have to be told twice. "The woman undid her blouse, now completely exposing herself," recalled another eyewitness. "His Highness Prince August von Hohenlohe used the occasion to risk a dance with the woman. Mr. Dajou felt inspired to take a wineglass and kneel down in front of her, sticking it between her legs from behind. He seemed to be suggesting that the woman fill it with piss. Then he stood up and pretended to drink the glass dry." On that evening, Dajou seems to have utterly abandoned his customary reserve. He went up to the jazz band, which had continued to play the entire time, and took a cucumber-shaped rumba maraca away from one of the musicians. "Mr. Dajou stuck the instrument between his legs, so that it resembled a gigantic organ, approached the woman, who was dancing with Mr. Dumke, from behind and made gestures simulating intercourse."

The Quartier Latin is a volcano, and patrons dance on its edge. For a few hours, it's as though the Third Reich doesn't exist. Leon Henri Dajou is a daredevil who refuses to acknowledge danger. But the noose is already around his neck—and during the Olympic Games it will be tightened.

Unprecedented effort in terms of technology and personnel goes into staging the Games in the Olympic Stadium. Jesse Owens becomes the undisputed star and fan favorite.

Monday, 3 August 1936

REICH WEATHER SERVICE FORECAST FOR BERLIN: Cloudy, occasional showers and a light breeze. Somewhat warmer. Highs of 21°C.

Mascha Kaléko isn't as famous a writer as Thomas Mann, who won the Nobel Prize for Literature seven years earlier, but she already has something of a reputation at the age of 27. Indeed, not long ago, Kaléko was considered one of the leading young hopes of German letters. Well-respected newspapers fought over her poems, which were lively, full of gentle melancholy and captured the spirit of the early 1930s. Kaléko's favorite subjects include the highs and lows of human interaction, the ups and downs of relationships and life in the big city. Her poem "The Next Morning" reads:

> We wake up. The sun barely shines
> Through the slits of our gray blinds.
> You yawn and I must admit.
> It sounded ugly, and it seems to fit
> That married people don't glow with love.

I lay in bed. You looked in the mirror
And lost yourself as you worked your razor.
You reached for your brush and hair cream
While I watched you silently.
The very definition of a husband.

How suddenly I loathed so much
The room, you, the faded bunch
Of flowers, the glasses we emptied yesterday
And the rest of the compote we ate.
Everything looks different the next morning.

At breakfast you stared at your bread silently.
That may be hygienic, but I find it not so keen.
I saw your fatty lips redden up
As you dipped the bread in your coffee cup.
I'd rather die than view scenes like this.

I got dressed, you inspected my legs.
The air smelled of coffee drunk to the dregs.
I went to the door. Work started at nine.
I only said this, though there was much on my mind,
"I think it's time to go."

Kaléko's poems about everyday life remained popular after
the Nazis' rise to power. In March 1933, Rowohlt published
a selection of her verse. The book sold so well that another
appeared in December the following year. But, at some point, the

officials at the Reich Writers' Chamber discovered that Kaléko was a Jew. Suddenly, one of the Third Reich's most promising authors is a *poeta non grata*. As if that weren't enough, her private life is also in turmoil. In short, by August 1936 the writer is going through an existential crisis.

Today Kaléko is in a hurry. She takes her keys, locks the door to her flat and walks down the staircase. Every time she leaves her building, the first thing she sees is the tax office in the North Wilmersdorf district. There it stands on the other side of the road, cold and forbidding as government buildings tend to be. Kaléko has lived at Lietzenburger Strasse 32 for almost a year now, and she's got used to the sight of this square, gray block. But today she doesn't notice her neighborhood. She's not only in a hurry—she's full of gleeful anticipation. She walks a few yards to the right, crosses Sächsische Strasse and enters Lietzenburger Strasse 35, which houses the post office serving postal code W5. She joins the queue for poste restante, tells the clerk her name and receives a letter. This has been going on for weeks. Usually, all the clerk hands over is a single letter, but sometimes if Kaléko hasn't had time to collect her mail for a while, it will be a whole bundle. Kaléko could have never imagined that she would feel such regular delight at visiting a post office, with its smell of linoleum. But the post office in Lietzenburger Strasse is where Mascha Kaléko picks up letters from her lover. What would Mr. Kaléko say, if he ever found out?

*

"Terse with Magda," Goebbels writes in his diary. "And that's for the best." The propaganda minister is burying himself in work, receiving numerous visitors including Crown Prince Umberto of Italy and his wife, the Italian propaganda minister, Dino Alfieri, the British diplomat's wife Sarita Vansittart ("a bigoted lady") and several actresses. Goebbels likes to play the womanizer, but as coolly as he treats his wife, he can't help thinking about her affair with Lüdecke. He keeps asking himself how Magda could have been so foolish as to get involved with such a dubious character.

It's not the first time that his wife has threatened to get Goebbels into political trouble. The 34-year-old Magda Goebbels is a woman with a past. Johanna Maria Magdalena Behrend came into the world in November 1901 in a hospital in the working-class district of Berlin Kreuzberg. Her family was poor and rather disreputable. Her mother, Auguste Behrend, was 22 when her daughter was born and worked as a servant for an affluent family on Bülowstrasse. Magda's father seems to have been unknown: no name is listed on her birth certificate. Auguste later claimed that the wealthy construction magnate Oskar Ritschel from Bad Godesberg was Magda's father; they were married, she maintained, but got divorced. But Auguste Behrend and Oskar Ritschel were never married, as Magda found out in late October 1931. "Magda sat there, devastated," Goebbels wrote in his diary at the time. "Her mother told her that she had never been married to her father. Magda knew nothing about this. Now she's inconsolable." But things would get worse for Magda. Ritschel was also not her real father.

The truth is complicated. Oskar Ritschel, the ambitious son of an industrialist, and Auguste Behrend, a young woman from a humble background, probably met each other at the Rheinhotel Dreesen in the stylish spa resort of Bad Godesberg, where Auguste spent one season working as a chambermaid. They seem to have been intimate, since Ritschel showed no surprise when Behrend announced that she was pregnant with his child. He volunteered to pay 300 marks (750 dollars) a month and later financed Magda's education. What Ritschel didn't suspect was that Magda's father was not himself, but probably the Jewish merchant Richard Friedländer, born in 1881, who married Auguste in December 1908. Friedländer's official residence registration forms, at least, list Magda as his daughter. The terrible truth, so feared in the Goebbels household, is that Magda's father was Jewish.

It's unclear whether and when Oskar Ritschel and Richard Friedländer saw through Auguste's murky romantic life. But in December 1931 the main newspaper of the German Communist Party, *Die Rote Fahne*, had no doubts as to whose loins had sired Magda. "She was born a Friedländer," the paper mocked. "This not exactly Aryan name fits perfectly with her husband's purebred Aryan face. We're no Jew-baiters, but we do take pleasure in noting that Goebbels married a woman born as a Jew." Goebbels had the Nazi Party newspaper *Der Angriff* deny the report, but he was still nagged by doubts as to whether Oskar Ritschel was truly Magda's father. He must have sensed that he had married into a difficult family. Goebbels considered his mother-in-law a "gruesome person," the sight of whom made him feel "nauseous," while he saw Ritschel as "a shabby egotist and wretched hypocrite." Then, in June 1934, Magda told Goebbels "the terrible matter." Goebbels was so shocked that he couldn't bring himself to write down what he heard, censoring his own diary. All he could commit to paper were vague hints: "Terrible scenes. I'm completely devastated...We've separated internally." Was this the moment that Goebbels learned that Richard Friedländer was Magda's real father?

Fast-forward to August 1936. Perhaps Goebbels has been thinking of his family by marriage—his mother-in-law, Oskar Ritschel and Richard Friedländer. And now there's the news of Magda's affair with Lüdecke. Goebbels writes in his diary: "It will take me a long time to recover from this." In fact his recovery takes exactly three days.

EXCERPT FROM THE DAILY INSTRUCTIONS OF THE REICH PRESS CONFERENCE: "Newspapers are requested to make clear that there is enough accommodation available in Berlin, even for one- or two-day visits."

*

For Adolf Hitler, the man of the hour may be Erich Borchmeyer, but the majority of the 100,000 spectators in the Olympic Stadium see things quite differently. For them, the star of the show is Jesse Owens, a spectacular 22-year-old American sprinter from Oakville, Alabama. At 5 p.m., after the qualifiers, the quarter-finals and semifinals, the final of the men's 100-meter race will be held. The original thirty-six competitors have been whittled down to the six fastest men in the world. Owens is the favorite, but the Führer is pinning his hopes on Germany's Borchmeyer.

The entire stadium watches, transfixed, as the six runners make their way to the starting blocks. Owens has drawn the innermost lane next to Sweden's Lennart Strandberg, Borchmeyer and the Dutchman Martinus Osendarp. The Americans Frank Wykoff and Ralph Metcalfe occupy lanes five and six. Then there is Franz Miller. With his white apron, he looks like a butcher or the owner of a successful pharmacy. But his job is unique: Miller is the race starter. With all the calm in the world, the corpulent man explains the starting command to the athletes. The Berlin Olympics are using a stop-motion camera system developed by the Zeiss Ikon and Agfa companies. When Miller fires the starting gun, he'll also send an electrical signal to start the race clock and the camera at the finish line. After around 10 minutes, the judges will be able to inspect visual images of the race.

It's almost 5 p.m., and the runners are about to take their positions. Osendarp looks nervous, scuttling to and fro, while Metcalfe crosses himself before kneeling down in the blocks. A dead hush has descended over the stadium. You can hear Miller's voice: "On your marks...get set..." Then the starting gun echoes through the arena. Just before the race Owens's coach told him to imagine he was running over hot coals, and he seems to have taken that advice. Owens's feet scarcely appear to touch the ground. He flies across the track, taking the lead immediately. After only half the race, he is a good 2 yards ahead of Osendarp and Wykoff. No one can compete with him, it seems, but suddenly Metcalfe makes up ground, and the two men run neck and neck over the final yards. Owens crosses the finish line in 10.3 seconds—Metcalfe and Osendarp follow at respective intervals of one-tenth of a second. Adolph Borchmeyer—Adolf Hitler's great German hope—comes in fifth.

There are wild celebrations in the Olympic Stadium, with the spectators chanting "Jesse!" The object of their admiration looks into the stands, as if he can't believe his eyes, and waves to his fans. In the Führer's box, however, the mood is as sour as a bad hangover. Hitler turns around and grumbles something to the men sitting behind him. The official Olympic newspaper will describe the hopes raised before the race in words that no doubt also applied to Hitler and his entourage: "Although we could see how dominant the Americans were from the times recorded in the qualifiers—could there not be a miracle? Could the 32-year-old Borchmeyer not by sheer willpower make it to the top three?" Obviously not.

There are various rumors about what happens next. Some people say that Hitler refuses to congratulate the race winner, but there's nothing to that story. After the Führer had received the winners of the women's javelin competition on his own initiative during the first day of the competition, the IOC informed him that congratulations from the head of state violated protocol. Hitler has therefore already ceased offering his personal congratulations to the winners.

Nonetheless, it's true that Hitler will have avoided a personal encounter with Owens at all costs. When Schirach suggests that he have his picture taken with the athlete, Hitler snarls: "The

Americans should be ashamed of letting Negroes win their medals. I'm not shaking hands with this Negro."

Hitler, the patron of the Berlin Olympic Games, has his own explanation for why Owens wins the day. His favorite architect, Albert Speer, will recall the following remark: "People whose forefathers came from the jungle are primitive—more athletically built than civilized white people," Hitler says, shrugging his shoulders. "They're not fair competition, and thus they should be excluded from future Games and other sporting competitions." But by no means will this day spell the end of the bad news for Hitler. The 100-meter race won't be the only event in which Jesse Owens wins the gold medal.

*

The news of Owens's triumph spreads like wildfire. In Southampton, England, a certain "J. M. Loraine" mails a letter to the sprinter. It asks Owens to say the following when he is presented with his gold medal: "It was an honor for me to represent my country and a joy to test myself against the best runners in the world. But I must refuse with loathing a prize from your government, which preaches racial hatred." Owens will never receive this letter. Mail to the athletes is intercepted and opened. The original letter is kept in a Gestapo file, and a copy sent to the Reich Security Main Office director, Reinhard Heydrich.

EXCERPT FROM THE DAILY INSTRUCTIONS OF THE REICH PRESS CONFERENCE: "As welcome as German victories are, it is not appropriate only to mention excellent German performances in the headlines. Foreign triumphs should not be downplayed. The racial perspective should not be applied in any form to discussions of sporting results, and in particular, Negroes should not be attacked on their sensitive points. Even less well-known members of the international and national Olympic committees should be mentioned occasionally."

*

A man of the world. That's what everyone thinks on meeting Mustafa El Sherbini for the first time. His shoes are polished to perfection, his stylish suit (double-breasted, as is the fashion in 1936) sits flawlessly, and his jet-black, slightly curly hair is cut neatly to the back. No question about it: the 28-year-old Egyptian makes quite the impression. If only he didn't wear that disturbingly sardonic smile all the time. On close inspection, you might take the young man for a gigolo, and that's by no means inaccurate. Like Leon Henri Dajou, Sherbini also began his career as a dance partner. We don't know when he left the city of his birth, Cairo, for Berlin. In any case, at some point he has arrived here, smiling his way into the hearts of the city's females. One of the many ladies who succumbs to the handsome young dandy's charms is Yvonne Fürstner.

Yvonne's parents, Alice and Solman, got divorced when she was young, and Alice married the extraordinarily wealthy Count Konrad von Frankenberg und Ludwigsdorf. The aristocrat had no children of his own, so he adopted Yvonne and her sister Lieselotte, making them into countesses and providing them with hefty allowances. Yvonne von Frankenberg, as she was now known, was a very eligible young woman, but she was incapable of settling down. Her marriage to merchant Robert Treeck ended in divorce, as did her union with the considerably older music publisher Otto Fürstner. Yvonne Fürstner was in her early 30s when she met Sherbini, and before long the two were a couple.

Sherbini dreamed of opening his own establishment—a chic place, preferably a bar and grill, as is all the rage right now. And of course, there had to be a stage for bands and amusing little variety acts. If Sherbini had his way, Berlin's high society would meet at his place. And together, his ambition and Yvonne Fürstner's money laid the foundations for the Sherbini Bar at Uhlandstrasse 18, an ideal location not far from Kurfürstendamm. The trendy art deco venue opened its doors in September 1933. By that point Adolf Hitler had been German chancellor for six months.

Hitler will never set foot in the Sherbini Bar, nor, almost certainly, will he ever learn of its existence. The things that go on there are abhorrent to the Führer. "Times haven't changed here," the Nazi newspaper *Berliner Herold* wrote. "Here the Kurfürstendamm world looks just as it did before 1933. Hot jazz, Negro dancing, exorbitant prices, foreign languages—you'd almost think you were in Montparnasse and not in Berlin." The hack who wrote these words for the *Herold* was condemning the Sherbini Bar, but Yvonne and Mustafa take his lines as a compliment. Although it was only established after Hitler's rise to power, the bar comes to symbolize the antithesis of the Nazi "people's community." In this tiny microcosm, a world that has gone extinct elsewhere in Berlin continues to flourish.

The Sherbini Bar's patrons are artists, actors, industrialists, diplomats and politicians. Ernst Udet frequents the place, as does tennis star Gottfried von Cramm and Martha Dodd, the socialite daughter of the American ambassador to Germany, who enjoys the male company she finds on Uhlandstrasse. The bar is also a meeting place for Egyptian expats, of whom there are quite a few in Berlin. People attached to the Egyptian embassy on Tiergartenstrasse regularly visit Sherbini and his establishment. Occasionally Ahmed Mustafa Dissouki, the owner of the ritzy Ciro Bar, will call in to see his friends Mustafa and Yvonne. Another good customer is the 22-year-old student Aziz de Nasr from Egypt's Gharbia Governorate. Aziz sublets a room from a certain Mrs. Luise Oppenheim and can't really afford such an expensive watering hole. But somehow he made his way to Sherbini's place, where he fell head over heels in love with Yvonne. He visits the bar as often as he can, tracking his beloved's every movement with stares of romantic longing.

From the very beginning, there's been a clear division of labor in the bar. Sherbini plays the role of *conférencier*, organizing the entertainment and being the face of the *établissement*. Yvonne runs the business in the background, keeping tabs on everything, and prepared to get tough when things get out of hand. Sometimes there is trouble when a customer loses control or refuses to pay his tab. For such occasions, Yvonne keeps a

thick rubber truncheon behind the bar. Thankfully she doesn't
have to use it all that much. Far more frequent are noisy argu-
ments at home. Sherbini has the looks of a dandy and the temperament of an Eastern potentate. Yvonne calls him her "wild
love," which sums up his two primary characteristics, for he can
be both lovable and savage. "As far as my wild love goes, I don't
think he'll ever change," Yvonne writes to her sister. "You have
to judge wild men by different standards."

In August 1936, the Sherbini Bar is one of the hottest
nightspots in Berlin. Although business usually declines in
the summer months, Yvonne hopes that the Olympic Games
will bring in more customers. Mustafa will greet patrons from
Germany and abroad, smile a lot, trade quips with the gentlemen
and gallantries with the ladies, while Yvonne stays close to her
truncheon and avoids the spotlight. Three years after the Nazis
assumed power, there are good reasons for Yvonne to take a back
seat. She's Jewish.

DAILY REPORT OF THE STATE POLICE OFFICE, BERLIN: "At
Salzburgerstrasse 6, a swastika flag hanging from a balcony
was set on fire, as was a poster featuring the Olympic flag
at Berchtesgadenerstrasse 14. Investigations have thus
far only revealed that the burning remnants of the flag
were used to try to set on fire a car with the registration
number IA 100 060. The suspected perpetrator is the
baker Hermann Ronne of Bornemannstrasse 3."

*

The "Magician"—which is what his children call the Nobel Prize–winning novelist Thomas Mann—hasn't been feeling well all day. Küsnacht near Zurich, where he resides, is enjoying better weather than Berlin, and Mann complains about the "oppressive sun." The "greenhouse air" spoils even his daily walk with his wife, Katia. Mann only recovers when things cool down late in the evening, which, as is his wont, he spends listening to the radio. He takes in a classical concert with works by Mozart and Schubert, paying particular attention to a short piano composition by Richard Wagner. The piece, *Albumblatt*, is "very authentic in its appropriately sensual indulgence," yet "rather impoverished in terms of content." Last but not least, Mann listens to the news from Berlin, noting in his diary: "Recordings of the 100-meter race, in which two American Negroes triumphed. Very nice!"

It is only thanks to enormous technological effort that Mann can follow the goings-on in Berlin's Olympic Stadium from far-off Switzerland. The 1936 Summer Games are a global media event the like of which has not been seen before. Eighteen hundred journalists from 59 countries are reporting on the competitions; in addition, 125 accredited photographers will produce around 16,000 images. Along with daily newspapers, radio plays a leading role in the coverage. The technological command center is located directly underneath the Führer's VIP box. A 65-foot-long switchboard can simultaneously handle eighteen connections throughout Europe and ten overseas. Twenty-four stations in total provide live coverage of the Games. Some of the reports are broadcast directly over the airwaves; others are recorded on shellac and later played back. All told, German stations will broadcast more than 500 reports—foreign stations will bring their audiences no fewer than 3,000.

Spectators in the Olympic Stadium will discover, next to the Führer's box, a 7-foot-long contraption that resembles an anti-aircraft gun. It's one of three electronic cameras allowing the brand-new medium of television to broadcast live from the arena. It takes two strong men to change the 110-pound lens with a diameter of 16 inches on the "iconoscope" built by the Telefunken company. Another novelty is the so-called intermediary film lorry of the Reich Post Office: a Mercedes transport vehicle with a cinematic camera mounted on the roof. Exposed celluloid runs through a completely darkened duct into the lorry's interior, where it is developed, fixed, dried and scanned. With a delay of only 58 seconds, Olympic competitions flicker across screens in twenty public television salons in Berlin, Potsdam and Leipzig. Three times daily—from 10 to 12 a.m., 3 to 7 p.m. and 8 to 10 p.m.—these primitive TV sets show film coverage. "Attention, attention!" goes the announcement. "This is the Paul Nipkow television station in Berlin with a special Olympic broadcast with sound at 7.06 meters and pictures on 6.77 meters in wavelength."

The National Socialists spare nothing in their attempts to impress the world. The more Thomas Mann in his exile in Küsnacht listens to radio broadcasts from Berlin, the more uneasy he becomes. The Magician knows that the enormous technological effort is being employed to intimidate, indeed

49

overwhelm the rest of the world. Hitler wants to demonstrate his power. The implicit message is that others should beware of messing with an industrial nation capable of such engineering feats. When Mann hears the recordings of the Olympic Games' opening ceremony, he feels physically ill. "An unpleasant business," he writes in his diary. "Fraught nerves. Worried about my appendix. But it's probably, as usual, my large intestine."

The American writer Thomas Wolfe experiences a summer of contradictions during the 1936 Berlin Olympics. "Thomas Wolfe came, and his effect was like an earthquake."

Tuesday, 4 August 1936

REICH WEATHER SERVICE FORECAST FOR BERLIN: Partly cloudy, with isolated light showers. Gradually lessening winds from the west during the day. Somewhat cooler, with highs of 18°C.

It's early in the morning, and Thomas Wolfe has only been in bed a couple of hours when his alarm clock goes off. German clocks sound different from American ones, he thinks. They're louder, and more pitiless and aggressive. Maybe, realizing how sleepy he still is, he just turns the damn nuisance off—or he throws it into the corner of his room in anger. The latter seems more likely, since when he's ripped from his sleep Wolfe is not just tired but also has a raging hangover. And yesterday evening began so harmlessly, with Wolfe being invited to dinner by Ernst Rowohlt. Slowly he begins to remember and realizes what happened.

The previous evening Wolfe left his hotel, glancing as always to his left up at the tower clock on the Kaiser Wilhelm Memorial Church. He walked across the street past the cosmopolitan Kakadu Bar, turned right down Joachimsthaler Strasse, then left onto Augsburger Strasse, then right down Rankestrasse. All in all he went no further than 500 yards. On the way, he bought some flowers for Rowohlt's wife, Elli.

Rowohlt lives at Rankestrasse 24 in a magnificent building constructed in 1898. When Wolfe got there and stared up at the ornate, imposing façade, a funny feeling came over him. It wasn't anxiety he felt at seeing his German publisher again, more like a mixture of caution and respect. Wolfe was on his mettle. He was all too aware from the previous year that being invited to dinner at the Rowohlts' is like confronting a force of nature. Born in Bremen in 1887, Rowohlt is a powerful giant of a man, with blond hair, blues eyes and a handshake that could crush stones. He's a man with the sort of energy that can set life spinning like a dizzying carousel. But for Rowohlt, Wolfe will later write, intoxicating excess is preceded by civilized understatement. "Today you'll come to my place for a meal," he told his guest earlier, nodding with satisfaction. "No one else will be there, just my wife and I. We'll have a quiet conversation and a peaceful evening. We'll eat and talk, but there'll be no drinks, no alcohol. You've had enough of that already. Or maybe…"—here he waved his massive fingers in a conciliatory gesture—"…we'll drink a simple wine. None of the hard stuff, just a simple, light Rhineland wine. I take the occasional glass for my kidneys. And we'll see that you get home early." The evening proceeded as announced. Elli had made a wonderful meal—the sort of simple, hearty German food Rowohlt is fond of—and they drank white wine for the benefit of their kidneys. Wolfe did indeed get home early—early in the morning, that is. It was 5 a.m. before he stumbled out of Rankestrasse, across Augsburger Strasse and

Joachimsthaler Strasse and back to Kurfürstendamm. As he did so, the Rowohlts' maid was disposing of "fourteen delicately thin empty bottles of splendid Rüdesheimer Riesling."

A few hours later, while Wolfe is beginning to recover with the help of an Alka-Seltzer, he contemplates what awaits him in the coming days in Berlin with a mixture of fascination and anxiety.

DAILY REPORT OF THE STATE POLICE OFFICE, BERLIN: "The Italian Olympic athletes arrived at Anhalter Station in ten train cars bearing images of Mussolini and the inscription '*Il Duce*.' On 4 August 1936, it was noticed that one of the Mussolini images had been indelibly defaced with a mustache, and that the words '*Heil* Moscow!' had been scrawled on one of the posters. It was impossible to discover when and where the graffiti happened, as this state of affairs was first discovered when the train wagons in question arrived at Tempelhof shunting yard."

*

"Will Owens win a second gold?" asks the front page of the tabloid *B.Z. am Mittag* the day after the American set a new world record in the 100-meter race. On the third day of competition, the focus in the Olympic Stadium is all on one man: Jesse Owens. At 10:30 a.m. the preliminaries for the long jump commence. Athletes have to record a jump of at least 7.15 meters to qualify for the finals in the afternoon. A little bit over 7 meters is child's play for Owens, who's been jumping that distance since he was in high school. The prospect of a second gold medal is nigh, but this time he has a serious competitor. Carl Ludwig Long—known as "Luz" from Leipzig is 23 years old, tall, blond and intimidatingly self-confident. For Owens, Long is a hated rival whom he watches with suspicion out of the corner of his eye. "How can he look so calm?" Owens growls at his coach. "Doesn't he know who he's up against?" Long is in fact well aware of the quality of the competition, but he is determined to keep his nerve and not betray the slightest hint of anxiety. Whereas Owens is visibly agitated, hectoring his coach, Long simply waits for his turn to jump, the very picture of calm.

The Owens versus Long duel will become the subject of various rumors and legends. Owens himself will later tell the world that during the morning qualifiers his first jump was a foul and the second too short, before Long gave him a decisive bit of advice about how to hit the board. The truth is that both athletes qualified with their second jumps. Decades later, when asked about his version of events, Owens will simply say that it was the sort of story people wanted to hear.

The showdown follows in the afternoon. More than 100,000 spectators eagerly await the beginning of the long jump finals. Among them are Hitler, Göring, Goebbels and the Italian Crown Prince Umberto. The weather has taken a turn for the worse. It's cooler, and an unpleasant wind is blowing through the stadium. The athletes are getting cold. Everyone in the arena is holding their breath. Long jumps first—7.54 meters. Then Owens—7.74 meters. Long improves his best to 7.84, but Owens bests that by 3 centimeters: 7.87 meters. Long positions himself for his third attempt, runs and also leaps 7.87 meters—a new European record. "Jesse immediately ran over and congratulated me," the German athlete will remember. As cheers break out in the stands, the two men embrace and laugh as they walk together for a few yards. Someone else in the arena is happy as well. "I looked up at the crowd which showed no signs of settling down and then up at the Führer's box," Long will recall. "The entire box was in a stir, and the Führer was applauding enthusiastically. I went over, stood below him and greeted my Führer with gratitude. And I could hardly believe it, but he got up and greeted me with his benevolent, paternal smile. I could tell from his eyes that his only wish was for me to win." But Hitler's joy is short-lived. In his final attempt, Owens sets a new world record of 8.06 meters. "I couldn't help myself," Long said afterward. "I ran up to him and was the first to congratulate and embrace him. He told me: 'You forced me to give my best!'"

During their duel a famous photograph was taken showing the two athletes lying on their stomachs on the ground of the stadium: two carefree, happy young men in their early 20s, seemingly inseparable. And then there's the presentation of the medals. The images captured by countless cameras go around the world. For the second time in as many days, Jesse Owens, a black student, has beaten all comers and is looking up at the American flag being hoisted into the Berlin sky to the tune of the "Star-Spangled Banner." Owens salutes the flag, while Goebbels seethes with rage. "We Germans earn one gold medal to the Americans' three, two of them won by a Negro," the propaganda minister will complain to his diary. "It's a disgrace. White humanity should be ashamed. But what does that matter in that country without any culture over there?'"

Goebbels is only too aware that Owens's second victory contains a strong political message. For the propaganda minister, it is an affront to the idea of white superiority. The American's extraordinary achievements might make even dyed-in-the-wool Nazis question the validity of the Aryan race's claims to a privileged position. Such concerns don't matter to Owens and Long. After the American national anthem has been played, they leave the athletics field arm in arm. This gesture of camaraderie will get Long into trouble. A short time later, he gets a visit from a representative of Deputy Führer Rudolf Hess, who tells him that he should never again dare to "embrace a Negro."

ORDER OF THE BERLIN POLICE PRESIDENT: "In many parts of Berlin, the drying of laundry and clothing, and the airing of beds from front balconies, loggias, roofs and street-facing windows has developed into a deplorable custom that elicits disgust and outrage among decent people. This bad habit can no longer be tolerated, especially not during the Olympic Games."

*

In the meantime, Thomas Wolfe has overcome the previous night's excesses and is waiting to be interviewed by a journalist for the *Berliner Tageblatt* newspaper. The Nazified German press is trying to put on an international face while the Olympics are going on. The *Berliner Lokal-Anzeiger*, for instance, is running articles about foreign and domestic cuisines. Readers can learn "How to make spaghetti and macaroni," while the Third Reich's foreign visitors are taught about the glories of traditional Berlin fare: "Pickled pork knuckle, known as *Eisbein*, when prepared properly, has always delighted diners, particularly Scandinavians, the English and the Dutch." The truth of such an assertion is debatable.

For its part, the *Berliner Tageblatt* is running interviews with notable visitors such as the Prince and Princess of Tripura, the Baltimore publisher William N. Jones and the top British diplomat Sir Robert Vansittart and his wife, Lady Sarita. Wolfe has become well enough known in Germany that Rowohlt has little trouble convincing the newspaper to interview him. Today, the interview is conveniently being held in Wolfe's hotel room and will focus on his relationship with Germany. The publisher rubs his hands. An interview with the *Berliner Tageblatt* is a fine—and cost-free—piece of advertising. Rowohlt knows that his author is very professional with journalists. Speaking, as they say, "in a polished style," Wolfe has it down to a T. The paper asked whether the interviewer can bring along an illustrator. Sure, is the answer. Why not?

When the knock comes at the arranged time at the door of his hotel room, Wolfe sees an unremarkable man, who introduces himself as the journalist from the *Tageblatt*, and a young woman who's obviously the illustrator. Politely, almost bashfully, she introduces herself as Thea Voelcker. Wolfe shakes her hand and looks her straight in the eye. The journalist seems oblivious to the chemistry between the two and gets straight down to business. Used to the routine, he asks the American writer the standard questions. How does he like Germany? "It's wonderful," answers Wolfe, who's having a hard time organizing his thoughts. "If Germany didn't exist, someone would have to invent it. It's a magical country. I know Hildesheim, Nuremberg and Munich, their architecture, their inner workings, the glory of their history and art." As Wolfe heaps praise on Germany, which seems to please the journalist, Thea Voelcker observes the whole scene attentively in the background, trying to memorize every feature of the writer's face while making her initial sketches. She'll flesh them out later.

Wolfe is telling the story of how he became embroiled in a fight at the Oktoberfest in Munich and had a beer stein broken over his head, which ended with him having to spend a few days in the local university clinic. Although the incident happened eight years ago, the writer can still remember the name of the doctor who treated him: Privy Councillor Lexer. Wonderful, the journalist tells Wolfe. Those are precisely the stories that interest the readers of the *Tageblatt*. But Wolfe is distracted. He keeps looking over at Thea Voelcker.

She's an impressive woman. A "Norse Valkyrie" is what Wolfe thinks when he first lays eyes on her, although he knows little about Nordic mythology and has never heard of Wagner's opera. "She had a mass of lustrous yellow hair braided about her head, and her cheeks were two ruddy apples," he will write.

"She was extremely tall for a woman, with the long, rangy legs of a runner, and her shoulders were as broad and wide as a man's. Yet she had a stunning figure, and there was no suggestion of an ugly masculinity about her. She was as completely and as passionately feminine as a woman could be." The appreciation is mutual. "I did not know your books, even not your name; but when I entered into your room and saw you, I stopped and said to myself: oh my God, here I am not afraid," Thea will later confess to Wolfe in a letter. "I felt: here is a friend."

Life hasn't been easy for Thea Voelcker. She's had to endure an unhappy childhood, early psychological problems, an unsuccessful attempt to study art at university and a joyless marriage that ended in divorce after only four years. All of this has made her an unstable, extremely vulnerable woman. But Wolfe has no way of knowing any of this. After the interview is over, he's obsessed by a single thought: how can he see Thea Voelcker again soon?

*

What does a woman of the world wear to the Olympic Games? The magazine *Die Dame*, a kind of 1930s German *Cosmopolitan*, has some important advice: "Particularly before noon, sporty clothing is just the thing in the various venues, from the stadiums to the Deutschlandhalle arena. Sporty from your hat to your shoes!" For the afternoon, too, the magazine recommends sporty attire—but with one caveat: "A skirt and blouse, worn without a jacket, are still not street clothes." Women are supposed to be role models, *Die Dame* cautions. "The impression made by a city or a country depends to a large extent on the women seen there."

*

Victor Müller-Hess has a job that gives many people the creeps, although he is an esteemed professor at the University of Berlin who is regularly invited to conferences, who publishes in respected journals and who has trained a whole host of students. What's off-putting about his calling is that it's focused on death—specifically the precise reason why someone left the here-and-now for the hereafter. Müller-Hess is a coroner.

The Institute for Legal Medicine and Criminology, of which Müller-Hess is the director, carries out around 500 court-ordered autopsies every year. In addition, a growing number of human dissections are performed for scientific purposes. In 1936, the employees at the institute cut open around 3,000 corpses, an average of ten a day, six days a week. To deal with these numbers, the institute procured seven new autopsy tables the previous year. At the start of the procedure, doctors examine the bodies externally. Then comes the internal inspection, which involves opening the skull, the chest and the stomach cavity.

The number of unusual deaths recorded in the autopsy reports in the first half of August 1936 is quite striking. The pensioner Herbert Fluder threw himself in front of a train in the Pankow district's main station on 1 August. Fifty-eight-year-old

August Heinemeyer was discovered hanging from a noose on 2 August, the same day that the medical doctor Wilhelm Iwan took an overdose of the sleeping tablet Veronal in Zehlendorf. Today, Tuesday, 4 August, Adolf and Erika Hahn succumb to gas poisoning in their apartment in Schöneberg. Mrs. Bertha Theil, née Haak, aged 37, will take her own life tomorrow. All in all, between 1 and 16 August 1936, twenty-seven people will die of gas poisoning, twenty-three from hanging, twelve will drown, six will be killed by firearms, four will be run over by trains, three will overdose on medication, and two will lose their lives to alcohol.

Coroners need a strong stomach, yet there are always cases that get to even the most hardened physicians. Among the autopsies Müller-Hess and his colleagues will carry out today are those on the bodies of Martha and Gertrud Geidel.

Martha Geidel is 36 years old, works as a seamstress and lives with her 9-year-old daughter Gertrud in a two-room flat on Scharnweberstrasse in the northern district of Reinickendorf. Several days ago she divorced her husband Ernst Emil, who earns his keep as a presser in a large launderette. Martha and Ernst Emil simply couldn't stand one another anymore—the love that once brought them together had given way to deep-seated antipathy. They fight whenever they're together—even in the divorce court there were ugly scenes between the two. The judge thinks Martha is unstable. More than that, he concludes that it's not in the best interests of the child, Gertrud, that Martha be awarded custody, which goes to the father.

Martha Geidel breaks down when the judgment is announced. Give up her child? Never! On the evening of 31 July she puts

Gertrud to bed. Perhaps she reads her a story or gives the girl a goodnight kiss: we don't know. We do know that she waits until the child is asleep, then goes into the kitchen, attaches a hose to the oven, opens the gas valve, takes the hose from the kitchen to the bedroom, shuts the door as best she can, fixes the hose to the head of the bed, gets into bed with her daughter and takes her in her arms.

The following day, 1 August, when the strong smell of gas can be detected throughout the building, concerned neighbors break down the door of Martha Geidel's flat. At the very same time, the opening ceremony of the Summer Games is coming to an end in the Olympic Stadium.

DAILY REPORT OF THE STATE POLICE OFFICE, BERLIN: "On 4 August 1936, his Majesty the King of Bulgaria and the Queen of Bulgaria arrived in Berlin by passenger car under the aliases Count and Countess Rylski. His Majesty the King took up residence in the Hotel Bristol, while the Queen checked into the Berlin University Gynecological Hospital at Monbijoustrasse 2."

*

At 5:30 p.m. the German team plays its first match of the Olympic football tournament. In the round of sixteen, national coach Otto Nerz and his men meet the team from the Duchy of Luxembourg. A crowd of 12,000 spectators in the Poststadium on Lehrter Strasse awaits kickoff. Among them is Deputy Führer

Rudolf Hess. It takes 16 minutes for Adolf Urban of Schalke football club to score the first goal, and on the half-hour mark, Munich's Wilhelm Simetsreiter tucks away a pass for a second. The outcome of the match still seems open. The Luxembourgers are spirited opponents. But that changes after the break. Referee Pál von Hertzka has hardly whistled for play to resume when Simetsreiter makes it 3–0 in the 48th minute. From then on Germany starts scoring for fun. Further goals come in minutes 50, 52, 74, 75, 76 and 90. The final score is Germany 9, Luxembourg 0. The hosts qualify for the next round of the tournament, while the visitors from Luxembourg are out. "It was a battle between a giant and a dwarf," writes the self-confident German press. "The Luxembourgers were brave, upstanding fighters who played out the game as best they could." But pride comes before the fall.

*

The first few days of the Olympic competitions have seen anything but typical high summer weather. It rains, and temperatures remain cool. But for anyone who still needs to wet his whistle, the *B.Z.* newspaper can recommend a thirst-quencher using Germany's famous brandy: "Asbach Uralt with sparkling water."

The Café Bristol on Kurfürstendamm is a popular spot for *flâneurs*. "The terraces of the cafés were always packed, and in these golden-sparkling days the air seemed to vibrate like music."

Wednesday, 5 August 1936

REICH WEATHER SERVICE FORECAST FOR BERLIN: Continuing cool temperatures and isolated showers. Partly cloudy, with stiff winds from the west. Highs of 18°C.

"Ledig, you lazybones, on the fifteenth it's the first of the month!" How often has Heinrich Maria Ledig heard these words from Ernst Rowohlt? Sometimes his boss will tower over him threateningly, sometimes he'll growl the words in passing, and sometimes he'll yell them across the office: "Ledig, you lazybones, on the fifteenth it's the first of the month!" It's Rowohlt's way of saying: Ledig, you're fired! Ledig answers meekly: "Yes sir, Mr. Rowohlt." Ledig, whom everyone calls Heinz, is an unremarkable man in his late 20s. His mother, Maria Ledig, used to be an actress in the theater in Leipzig who performed under the name Maria Lee; nothing is known, at least officially, about his father. Ledig has worked for the Rowohlt publishing house for a good five years. At first he was in charge of sales, then the press department, and gradually he's made his way through all the company's departments. No matter how often Rowohlt threatens to show him the door, he can't do without the young man's services.

Ledig is not only Rowohlt's most important employee. He's also his illegitimate son. Both of them guard this secret carefully—especially from one another. "Of course, he has no idea he's my son," Rowohlt assured the writer Ernst von Salomon. "Promise me you'll keep your mouth shut!" Salomon complies. A short time later, Ledig takes Salomon into his confidence. "Of course, he has no idea that he's my father," the young man tells the writer. "Promise me you'll keep your mouth shut!" Salomon gives his word again. Last but not least, Salomon's fellow writer Hans Fallada brings up the curious relationship between Ledig and Rowohlt. Salomon will write: "'Do you know that Ledig is Rowohlt's son?' Hans Fallada asked me. I said: 'You're joking!' Fallada replied: 'No, I'm not. Rowohlt told me. He thinks Ledig doesn't know. Then Ledig told me that he thinks Rowohlt doesn't know. I had to swear on a stack of Bibles not to say anything. But the entire publishing house knows. And they laugh about the fact that neither man is aware that they all know the truth.'"

*

At 11 a.m. the venerable Prussian Academy of Sciences is welcoming a prominent visitor. Sven Hedin, the famous Swedish explorer and traveler, is scheduled to hold a talk at the invitation of the Olympic Organizing Committee. Originally, scholars from each of the continents taking part in the Games were supposed to speak, but this plan was canceled early on. The only speaker left is Hedin, who is considered a friend to

Germany and admirer of Hitler. Goebbels's Propaganda Ministry has declared the visit by the 71-year-old to be a sensation. Yesterday the aging explorer gave a rousing address to "the youth of the world" at the Olympic Stadium during a break in the competition. His topic today, however, is considerably less spectacular: the role of the horse in Asian history. Hitler and Goebbels politely excuse themselves for not being able to attend—important commitments have got in the way. At the end of Hedin's lengthy lecture, Theodor Lewald makes an unintentionally funny remark. He is certain, he tells the visitor from Sweden, that in 2,000 years people will still remember Hedin's talk to the Prussian Academy of Sciences.

*

Austria's ambassador to Germany, Stephan Tauschitz, writes to the state secretary for foreign affairs in Vienna: "The leader of the Austrian team, Baron Seyffertitz, is unhappy about the athletes being overly pampered in the Olympic Village. Their every wish—perhaps without intent—is being read from their faces."

*

That morning, Thomas Wolfe drinks his first beer in Café Bristol. It won't be his last drink of the day. He prefers beer in the morning, switches to white wine over lunch, takes whisky during the afternoon and goes back to white wine in the evening. But sometimes he alters the sequence. It's easy to think that

Wolfe has a drinking problem, but he doesn't look at it that way. As he sees it, he drinks purely to celebrate life. Since last year, he knows a number of Berlin cafés, restaurants and bars, which he visits regularly. Of the city's cafés, Wolfe loves the Bristol above all. It's only a few hundred yards from his hotel and has a large terrace giving out onto the street. For Wolfe, it's like sitting in a theater box with a perfect view of the action on stage, and the piece being performed is "Kurfürstendamm in Summer." Every minute, hundreds of people pass the Bristol's terrace, coming from the left and the right, mingling, avoiding one another and stopping. There are the young and the old, women with prams, businessmen hurrying to appointments, Hitler Youths, *flâneurs* and countless tourists from every country under the sun.

For the duration of the Games, loudspeakers have been mounted in the trees lining Kurfürstendamm so that people can follow the action in the Olympic Stadium. As Wolfe sits on the Bristol's terrace and drinks his beer, it's as though the trees were talking to him. The traffic noise and the murmurings of passersby merge with a tinny voice bringing people up to date on preliminary, intermediate and final races, spitting out names of athletes all the while. The activity on Kurfürstendamm and the talking branches exercise a special magic that Wolfe cannot resist.

He is being joined now by Heinz Ledig. Rowohlt has charged his son and employee with taking care of the publisher's American visitor during the Games. Rowohlt's solicitousness is pragmatic. Wolfe may love Germany with a passion, but his knowledge of the language is limited. His "taxi driver's German," as he calls it, is sufficient to order a drink or to give directions in a cab, but nothing more. Heinz speaks good English, albeit with a strong accent that Wolfe can imitate to comic effect: "Zis little man with hiss pipe—do you not s'ink it str-a-a-nge?"

But Ledig is more than just Wolfe's interpreter. The two men met the previous year and quickly struck up a friendship, although on the face of it they're complete opposites. On the one hand, there's Wolfe, a physical giant with boundless energy and an unquenchable thirst for life. On the other, there's Ledig, eight years Wolfe's junior, spindly, shy and rather nondescript. But it's precisely their differences that bring the two men together. When Wolfe and Ledig sit in the Café Bristol, stroll down Kurfürstendamm, visit a restaurant or drink their way through Berlin at night, they're like two very different brothers.

In the bustle in front of the Café Bristol, Ledig spots a newspaper boy. "*Tageblatt*... get your *Berliner Tageblatt*," the kid cries, waving a copy of the paper in the air. Like a fishwife hawking her wares at a market, the boy reads out the front-page headlines: "Six gold medals. Four for the U.S., one for Germany, one for Italy! The Führer again present in the stadium." Ledig motions for the boy. "One *Tageblatt*, please." "That will be 20 pfennigs, sir." Ledig opens the paper, excitedly flipping through the pages until he finds the interview with Wolfe. He scans the article. The anecdote about Wolfe's visit to the Oktoberfest is there, as is his praise of German introspection. Very nice, thinks Ledig, every inch a publisher. The article is good advertising for the Rowohlt author and his books. Satisfied, Ledig folds up the paper and slides it over to Wolfe. But the writer isn't interested in the interview and puts the paper in his jacket pocket without a word. Wolfe would rather listen to the trees. In any case, he hasn't got much time. That afternoon, Wolfe has an appointment in the Olympic Stadium.

*

At 3 p.m. the finals of the women's fencing begin. Each of the eight athletes who qualified for the last round of the competition face one another—there are seven bouts in all. With six wins and one loss, Hungary's Ilona Schacherer-Elek is at the head of the pack. But one of the most intriguing bouts is still to come: Germany's Helene Mayer against Austria's Ellen Preis. In the Domed Hall, you can hear a pin drop. The competition's outcome is still uncertain. If Mayer wins, she'll draw level with Schacherer-Elek, and there will be a tie-breaker. If Preis wins, the Hungarian will take the gold medal. Eighteen years after the demise of the Austro-Hungarian Empire, the Habsburg monarchy is briefly reborn in the sporting arena. The Austrian Preis beats Mayer, helping the athlete from Budapest to top honors. "Helene Mayer lost the decisive bout," the *Olympia-Zeitung* newspaper writes. "Oh well, silver for Germany is nothing to turn your nose up at." Indeed, second place is perfectly respectable. But was the medal really won for Germany?

Many years ago, Helene Mayer was one of Germany's top fencing prospects, winning the first of many gold medals at the

1925 German championships at the age of 14, and finishing first every year between then and 1930. In 1928, she won her first Olympic gold medal at the Amsterdam Summer Games. Two years later she enrolled at the University of Frankfurt and began studying law. When her sporting days are over, she once said in an interview, she wants to become a diplomat. By that point Helene Mayer is already a star. She possesses something you can neither buy nor learn: charisma. You can feel it when she enters the sports arena. And in her white fencing outfit, her hair done up in fashionable blond plaits, she also looks stunning.

For a long time, Mayer is the pride of Germany. She's presented with the Honorary Prize of the Reich Government over tea by German President Paul von Hindenburg. But then comes 30 January 1933. Within less than three months, the fencing club of Mayer's hometown of Offenbach strikes her name from its rolls. According to the ideology of the new regime, Helene Mayer is a "half-Jew." She learns of her club's decision in California, where she has a scholarship as an exchange student. She decides not to return to Germany, and at her college in Oakland she is given an unexpected career opportunity. In the autumn of 1934 she begins teaching German and fencing.

That could have been the end of the story. Helene Mayer could have stayed in the United States, received American citizenship and continued her career under the Stars and Stripes. But things turned out differently.

*

In Venice, Mitja Nikisch says farewell to life. Once upon a time in Berlin, Mitja was a star who performed with his dance orchestra in the most elegant clubs in the city. Under normal circumstances, he would be enjoying a series of triumphant engagements in the German capital during the Olympics. But what's normal when Adolf Hitler is Reich chancellor and you yourself are dying?

Mitja is the son of Arthur Nikisch, the former main conductor of the Berlin Philharmonic. Under his father's strict gaze, Mitja was trained as a pianist at the Leipzig Conservatory. His debut in 1917 at the age of 18 with the Berlin Philharmonic, with his father wielding the baton, marked the beginning of a meteoric career. Mitja played with all the great musicians of his time. His speciality was the grand works for piano—the concertos of Liszt, Brahms, Tchaikovsky and Rachmaninov. Many a female heart melted when the young man with his aristocratic good looks and dreamy, melancholy eyes took to the stage.

In the mid-1920s, Mitja discovered jazz and enjoyed a run of success with the Mitja Nikisch Dance Orchestra. For many fans, he was Berlin's best bandleader in the early 1930s. But the group fell apart when the Nazis came to power in 1933. Many of the members were Jews, who were forced to emigrate. Mitja returned to playing the piano, hoping to pick up where he had left off with his career as a concert performer. Initially, things looked good. In December 1933, Mitja played again for the first time with the Berlin Philharmonic. The conductor was none other than Wilhelm Furtwängler. A short time later, he and the orchestra recorded a Mozart piano concerto for Telefunken. His private life was also looking up. He had fallen in love with a woman from Moscow called Alexandra Mironova. Twelve years his junior, she had made a name for herself as a soubrette in Berlin's Schillertheater under the pseudonym Barbara Diu. Mitja was utterly enamored, but he didn't like his lover's Russian name and called her Barbara instead. The two planned to get married. Then destiny intervened.

On summer holiday in northern Italy, Mitja was diagnosed with lymphatic cancer. He knew he didn't have long to live, but nonetheless he began to compose a piano concerto. His illness released enormous amounts of energy, and working in an intoxicated frenzy, he devoted several hours a day to his magnum opus. The result is a 40-minute piece in three movements: *andante et romanza*, *scherzo* and *fantasie pathétique*. You don't need much imagination to spot the biographical elements in this work.

The introductory *romanza* is a love letter to Barbara, with the music coming in strings of gentle, contemplative pearls. In the *scherzo* the composer calls to mind his rich musical career and many triumphs. Lasting only four minutes, the movement is a musical recollection of an all-too-brief life. The concluding *fantasie pathétique* begins with cutting dissonance that can be interpreted as Mitja's cancer diagnosis. What follows is a masterpiece of sorrow. At times, the music could hardly be any more downbeat before surging aggressively. At other times, it's full of pained tenderness. Mitja's desperation becomes palpable as chords come together to form cascades, seemingly asking: Why? Why me? A wild solo piano cadence introduces the finale. Kettledrum and snare drum provide the orchestra with an unrelenting beat, the cellos and violas intone a mysterious melody, and the piano joins the action with some arabesque figures. At this point in the score, Mitja wrote the word "maestoso." The drums beat out the tempo as loudly as they can, there are layers upon layers of sound, and the music seems to march inexorably toward a dark ending. Here, the composer literally loses his composure.

Today, Mitja Nikisch finishes his piano concerto and dies. He is 37 years old. In Berlin, the newspapers are full of reports about sporting achievements and tips for entertainment. The journalists won't spare a single drop of ink for the death of the most gifted and best-known musician the city had before 1933. Barbara is in London on business when her fiancé passes away. When she returns to Venice, she'll find the handwritten score of the piano concerto with the following dedication:

For my wife Barbara Nikisch

Pause for a bit, wanderer,
I am home.
In my sphere
The stars shine bright.
Think of me,
You are only a guest
On this earth,
Where everything is in vain.
Take your ease, pick a flower
And continue on your way.

DAILY REPORT OF THE STATE POLICE OFFICE, BERLIN: "The trains that arrived at 3:30 and 8:45 p.m. at Anhalter Station were subjected to a thorough search. No stickers or inflammatory pamphlets were found."

*

"Afternoon. Stadium. Running and jumping events," Goebbels records in his diary. "No rewards for us. I put that Riefenstahl woman in her place. She behaved indescribably badly. A hysterical woman. Nothing like a man, that's for sure." Leni Riefenstahl is directing the official film about the 1936 Olympic Summer Games. She was commissioned a year ago by Hitler himself to fulfill the duty of the host country, as per IOC stipulations, to capture the sporting event on celluloid. The 33-year-old Riefenstahl is Hitler's go-to solution when he needs a film made. She has already shot three documentaries about Nazi Party rallies in Nuremberg to the dictator's great satisfaction and is practiced in the art of stylizing the Führer as a semidivine figure. The Olympic film will, of course, have to serve the interests of propaganda, but at the same time, with an eye toward viewers abroad, the political message shouldn't be too transparent. Hitler wants the film to present the rest of the world with a seemingly objective picture of an open-minded, cosmopolitan and peaceful Germany. He's given Riefenstahl a blank check to this end. No one—not even Propaganda Minister Goebbels—is allowed to interfere in the project. The jealous Goebbels naturally chafes under this restriction and keeps a sharp eye on the director.

Riefenstahl will eventually receive the enormous sum of 2.8 million reichsmarks to shoot her film. She herself is initially paid 250,000 marks—a sum that will be increased to 400,000. To conceal the fact that the Reich government has commissioned and is paying for the film, a holding company called Olympiade-Film has been formed; its managing partners are Riefenstahl and her brother Heinz. Some 200 people, including 45 cameramen, are part of the film crew, and over the course of the Games they will shoot more than 400,000 yards of celluloid. Riefenstahl has towers constructed and foxholes dug in the Olympic Stadium to capture the action from unusual perspectives. A specially built catapult camera races on tracks alongside the sprinters, yielding unprecedented images. Riefenstahl also uses handheld cameras to get up close to the athletes. She ties other cameras to balloons to get aerial shots, employs underwater equipment for the swimming events and experiments with slow-motion footage.

This gigantic amount of effort comes at a price that's more than just financial. Riefenstahl's cameramen often get in the way, hindering athletes and referees, and blocking the view for the general public and even the guests of honor with their massive equipment. Riefenstahl doesn't care whether her spotlights and flashbulbs blind the sportsmen and -women and spook the horses in the equestrian events. On numerous occasions she and Goebbels quarrel loudly. The propaganda minister may claim to have read the director the riot act, but she doesn't put up with any nonsense and fights back. Indeed, Riefenstahl seems to enjoy conflict. She wears long gray flannel trousers, a stylish blazer and a kind of jockey's cap, making her look like a Hollywood star. Two photographers follow her every step; their only task is to capture images of her at work. Leni Riefenstahl knows what she's doing.

"Every now and then she'd sit down next to the Führer," the Jewish journalist Bella Fromm will recall. "She had a curdled smile like on the cover of a glossy magazine, and her head was crowned by a halo of importance." When the director isn't ostentatiously posing at Hitler's side, she runs from camera team to camera team, barking instructions and gesticulating wildly. The people who work for her grin and bear Riefenstahl's vanity. Whenever she discovers photographers in the press section threatening to steal her show, she sends a messenger with one of her feared notes: "Leni Riefenstahl calls upon you to remain in your spot when you take images. Do not move around. If you ignore these instructions, your press pass will be revoked." It's no wonder that the director isn't very popular in the Olympic Stadium. Members of the audience seem to enjoy mocking her personal vanity. "Leni, Leni, show yourself," they chant, only to sneer when the director poses and gives them a wave: "Boo, you old cow, you old cow."

The writer Carl Zuckmayer calls Riefenstahl the Reich's "glacial crevasse" in reference to the fact that she originally made her name with films about mountain climbing and skiing. "In her defense, you must admit she's no apostate," Zuckmayer will write from American exile in 1943–44. "She always believed in Hitler as a savior. When he awarded her the Golden Laurel or something similar for her work on the Olympic film or one of the films about the Nuremberg Rallies, she nearly fainted from excitement.

Although she didn't succeed in collapsing into the Führer's arms. Instead she sank to the ground at his feet, whereupon he, visibly disgusted, had to step over her and make his exit."

*

Good things come in threes. Jesse Owens doesn't doubt for a second that he'll win his third gold medal. The final of the 200-meter race is set for 6 p.m. Owens only has two serious competitors in the discipline, Eulace Peacock and Ralph Metcalfe. Peacock is recovering from a thigh injury 3,500 miles away in New Jersey, while Metcalfe had failed to qualify for the event. So what could go wrong? Owens's only concern is the weather. It's already rather chilly early in the evening. When one of the race marshals checks the thermometer shortly before the race, it reads 13.3°C (55°F). The ground is also wet after a brief afternoon shower. Not the best conditions for the 200-meter race.

Thomas Wolfe has arrived in the stadium, accompanied by a pretty brunette. Wolfe met Martha Dodd, the daughter of the American ambassador to Germany, when he was in Berlin last year. Martha has been living with her parents in the German capital for three years. William Edward Dodd, her father, is an intellectual—a renowned historian and university professor— but not a seasoned diplomat. After a number of candidates had declined President Franklin D. Roosevelt's offer to take over the U.S. embassy in Berlin, the choice fell to Dodd, who had studied in Leipzig, spoke fluent German and was a great admirer of German culture. Ernst von Salomon, who worked for Dodd at the embassy, has quipped: "Across the pond he's considered one of the world's leading experts on German history—pre-1870, that is." It's hardly a disservice to Dodd to term him a last-ditch diplomatic solution. He felt much the same way himself. Instead of coming to Berlin, he would have vastly preferred to stay on his small farm in Virginia and write his multivolume history of the American South.

Twenty-seven-year-old Martha accompanies her father on social occasions. She enjoys hosting parties and receptions in the embassy, which always attract a colorful array of journalists, artists, military officers, diplomats and secret service agents. Much to her father's dismay, Martha has a reputation of being open to advances from the male sex. Her lovers are said to include dubious figures like Rudolf Diels, the first head of the Gestapo, as well as Hitler's friend and the Nazi Party's foreign press secretary Ernst "Putzi" Hanfstaengl. It was he who arranged a meeting between Martha Dodd and Hitler in Berlin's Hotel Kaisershof. "Hitler needs a woman," Hanfstaengl told her. "And Martha, you are that woman!" But Martha felt differently. Instead of getting involved with Hitler, she started a passionate affair with Boris Vinogradov, the first secretary at the Soviet embassy.

On this Wednesday evening in August 1936, Wolfe and Martha Dodd take their places in the diplomats' box, to which the ambassador's daughter has access. William Edward Dodd is returning from a trip to the United States and won't be back for a few days. Without her paternal chaperone, Martha is hanging all over her "Tommy," as she calls the writer. Wolfe seems to have no objections. Martha, he will later joke to a friend, fluttered around his groin like a butterfly. And for the moment, he seems to have forgotten all about his Valkyrie Thea Voelcker.

It's Wolfe's first time in the Olympic Stadium, and he's overwhelmed by it all. He tells Martha Dodd that it's the most perfect and beautiful arena he has ever seen. From his seat, Wolfe has a prime view not only of the sporting competitions but also of the more elevated Führer's box. If he cranes his neck slightly, he can make out Hitler fidgeting in his seat. The little fellow to Hitler's left, Wolfe thinks, must be Joseph Goebbels. The man in the white suit sitting behind the Führer, Martha Dodd says, is Reich Sports Leader Hans von Tschammer und Osten. And who's the old guy with no hair? Wolfe asks. That's Theodor Lewald, and he's the chairman of the German Olympic Organizing Committee. Wolfe can't help staring at Hitler. Then the loudspeakers announce the start of the next event, and he turns his attention back to what's happening in front of him.

Two Americans, two Dutchmen, a Swiss and a Canadian are competing in the final of the 200-meter race. Again the spectators fall completely silent and you can hear the proverbial pin drop. Then the starting gun fires, and immediately a cheer goes up. Jesse Owens takes an early lead and maintains his advantage until the home stretch. He breaks the tape at the finish line 4 yards ahead of his compatriot Mack Robinson. The entire stadium anxiously waits for the winning time. After a few seconds, the speaker intones: 20.7 seconds—a new Olympic record. Wolfe jumps from his seat and cries out in celebration. His jubilation is so loud, his enthusiasm at Owens's third gold medal so primeval, that people sitting nearby start to stare, half in fear and half in amusement. With the Führer's box only a few yards away, Hitler, too, can hear Wolfe's joyous whoops. Martha Dodd watches Hitler rise, bend slightly over the balustrade and search with furrowed brows for the miscreant. Wolfe is a giant of a man anyway, and you can't miss him now, standing in the diplomats' box. For a few seconds the two men's gazes meet. Hitler glares at the writer as if to punish him with his eyes, but Wolfe couldn't care less. "Owens was black as tar," he will say later, "but what the hell, it was our team and I thought he was wonderful. I was proud of him, so I yelled."

The president of the International Olympic Committee, Henri de Baillet-Latour, at the Reich government's official reception at the Berlin State Opera. "The Olympians look like the directors of a flea circus."

Thursday, 6 August 1936

REICH WEATHER SERVICE FORECAST FOR BERLIN: Gradually settled conditions as westerly winds die down. Temperatures remain cool, and skies increasingly overcast. Possible light showers in the afternoon. Highs of 18°C.

The usual hustle and bustle is already underway on Kurfürstendamm when Thomas Wolfe draws back the curtains of his hotel room and opens the window. He loves it when the noise blows into the room like a breeze. Every city has its own sound. Berlin is different to New York, and New York different to Paris. Wolfe possesses a fine ear for urban acoustics, such as the sounds of the three trams that pass by the hotel every few minutes. As Wolfe stands at his window, watching the cream-colored tramcars, it occurs to him that they are almost silent. Every now and then sparks crackle on the wires above, but that's it. The cars glide along the tracks as though part of a model railway set. There's nothing like the din created by American streetcars. Everything works perfectly in Germany, he says to himself with a smile: "Even the little cobblestones that paved the space between the tracks were as clean and spotless as if each of them had just been gone over thoroughly with a whisk broom, and the strips of grass that bordered the tracks were as green and velvety as Oxford sward."

If Wolfe leans only slightly out of his window, he can see the terrace of the Alte Klause, a popular watering hole and restaurant right next to Hotel am Zoo. He'll be meeting Heinz Ledig there in the afternoon for a couple of drinks. The new day in Berlin can get underway. Wolfe takes a deep breath as if to inhale something of the big city. There's a knock at his door. Wolfe shuts the window and calls out, "Come in!" It's the same procedure every morning. After a couple of seconds the door opens, and a room waiter pushes a gently clinking service trolley into the room. "Good morning, sir!" he says. The young man speaks in the firm voice of someone who's proud that he knows a couple of words of English, even though his German accent brings a smile to Wolfe's face. Politely bowing, the waiter transfers a plate, a coffee cup, silverware, a serviette, a pot of hot chocolate, a basket of rolls and croissants, and butter and jam from the trolley to Wolfe's table. The young man must have practiced these moves quite a lot: he always positions everything in exactly the same place. The serviette and silverware are in their appointed spot to the right of the plate, the bread basket is in the middle of the table, and next to it is the hot chocolate. It would never occur to him to place the rolls to the right of the plate or position the jam where the butter is supposed to go. The whole procedure only takes two minutes, and always concludes with a polite "If you please, sir." The waiter leaves the room as unobtrusively as he had entered it. Just before he closes the door he says, "Dank you ferry much, sur," which never ceases to amuse Wolfe.

He has finished breakfast and his morning toilet routine and is getting ready to leave the hotel, when he comes across the newspaper that Ledig gave him the day before in Café Bristol. Flipping through it, he finds the interview, but before he can start to decipher the German text, he can't help but mutter "*Sweinsgesicht*." He's appalled: Thea Voelcker's portrait makes his face look like a pig's—and upset as he is, he doesn't realize that his German now sounds as amusing as the waiter's English a short while ago. In a foul mood, he makes his way over to the Alte Klause, where Ledig is already waiting for him. Normally Wolfe always has a friendly word for the lady at reception and the bellboy who holds the door open for him. But today he passes by in stony silence. America is not amused.

In front of the Alte Klause, Wolfe scans the people sitting on the terrace, locating Ledig after a few seconds. Wolfe asks him whether he's seen Voelcker's sketch. Before Ledig can answer, he blurts out that in the considered opinion of his mother, he's the best-looking one in his family. How dare that blond woman depict him like that? He has no interest whatsoever in seeing the Valkyrie again. Gesticulating and cursing loudly, he drags Ledig by the hand in front of the reflecting glass of a shop window and asks: "Do I have a *Sweinsgesicht*?" Ledig would love to calm his friend down and reassure him that no, he doesn't have a *Sweinsgesicht*. He'd love to agree that the sketch is a bad likeness and that the blond woman is a poor artist. Last but not least, he'd love to point out that they shouldn't overdramatize the situation, that it's only a drawing and that the interview, in which Wolfe cut a good figure, is the main thing. But Mr. Wolfe doesn't want to hear any of this. Suddenly, he starts blaming the Gestapo: yes, he is convinced that Himmler or some other sinister figure must have forced Voelcker to depict him in such an unflattering fashion. You couldn't put anything past the Nazis, Wolfe rants. Maybe they're blackmailing Thea? Now Wolfe's mood changes completely. Poor Thea, he wails. What have they done to her? Wolfe insists that she be invited to the party Rowohlt is throwing tomorrow in his honor. Ledig promises that she will be, shaking his head as he does. He's used to Wolfe's mood swings, but this rapid-fire back and forth is too much for him.

As if that wasn't enough, Wolfe now wants to go to Potsdam with Ledig and his girlfriend. He's never been to Potsdam, Wolfe says in a stentorian tone, and today's the perfect day for a trip. So off they go. But the trip turns into a disaster. "He was in inner turmoil, and he took it out on us," Heinz will recall. "He showed no interest in anything, and in the end he asked us why we had dragged him along to see all this austere royal Prussian pomp."

*

Whenever the National Socialists want to impress a foreign guest, they put him up at the Hotel Eden. The establishment on the corner of Budapester Strasse and Nürnberger Strasse is one of the most luxurious and expensive places to reside in Berlin. The formal five o'clock tea on the rooftop terrace, where dance bands from Germany and abroad play their tunes, is legendary. There, waiters in white tuxedos serve tiny triangular cucumber sandwiches and opalescent cocktails. There's a minigolf course on the terrace too. Dancing or playing minigolf high above the roofs of the surrounding houses is the height of cosmopolitan swank in the summer of 1936.

Sir Henry Channon and his wife, Lady Honor Guinness, who arrived at the Eden yesterday, have just left their suite. The couple are the guests of Hitler's foreign policy adviser Joachim von Ribbentrop, who is sparing no effort to spoil them. Channon has even been assigned a personal aide-de-camp as well as a limousine with a ranking member of the SA for a chauffeur. Channon and his wife are very susceptible to such expressions of thoughtfulness.

Sir Henry – his nickname is "Chips" – is no ordinary visitor. Born in Chicago, he distanced himself from America at an early age and pledged his loyalty to the British Empire. He's been a British citizen since mid-1933. In 1935 he was elected to the House of Commons. The Tory politician also dabbles in writing. His biography of the Wittelsbach dynasty, *The Ludwigs of Bavaria*, was even translated into German and garnered positive reviews. The aristocrat is a man of culture and education, and a polished, intelligent conversationalist, full of charm and wit. Some people dismiss Channon as a perfumed dandy and a lounge lizard – an impression that's not entirely false. His marriage to Lady Guinness, twelve years his junior and from the Irish brewing dynasty, is probably nothing more than a smokescreen. It's a safe bet that Sir Henry is homosexual.

"Chips" isn't the only influential Englishman who's accepted Ribbentrop's invitation to the Olympic Games. Press magnate Harold Harmsworth, owner of the *Daily Mail* and the *Daily Mirror*, his competitor Max Aitken, owner of the *Evening Standard* and the *Daily Express*, and the highly decorated General Francis Rodd have all taken up residence in the Eden. The presence of these Englishmen in the German capital reflects Hitler's political ambition. The Führer dreams of an alliance between London and Berlin. Hitler not only wants to drive a wedge between the British and the French, he also hopes to gain the necessary leeway to carry out his plans for expansion in eastern Europe. The winds seem to be blowing in his favor. A number of British Conservatives are pleading, in the aftermath of the Depression and in the face of the crisis in Spain and the incipient civil war there, for a rapprochement with Germany. And one of the leading Germanophiles on the Thames is Sir Henry "Chips" Channon. It's no wonder that Ribbentrop has rolled out the red carpet for him and his wife.

As a so-called appeaser, Channon is the polar opposite of Robert Vansittart. The 55-year-old Sir Robert, nicknamed "Van," has served as permanent undersecretary of state for foreign affairs and is regarded as one of the most influential British diplomats. He is utterly mistrustful of the Third Reich. For many years, Vansittart has warned against Hitler, arguing that he is not a man to be trusted and that he will plunge Europe into war sooner or later. It is therefore considered a great coup that Ribbentrop has been able to lure Vansittart and his wife, Sarita, to the Berlin Olympics. No one had reckoned with that. Paris views the Vansittarts' visit with great concern.

Officially Lord and Lady Vansittart are on a private holiday. Cecil, her son from a previous marriage, is an absolute sports fanatic, Sarita states in an interview, and was particularly keen on coming to the German capital. What's more, the trip is an opportunity for her to see her sister Frances, the wife of the British ambassador to Germany, Sir Eric Phipps. Whatever the reasons given, Van's fourteen-day visit to Nazi Germany has enormous political significance. He may be officially on holiday, but the diplomat is meeting for personal talks with Hitler, German Foreign Minister Konstantin von Neurath, Rudolf Hess, Hermann Göring and Ribbentrop. Vansittart sees his counterparts from the German Foreign Ministry, receives entrepreneurs and journalists, visits the Olympic Stadium and attends numerous receptions and parties. The Vansittarts' presence in Berlin is the political talk of the town.

This afternoon, Sir Robert is scheduled to meet Goebbels. The propaganda minister is initially skeptical about his visitor. "He was an overly nervous gentleman who was clever but not particularly energetic," Goebbels will write in his diary. "We still have a lot of convincing to do with him, but without doubt he can be won over. I worked on him for an hour." At the end of their meeting, Goebbels was sure, Vansittart had been "deeply impressed...I enlightened him."

Hitler's chief ideologue, Alfred Rosenberg, claims to have been told extraordinary things by Vansittart: "Along with all Britons, he's very angry about the Negroes from the United States, as they're also putting the English to shame at the Olympics. I laughed and asked: 'Why do you have these "racial prejudices"?' With good reason Vansittart has always been and is still considered our enemy. Catholic and Francophile. Now, because of Spain, this smug gentleman seems to have some doubts about the wisdom of his views. I tried to get something out of his wife concerning rumors of Jewish ancestry. When she too bitterly complained about the black runners from the United States, I said that they represented a general danger for the USA: a pool of reserves for the Communists. And that the Jews would finance this black, Communist revolt. I was astonished when she answered: 'You're right.'"

Is this a case of trickery? Is Vansittart flattering his hosts? What is certain is that Sir Robert is genuinely impressed by what he sees in Berlin. The organization of the Games, the athletics field with its many newly constructed buildings, the athletic achievements of the German team, the brilliant receptions and the many expressions of regard, large and small, make quite an impression on the diplomat. "These tense, intense people are going to make us look like a C nation," Vansittart writes in a confidential report. Of all the Nazi leaders, he gets along best with Goebbels. "I found much charm in him—a limping, eloquent, slip of a Jacobin, 'quick as a whip,' and often, I doubt not, as cutting," opines the diplomat. Vansittart also believes that Goebbels is a calculating fellow and thus someone with whom Britain can negotiate. "My wife and I liked him and his wife at once."

The Nazis are at great pains to portray their regime as peace-loving and reliable. This illusion is so seductive that Vansittart begins to question his original stance. Perhaps he's been wrong about Hitler? What if the leaders of the Third Reich aren't really warmongers? Vansittart is pensive—and in this respect what Goebbels and Rosenberg write about the visitor from Britain is true. The regime's elaborate charm offensive seems to be paying off. But then there's an incident that allows the British diplomat to see through the carefully constructed façade. Vansittart and Ribbentrop are having lunch. They chat, eat, drink and discuss the possibilities for future cooperation. But in the middle of the conversation, Ribbentrop seems to lose control of himself for a couple of minutes and blurts out what he really thinks. Vansittart will describe this moment as follows: "He remarked on one occasion that 'if England doesn't give Germany the possibility to live,' then there would eventually be war between them, and one of them would be annihilated. I was wise enough not to ask him what he meant by it."

EXCERPT FROM THE DAILY INSTRUCTIONS OF THE REICH PRESS CONFERENCE: "We urgently warn against burdening reports on the Olympic Games with racial perspectives."

*

The Goebbelses have put their marital crisis behind them. Not for the first time, Adolf Hitler is the one who has mediated between them. "Afterward a long time with the Führer," Goebbels writes in his diary. "He praises Magda a lot. He finds her enchanting, thinks she's the best woman I could find anywhere." Hitler's concern is entirely selfish. He himself is a source of tension between the couple. The Goebbelses have a complicated triangular relationship with the Führer, in which private and public affairs are closely intermingled. When Hitler met Magda Goebbels in 1931, he seems to have fallen in love with her. After she married his paladin Goebbels, he was disappointed, which made the future propaganda minister fear for his future. "Poor Hitler!" he wrote in his diary. "I'm almost ashamed that I'm so happy. Hopefully, it won't cloud our friendship." But the very next day, Goebbels has been reassured: "He loves Magda. But he's happy for me." Goebbels concluded his diary entry with a telling sentence: "All three of us will be good to one another." An arrangement is agreed. Hitler gives his blessing to Joseph and Magda's marriage, and Goebbels allows his wife to have a platonic relationship with Hitler, which in turn brings the two men closer together. At the same time, Magda Goebbels slips into the role of the First Lady of the Third Reich. She offers Hitler advice and spends significant time alone with him. Goebbels, for his part, is completely dependent on Hitler. The Führer is not only the "boss," as Goebbels calls him in his diaries, but the secret head of the family. Goebbels seems to realize this but idealizes his relationship to Hitler to the point of kitsch. "He is very charming with me," Goebbels gushes on one occasion. "If I speak with him alone, he talks to me like a father. That's the way I like him best."

The Lüdecke affair is now dead and buried. The first week of the Olympic Games is nearing its conclusion, and this evening Goebbels will be in the spotlight at a ceremonial reception at the State Opera. The propaganda minister is very satisfied with himself. Everything seems to have returned to normal.

Nonetheless, in a few days, Joseph Goebbels will meet a woman who will completely derail his and Magda's lives.

*

"Short sentences express more than long ones, and complex sentences are alien to the German language," declares Interior Minister Wilhelm Frick in the *Berliner Lokal-Anzeiger* newspaper. "Especially today, when a word is once more a word, a command is a command, and countless facts of our modern life have to be communicated and understood quickly, concisely and unambiguously, our language must be particularly transparent." Frick was awarded his doctorate in law from Heidelberg University in 1901. Back then, a doctoral thesis wasn't necessary to obtain the title.

*

There's not a day of the Olympics that doesn't feature a distinguished reception, a fashionable party or some other social event. Every representative of the Third Reich who's anyone is hosting their own festivities during the Games. Frick invites guests to the Pergamon Museum, and Sports Leader Tschammer und Osten uses his official villa as a venue. Hitler is staging a number of receptions in the Chancellery, and Foreign Minister von Neurath is opening the doors of Charlottenburg Palace, while Berlin's police president, Wolf-Heinrich von Helldorff, uses the Prussian parliament building. The coming days will feature private receptions hosted by Göring, Ribbentrop and Goebbels, but tonight everyone is heading to the State Opera, where the Reich government and the government of Prussia are holding an official function.

In the building, preparations for the event have been going on for weeks. A purpose-built, free-standing staircase now connects the vestibule with the stalls, and this has required parts of the opera house's first and second balconies to be dismantled. Historical conservation standards are simply ignored. The loggias and boudoirs have been covered in cream-colored silk. The seating area for the audience has been raised and converted, along with the stage, into a huge banquet- and ballroom. Servants dressed in red tailcoats, knee breeches and powdered wigs are everywhere holding torches affixed to long staffs. "Foreigners are spoiled, indulged, flattered and fooled," the journalist Bella Fromm writes in her diary. "The propaganda machinery is trying to give visitors a positive impression of the Third Reich using the Olympics as camouflage." It's a classic case of bread and circuses.

Göring, in his capacity as Prussian state premier, and Goebbels, representing the Reich government, greet the waves of people arriving, which include almost the entire diplomatic corps, representatives of the Nazi Party and government, and members of the German and International Olympic Committees as well as numerous artists and guests of honor. To avoid fighting over territory, the two hosts have claimed two impressive loggias directly across from one another, where they hold court with their respective entourages. The actress Jenny Jugo can be seen at Goebbels's side, while her colleague Carola Höhn rubs shoulders with Göring. The actor Gustav Gründgens and the conductor Wilhelm Furtwängler are clever enough to visit both loggias.

The evening begins with music. After a fanfare march, played by the band of Hitler's house guard "Leibstandarte Adolf Hitler," the Berlin Philharmonic plays—what else?—the prelude to Wagner's *Meistersinger*. "Göring and I spoke," writes Goebbels in his diary. "Three minutes each. I was in top form. Every sentence hit its mark." Indeed, Goebbels's short address is a masterpiece of demagoguery and manipulation. It isn't easy for him to open his heart to foreign guests, Goebbels purrs, because a lot of people outside Germany treat whatever he says as propaganda. And yet propaganda is the furthest thing from his mind this evening. Germany, he says, has invited its guests to a "festival of joy and peace." Goebbels adds: "My impression is that this festival is perhaps more important than many of the conferences that were held in the postwar period...We want to get to know and appreciate one another and build a bridge with which to unite the peoples of Europe." Adolf Hitler's Germany as a motor for peace in Europe? Goebbels is all aglow with his own verbal gymnastics, but he reveals his true intention in his diary that day: "It was a major feat of propaganda."

*

And Hitler himself? The Reich chancellor doesn't attend the reception hosted by his government. Like everything else during the Olympics, his absence too is calculated: it is supposed to reinforce the image of the Führer who labors tirelessly and the faithful patriarch who doesn't care for leisure-time amusements and social events. Hitler's popularity reaches its zenith in the summer of 1936, penetrating deep even into the working classes. Willy Brandt, later chancellor of West Germany, who has traveled in secret from his Norwegian exile to Berlin, asks: "Why can't we admit that even people who used to vote left are impressed?"

In terms of foreign policy, up to the summer of 1936 Hitler's regime has been characterized by risk, political provocation and blackmail. In mid-October 1933, Germany announced it was quitting the League of Nations and the Geneva Convention, signaling the start of a massive rearmament initiative. Less than two years later, in mid-March 1935, Hitler introduced universal conscription, violating one of the most important provisions of the Treaty of Versailles. Instead of the agreed-upon 10,000 men, the reconstituted Wehrmacht will have a strength of 550,000 soldiers. In March 1936, Hitler achieved his greatest coup to date as he sent troops into the demilitarized Rhineland, calling this violation of international agreement a "restoration of the national honor and sovereignty of the Reich." The treaties of Versailles and Locarno both forbade Germany from stationing troops in the Rhineland, which was conceived as a buffer zone with France. According to the agreements, a German violation of this provision would be regarded as a hostile act and a disruption of world peace. In other words, the German government has given the rest of Europe a casus belli.

Hitler wagered everything on a single card in the spring of 1936, and he was correspondingly nervous. "The 48 hours after the troops marched into the Rhineland were the tensest time in my life," he will admit years later. How would Paris react? Would the result be war? Hitler later says: "If the French had pushed forward into the Rhineland, we would have had to withdraw with our tails between our legs. The military forces at our disposal would not have sufficed to put up even moderate resistance." But nothing happened. London and Paris exchanged notes of protest—and that was the end of it. Hitler has exposed the indecision of the Western European powers. He has humiliated them, leading them around by the nose in the political arena. A few weeks later, at the Berlin Olympics, he's putting forward what is presumably his best face. Following up provocations and broken promises with gestures of reserve and reliability was typical of the early years of the Nazi dictatorship. Thus the sporting festival in Berlin is the icing on the cake of the violation of international law in the Rhineland.

The Olympics are the high point of Hitler's massive hypocrisy. Despite the crass contempt he has displayed for agreements in the preceding months, he's able to assume the mantle of the peace-loving statesman. But the dictator puts down his true intentions in a memorandum sometime in August 1936. We don't know precisely when it was composed, but it's possible that Hitler is formulating his monstrous plans at the same time as Goebbels is pompously invoking peace between nations in the State Opera. In any case, Hitler already sees war with the Soviet Union as inevitable. Germany, he believes, is "overpopulated" and needs "living space." The top-secret memorandum concludes with some ominous words: "I hereby define the following tasks: (1) The German army must be ready for deployment within four years. (2) The German economy must be capable of war within four years." In three years, the Second World War will begin.

DAILY REPORT OF THE STATE POLICE OFFICE, BERLIN: "At 10:10 p.m. a Communist Party propaganda flyer measuring 3 × 8 centimeters was discovered stuck to the telephone booth on the corner of Kantstrasse and Wielandstrasse in the Charlottenburg district. In addition, an Olympic telephone directory was torn off. Flyer removed. No culprit located."

*

That evening Thomas Wolfe, Heinz Ledig and his girlfriend are still in Potsdam. They've left Sanssouci Palace and have settled down in a rustic restaurant. The three of them are devouring a platter of hearty sausage specialities, drinking beer and laughing. Wolfe's mood has apparently improved. "Still," Ledig will recall, "on the way back to the train station he stopped in front of shop windows and the reflective surfaces of advertisements for minutes at a time. Pensive and irritated, his neck comically stretched, he compared his powerful, handsome head with the '*Sweinsgesicht*' with which the lady illustrator had contradicted his mother's opinion."

EXCERPT FROM THE *BERLINER LOKAL-ANZEIGER*: "Olympics spectator from Denmark, in her thirties, widow, medium build, fashionable, domestic, nice home, seeks to marry a well-situated cosmopolitan man of similar age who lives in Berlin. Serious, personal answers only."

The publisher Ernst Rowohlt loves hearty German food. "Suddenly beads of sweat appeared on his forehead of the sort he would get after consuming several plates of pork belly with carrots."

Friday, 7 August 1936

REICH WEATHER SERVICE FORECAST FOR BERLIN: High pressure, mostly sunny, with temperatures rising throughout the day, slight winds, dry. Highs of 23°C.

There's chaos in the offices of the Rowohlt publishing house at Eislebener Strasse 7. Since early morning, boxes are being packed, moved around and stored. Piles of books covering almost every square foot of office space, which takes up a whole floor of the pre–First World War building, have been pushed to one side or fashioned into makeshift seats. Even the desks, where editors read manuscripts or correct page proofs, are being requisitioned for different uses. Ernst Rowohlt is visibly nervous. He paces throughout the various offices, searching desperately for some important papers he's unable to find in all the confusion and repeatedly barking: "Ledig, you lazybones, on the fifteenth it's the first of the month!" Heinz Ledig and the other Rowohlt employees know their boss and don't take his moods too seriously. At some point Rowohlt murmurs that this will all be the death of him. Then he leaves to have lunch. In the meantime, his secretaries Fräulein Seibert and Fräulein

Ploschitzky, the editors, the apprentice and Ledig get things straightened out.

Rowohlt isn't moving house. All the activity is in preparation for an event that is as regular as the weather, and just as disruptive: the "authors' evening" Rowohlt hosts every three months. The events are little more than boozed-up parties, although Rowohlt prefers the term "authors' evening" because that sounds more important. Plates, glasses and silverware are now piled up where, a few hours ago, manuscripts were being polished. A giant barrel of beer is at the ready in one corner, and cases of wine are stacked in another. Rowohlt orders the food from the Schlichter restaurant on nearby Augsburger Strasse. If the publisher had his way, pork belly with carrots or broad beans with bacon would be on the menu, but the boss takes pity on his guests' more delicate palates and has ordered lighter fare: salad, vegetables, ham and roast beef. But before Schlichter arrives and begins to arrange his many bowls and platters into a sumptuous buffet, Ledig and the others have to finish making space. The race is on.

*

"Sven Hedin visits a Labor Service camp," reads the headline in the *Berliner Lokal-Anzeiger*. The accompanying article contains hardly any information beyond that, but Joseph Goebbels is prepared to exploit the famous Swedish explorer's visit to Germany any way he can. In the small town of Werder near Potsdam, the Reich Labor Service has set up a work camp, Elisabethhöhe, for young women. The girls who live there, or "labor maidens," as the Nazis call them, work in gardens and fields, feed livestock and look after children. "Voluntary service for the German people" is what the Nazis call it. It's impossible to tell from the articles what Hedin and the girls discussed. In any case, the naively idealistic intellectual fits the role of the "useful idiot" to perfection. "It was a pleasure I won't forget to see and meet the girls in Elisabethhöhe," the Swedish scientist writes in the guest book. "Long live the maidens of Germany!"

Around 35 miles from Werder is the small city of Oranienburg. There, the authorities are building a camp that won't under any circumstances be shown to international guests like Hedin. There are no visitors and no guest books here. Since mid-July, prisoners from the Esterwegen concentration camp in western Germany have been clearing an expanse of forest between Oranienburg and the neighboring community of Sachsenhausen. Using primitive tools, the prisoners are felling massive trees and digging up their roots. They are also being forced to build roads, barracks and watchtowers and erect barbed-wire fences. In the coming weeks, a monstrous facility will sprout from the ground. Over the coming years, more than 200,000 people will be interned in the Sachsenhausen concentration camp that is being built in the summer of 1936.

From the very beginning, conditions there are inhumane. "At night prisoners weren't allowed to leave their barracks," one early prisoner will recall. "And because there was no latrine in the barracks, in one of the small empty rooms in between the building's two halves there were tubs from marmalade, margarine and things like that, which were often overflowing by the morning. These had to be carried more than 100 yards to the next latrine trench—a disgusting job no one did voluntarily." There's no direct water supply to the camp in August 1936, so water has to be brought in barrels from nearby Oranienburg. The helpless prisoners are subjected to their SS guards' every whim. Abuse and torture are everyday occurrences. For the most minor of infractions, prisoners have to stand at attention for hours, exposed to the elements. They're beaten with sticks and hung from hooks with their hands bound behind their backs. A fair number of them collapse physically from the hard labor and their terror of the SS. All of this is taking place 5 miles away from the city limits of Berlin—a 40-minute local train ride from the city center.

It's tempting to blame the blanket of National Socialist propaganda during the Olympic Games for the fact that Germany can build a concentration camp without attracting any international outrage and protest. But Hedin and countless other visitors from abroad could easily get a more realistic picture of Adolf Hitler's Germany in the summer of 1936. The free German press in exile, for instance, runs extensive reports about despotism and injustice in the Nazi state. In July, the *Arbeiter-Illustrierte-Zeitung* (Workers Illustrated Newspaper), published in Prague, smuggled into Germany a 16-page pamphlet with the seemingly harmless title "Get to Know Beautiful Germany: An Indispensable Guide for Every Visitor to the Olympic Games in Berlin." The cover featured an idyllic German landscape, but inside a map pinpointed almost all of the then-existing concentration camps, penal facilities and court prisons. "SA torture chambers have not been included," a foot-note read. "They are too many in number."

*

"That's Cádiz," says the captain of the *Usaramo*, pointing straight ahead. On the ship's bridge, Hannes Trautloft stares out at the coastline before him. The sun dances over the surface of the water, blinding him, so that he has to squint to make out anything at all. In the distance, he sees countless white houses, with an eighteenth-century cathedral rising from their midst. So that's Cádiz, Trautloft murmurs, the gateway to Africa. After a full week at sea, he, Max von Hoyos and the other members of the Travel Club Union will shortly begin their Spanish mission. The rest of the passengers have disembarked, and the crew is beginning to unload the hold. Trautloft watches as a crane lifts one crate after another from the belly of the *Usaramo* and deposits them on the quay. Suddenly, one big piece of cargo comes loose and plummets 30 feet to the harbor cobblestones below. When it breaks open, it reveals a gigantic, 550-pound aerial bomb. The deadly device lies there in the Spanish midday sun as if being presented on a plate. It's lucky that the bomb didn't explode and cause a massacre in the crowded harbor. "After this little incident, we sat by the radio and listened to the results from the Olympic Games in Berlin," Trautloft will remember.

After the accident at Cádiz harbor, there's no longer any doubt that the Travel Club Union consists of something other

107

than a bunch of tourists with nothing more in their luggage than summer clothing. Trautloft, von Hoyos and the others are part of a group of German soldiers who will later be known as the Legion Condor.

Spain saw a military putsch in mid-July. Under the leadership of General Francisco Franco, large parts of the Spanish army have risen up against the government of the Second Republic, which had just been elected in February. In late July, while attending the Wagner Festival in Bayreuth, Hitler decided that Germany would help transport Spanish soldiers from the colony of Morocco to the Spanish mainland. To this end, he sent sixteen German aircraft along with other military hardware to the Iberian Peninsula. Hitler saved the nationalist rebellion from defeat, leading to the start of the Spanish Civil War.

The putschists get even more support from the Italian government, while the Republic receives help from countries as diverse as the Soviet Union and Mexico. Hitler is pursuing selfish aims in Spain. With Mussolini, he wants to forge a right-wing alliance against the European Left. In addition, Spain has raw materials needed by the German arms industry. Initially, this looks like a limited political adventure. The Germans keep their activities supporting the putsch secret—nothing can be allowed to contradict the staged image of Nazi Germany as the peace-loving host of the Olympic Games. "After the Olympics, we'll get ruthless," Goebbels confides in his diary on 7 August. "Then there will be some shooting."

*

In the Olympic Village people are constantly coming and going. New athletes move in, while others, whose competitions have finished, leave the facility. Today, the Village's population has reached its peak with 4,275 athletes. In addition there are 1,241 staff who work in administration, in the kitchens, in cleaning and in medical services. All in all, 5,516 people have to be provided for, and that demands precise logistics. Decentralization is key. Every participating nation brings along its own kitchen, and some even provide the cooks, so that the broad spectrum of national preferences and tastes can be satisfied. Peruvian athletes eat as many as ten eggs a day, while athletes from the Philippines don't like cauliflower, honey or cheese. Poles love cabbage, Hungarians prefer pork, Turks eat lots of lamb, and Luxembourgers consume a conspicuous amount of vegetables. Americans devour all sorts of meat—including rare steaks before they're set to compete—but won't touch smoked fish. As side dishes, Jesse Owens and his countrymen favor baked potatoes and vegetables, and for dessert it's custard or ice cream. The Japanese eat 10 ounces of rice a day and a lot of fish—they've brought their own soy bean products with them. For Argentinians, meat is all-important. To be on the safe side, they've shipped more than 8,000 pounds of their best beef to Berlin so that they can daily enjoy *bife a la plancha* and *empanadas criollas*. For breakfast, German athletes get four eggs, milk with glucose, tomato juice, quark with linseed oil, and bread with lots of butter. They also eat lots of meat (such as minced raw liver), potatoes and vegetables bound with flour. There's no ban on alcohol in the Village, but the athletes don't drink much. Only the Italians and French refuse to do without their Chianti and *vin rouge*. Athletes from *la grande nation* in particular are discriminating diners and insist on the finest-quality filets and ragouts. The chefs at the Olympic Village cater to their every wish.

All in all, over the course of the Games, the athletes will consume 175,000 pounds of meat, 6,500 pounds of fresh fish, 20,000 pounds of pasta, 130,000 pounds of bread, 130,000 pounds of fresh vegetables, 120,000 pounds of potatoes, 5,500 pounds of coffee, 19,000 gallons of milk, 232,029 eggs, 24,060 lemons and 233,748 oranges.

NATIONAL SOCIALIST PARTY PRESS SERVICE REPORT: "Ministers Nenné and Cale serving the maharaja of Baroda (India) paid a visit to the NSDAP's Office for Racial Policy to inform themselves about the National Socialist standpoint on the race question and racial legislation in the new Germany. The two visitors were particularly interested in the laws concerning Aryans. There was agreement on basic questions."

*

The Poststadium on Lehrter Strasse is bursting at the seams. Twenty-five thousand people have turned out to watch the football quarter-final match between Germany and Norway. The German national team under coach Otto Nerz is considered one of the tournament favorites, and after the sensational 9–0 victory over Luxembourg, no one has any doubts that the Germans will beat the Norwegians as well. Looking ahead to the semifinal, Nerz has elected to rest many of his regular starters, fielding a team of reserve players instead. At exactly 5:30 p.m., referee Arthur Barton from England blows the opening whistle, and the drama begins.

In the first few minutes a defensive blunder by the Germans sends Norwegian winger Odd Frantzen clean through on goal. Alf Martinsen takes the ball, then passes it to Reidar Kvammen, who finds Magnar Isaksen. The stadium clock reads 5:37 when Isaksen puts Norway ahead 1–0. Conceding such an early goal shocks the Germans. Their defense is tentative, and in attack they're out of luck. Time is beginning to run out in the second half. In the 83rd minute, Isaksen—again assisted by Martinsen and Kvammen—scores his second goal. The 2–0 victory sends Norway through to the semis; Germany is out of the competition. "The Führer is very upset, and I can hardly control myself," Goebbels writes in his diary. "It was a real test for the nerves. The spectators went berserk. A battle never seen before. A game as a piece of mass suggestion."

As is so often the case, disappointed fans blame the coach. Nerz is fired, and his former assistant, Sepp Herberger, takes over the national team.

EXCERPT FROM THE DAILY INSTRUCTIONS OF THE REICH PRESS CONFERENCE: "The Italian gold medalist is named Georg Oberweger, not Giorgio Oberweger. Sports reporters are to take care not to de-Germanify athletes' first names."

*

Back at Eislebener Strasse, the publisher's offices have been transformed, and the guests are arriving. Rowohlt's authors' evenings are very popular, and it's not unusual that as many as a hundred people show up. Aside from Rowohlt writers, authors with other publishers, journalists, artists, scientists and businesspeople often attend, as well as various others connected with or somehow deemed useful to Rowohlt.

Tonight's guest of honor is Thomas Wolfe. Rowohlt is proud of his best-selling American author and wants to show him off to his guests. In garbled English, Rowohlt welcomes all his guests and launches into a short speech, beginning with the remark that he and his "husband" are happy everyone has come. Wolfe grins, while Ledig shakes his head in despair. He's told the publisher over and over that the word is "wife" and not "husband," but Rowohlt can't seem to get that into his head. He's sure, the publisher continues, that some day Wolfe, too, will find himself a good husband, pronouncing the word as "hosenband." After a few other malapropisms, he opens Schlichter's buffet, which the guests greedily pounce upon.

At Wolfe's request, Rowohlt has invited Thea Voelcker, with whom the author is no longer angry, Martha Dodd, and Mildred Harnack and her husband, Arvid. Mildred comes from Milwaukee, Wisconsin, and works as a literary scholar and translator in Berlin. Arvid is an economist in the service of the Reich economics minister. Wolfe likes the Harnacks, particularly appreciating Mildred's calm, collected manner, which differs so greatly from his own impulsive temperament. In fact, in a number of ways Mildred exerts an exotic attraction over the author. She is a relatively large woman with slicked-back hair and a severe look to her face. Since she invariably wears gray, she looks a bit like a nun. What Wolfe doesn't know is that for more than a year the Harnacks have been working as spies for the Soviet Union.

Strangely, the conversation at Rowohlt's authors' evenings almost never turns to literature. Mostly people talk about current social issues or politics, and of course tonight the Olympics are on everyone's minds. Wolfe is fulsome in his praise. "With no past experience in such affairs," he'll write later, "the Germans had constructed a mighty stadium which was the most beautiful and most perfect in its design that had ever been built. And all the accessories of this monstrous plant—the swimming pools, the enormous halls, the lesser stadia—had been laid out and designed with this same cohesion of beauty and of use. The organization was superb. Not only were the events themselves, down to the minutest detail of each competition, staged and run off like clockwork, but the crowds—such crowds as no other great city has ever had to cope with, and the like of which would certainly have snarled and maddened the traffic of New York beyond hope of untangling—were handled with a quietness, order, and speed that was astounding." Mildred Harnack listens to Wolfe's paean to German organizational talent without batting an eyelid, but her gaze must contain the hint of an objection, because Wolfe suddenly falls silent. You have to be very careful, Mildred begins, but before she can finish her sentence, they're joined by other guests who want to talk to the famous author. As they tell Wolfe how much they admired his last novel, *Of Time and the River*, he thinks about Mildred's warning. What was she trying to tell him?

The evening takes its course, and the mood grows ever more relaxed. Suddenly, Ernst Rowohlt's booming voice breaks into a song: "I have a little Mosel...a little Mosel." Thus far there's only been beer and schnapps, but now the publisher serves up some of his precious white wine. Every bottle that is uncorked, and there are quite a few of them, is welcomed with a joyful "I have a little Mosel..." Rowohlt is greatly amusing himself by teaching Wolfe the words to obscene German songs. One of them goes "Lick, lick, lick the cat's arse," and Rowohlt, swinging a bottle of Mosel, gleefully performs it for his star author. Wolfe has no idea what the words he parrots back mean. Ernst von Salomon will later write that like the hours "in which fraternization took place on the battlefield, these were times in which people freely admitted the deepest truth about themselves and embraced one another in a spontaneous way that lasted a lifetime."

The only one who isn't enjoying the festivities is Thea Voelcker. It's only the second time she has met Wolfe. In essence, she doesn't know him at all, and now she's being forced to watch him exchange intimacies with Martha Dodd. She's a stranger here, and she finds Mildred Harnack's stern appearance, Rowohlt's lack of inhibition and the generally boisterous mood thoroughly unsettling. They all make her feel like an intruder who doesn't belong amidst the other guests. And on top of that she increasingly comes to believe that Ledig is following her every move suspiciously. Once, their gazes cross, and she instinctively recognizes deep animosity in his eyes. At least she thinks she does. For Wolfe this is just silly. In his eyes it's typically German that two people who aren't acquainted at all should immediately mistrust one another. At least he's never encountered anything similar anywhere else in the world. But what if this is not a case of individual animosity? What if Germany has been infected with an insidious disease that has eaten its way into society and poisoned relations between people? Before Wolfe can ponder the thought, Ernst Rowohlt strikes up his Mosel song once more and tugs him back into the whirl of the authors' evening.

Dawn is breaking by the time the final guests leave Eislebener Strasse. Wolfe only has a few hundred yards to walk to his hotel. While he strolls through the streets of a city that is beginning to wake up, he can't help but think about Mildred Harnack's mysterious warning.

*

"Early to bed," Goebbels writes in his diary. "Today the Olympics are one week old. Hopefully they'll be over soon."

A glance into another world. The Ciro Bar seems to be a sanctuary from Nazi terror.

Saturday, 8 August 1936

REICH WEATHER SERVICE FORECAST FOR BERLIN: Heavy clouds, with isolated thundery showers. Somewhat cooler, with weak northwesterly winds. High of 21°C.

EXCERPT FROM THE DAILY INSTRUCTIONS OF THE REICH PRESS CONFERENCE: "It is requested that special care be taken when translating German articles and special supplements. Foreigners have repeatedly complained that the English and French versions of articles have been extraordinarily bad."

Elisabeth L. is 10 years old and, until recently, she lived with her parents in a lovely flat. The Ls owned tables, chairs, beds, wardrobes, a sideboard and many other things. There was also a small kitchen where Elisabeth's mother cooked for the family. A cross was nailed above the kitchen door—the Ls are Catholics— and pictures hung on the walls. There were cushions on the sofa, the windows had curtains, and flowers decorated the tables. The parents worked during the day while their children were at school. Most people would think that Elisabeth, her parents and her siblings were a completely average German family. Not in Interior Minister Wilhelm Frick's view. For a while now, he's trained his sights upon people like Elisabeth. For him the 10-year-old girl is an irritant, even a personal affront. As far as the Nazis are concerned, the Ls are "gypsies," and there's no place for gypsies in the Olympic city of Berlin. With his decree "For Combating the Gypsy Plague" of June 1936, Frick charged the police president in Berlin with carrying out a "gypsy manhunt day." The goal was to remove all of the capital's Sinti and Roma from their apartments or camping sites and intern them in a single spot outside the city center.

On Thursday, 16 July 1936, two weeks before the Olympic Games get underway, the initiative begins. Early in the morning, with 600 other Sinti and Roma, the Ls are arrested and taken to the outlying district of Marzahn. Marzahn has been part of Greater Berlin since 1920 but it's retained much of its original small-town character. There's a small nineteenth-century church and a picturesque school from the late Wilhelmine Empire. But not everywhere in Marzahn is so idyllic. Next to the rail line to Ahrensfelde and Werneuchen there are sewage farms where Berlin's waste water is processed. Trucks arrive constantly and pump sewage into the fields, causing a terrible stench. Here, between the train tracks, the septic fields and the municipal cemetery, is where the new Sinti and Roma camp is located. Families like the Ls who have always lived in apartment buildings suddenly find themselves deposited on a damp field. "In Marzahn there were a couple of wooden barracks and a couple of caravans with no wheels that had been propped up on stones," Elisabeth will remember. "We were taken from our lovely flat and put into an old caravan. That was where we were supposed to live, the entire family. We weren't allowed to take anything with us from our flat. Even if we had been, there were no flats in Marzahn where we could have put our things. There was nothing."

Living conditions in the camp are catastrophic, with the 600 inmates having only two toilets at their disposal. Immediately after the camp opens, there are outbreaks of skin diseases and infections. The inmates are completely abandoned, not provided for in the slightest. The Sinti and Roma have to buy their food from local shops. The camp has no source of drinking water, so Elisabeth and the others are forced to walk a mile and fetch water from Marzahn town center. When they arrive there, they're often met by waves of hatred. Many shopkeepers refuse to sell them anything but scraps. Elisabeth becomes familiar with a completely unknown sensation: hunger.

In August 1936, the camp isn't yet fenced, but local police diligently monitor everyone who comes and goes. People are only allowed to leave the camp to go to work and buy food. Internees are required to check in and out of the place, and there's a curfew at 10 p.m. Anyone violating the rules faces rubber truncheons and guard dogs. "Basically we lived in constant fear," another of the internees later recalls. "We were afraid of the police, the local residents, anyone and everyone."

The Olympic Stadium is 15 miles away from Marzahn. Elisabeth has heard that many happy people from all over the world are celebrating a gigantic festival—a festival of friendship and peace between nations. She doesn't experience any of that in her rickety caravan. The camp is located on the other side of the city, in an out-of-the-way location where no tourists ever stray to share their celebrations with a little girl. Elisabeth doesn't feel like celebrating, anyway. She doesn't fully understand what "peace between nations" means, but if it entails innocent people being taken from their homes and dragged to a place like this, it can't be anything good.

Elisabeth wants to go back home with her parents to their flat. She wants to sleep in her own bed again. Little does she know that things are about to get much, much worse for herself and her family.

*

In the Stadium am Gesundbrunnen, the last football quarter-final begins at 5:30 p.m.: Austria versus Peru. Although the stadium has a capacity of 36,000, only around 5,000 people turn out for the match. The duel between the Austrians and the Peruvians obviously hasn't caught the popular imagination. Perhaps that's because it's the first time the national team of the Andean nation is taking part in a tournament outside South America. Peru is an unknown quantity, but opponents underestimate them at their peril. In the round of sixteen, the Peruvians dispatched Finland 7–3.

After telling both teams' captains that he expects a fair match, the Norwegian referee, Thoralf Kristiansen, punctually blows the opening whistle. After the 90 minutes the score is 2–2, meaning extra time. It's a festival of the unprecedented. After Kristiansen disallows three goals in the first half, Peruvian fans storm the pitch and attack an Austrian player in the second. The referee later testifies that one of the pitch invaders had a revolver in his hands, and the British newspaper the *Daily Sketch* will write that the roughly 1,000 Peruvians carried "iron bars, knives and even a pistol." The stadium descends into anarchy. Kristiansen is completely at a loss—he's never experienced anything like this. Before he can restore order and suspend the match, the Peruvians score two more goals. The scoreboard reads 4–2, but the Austrians immediately lodge a protest. And they succeed. Football's world governing body, FIFA, which has organized the Olympic tournament, nullifies the result and orders a replay at which spectators are banned. *Tu felix Austria*, as the old saying goes—Austria, it's your lucky day!

And the Peruvians? They smell a conspiracy. Nazi Germany has pressured FIFA to cheat Peru's national team, which includes five black players, of victory. The whole story of the pitch invasion, they say, is just a cock and bull story. "An embarrassing incident with Peru," notes Goebbels in his diary. "But Germany is completely innocent." IOC President Henri de Baillet-Latour also dismisses the Peruvian allegations as nonsense. Responsibility for the decision to replay the match rests entirely with FIFA, he declares in an interview. Germany isn't even a member of that body.

The Peruvians boycott the replay, ending their participation in the Olympics, and leave Berlin. They're joined in a show of solidarity by Colombia, whose team of five athletes has yet to win a single event. Austria move on uncontested into the football semifinals, and the 1936 Olympics have their first scandal.

*

Der Angriff, the daily newspaper of the NSDAP in Berlin, publishes its thoughts on a new Olympic event: "Basketball is on the Olympic Games program for the first time and is still something of a 'dark art' for many of us here in Germany. That's a shame, because this sport is not only good physical exercise. It's full of competitive ups and downs and always offers enough possibilities to captivate not just the players but spectators too."

*

Eduard Duisberg, the artistic director of the Scala, Berlin's famous variety theater, is clearly a very practical fellow. The city is crawling with Americans, he thinks, so let's offer them some American entertainment. Under the rather grandiose title "Marvelous World," Duisberg is presenting a large-scale, deliberately international revue for the Olympic month of August. Along with the always popular Scala girls, a group of twenty-four scantily clad female dancers, the bill features a conspicuous number of American artists: the dancer Mathea Merryfield from California ("America's prettiest chorus girl"); the diminutive mime artist Fred Sanborn, who also plays a mean xylophone; the Four Trojans, a quartet of acrobats performing dizzying tricks at dizzying heights; and Jack and George Dormonde, two slapstick artists on unicycles. The dancer Dinah Grace— despite the sound of her name—is not an American. Her real name is Käthe Gerda Johanna Ilse Schmidt and she's an officer's daughter from Berlin.

Twice a day, at 5:15 and 8:45 p.m., the actors and cabaret artists Georg Alexander, Anita Spada and Trude Hesterberg introduce the show. As expected, the Berlin press is full of praise—the Nazis want to show that Germany is also a world leader in variety theater. A reporter for the *Berliner Lokal-Anzeiger* probably unintentionally displays some political humor when he gives his article about the current Scala season a headline that could apply to the entire Olympic Games: "Marvelous World of Illusions."

*

Beer and weapons. If you were to ask Clara and Paul von Gontard how they came by their enormous personal fortune, they would have to say "beer and weapons." People don't ask multimillionaires like the Gontards such trivial questions, of course, but the fact remains that they're among the richest people in Germany. Clara is the daughter of brewing magnate Adolphus Busch from the German-American beer dynasty Anheuser-Busch. Adding to those family millions, she married Paul von Gontard, who has been the director of the German Weapons and Munitions Works for over twenty-five years and sits on the boards of a number of leading German companies. Wherever there are military conflicts in the first third of the twentieth century,

Baron von Gontard profits. To keep business simple, he doesn't discriminate between customers, selling his wares to anyone with the means to buy them. Thus, Gontard is always on the winning side. Commissions—7 percent of net profit—keep rolling in.

Clara and Paul's 26-year-old daughter Lillyclaire is the 1930s equivalent of an "It girl." When Miss Lillyclaire married the merchant Werner Schieber in December 1930, the tabloids celebrated the event as that year's dream wedding. The only critical note came from the journalist Carl von Ossietzky, who wrote that Gontard "gave his daughter a wedding that cost a rumored 40,000 marks (100,000 dollars) and featured the sort of ostentatious luxury favored by people with bad taste after they study swank magazines." But despite the spectacular wedding, the marriage didn't last long, and her father seems to have handpicked Lillyclaire's next husband: the strapping Nazi and successful entrepreneur Bernhard Berghaus, who has excellent connections with both the regime and Himmler's SS. Berghaus owns a number of metalworking companies, and in the summer of 1936 he founds the Berlin-Lübeck Machine Factory, which will play a leading role in the rearmament of the Third Reich. In Lübeck, the firm manufactures the standard rifle of the German army, the Karabiner 98k, earning untold sums of money. Berghaus is just the sort of fellow Paul von Gontard originally envisioned his daughter marrying: wealthy, ambitious and completely unscrupulous in business. That wedding took place in 1935.

If there's any such thing as Third Reich high society, it's the Gontards. The family regularly hosts elegant receptions in their pompous villa on Bendlerstrasse in the Tiergarten district. But during the Olympics, Clara and her daughter can most often be seen in the Ciro Bar. Along with the Quartier Latin and the Sherbini Bar, this small establishment on Rankestrasse is one of the most fashionable nightspots in Berlin, frequented by film stars, diplomats, politicians and businesspeople. Many of the patrons come for the excellent jazz music. The pianist of the Ciro Bar's house band recalls: "We had a certain amount of license because we attracted an international crowd, and they wanted the same repertoire as they heard abroad. We had trouble keeping up with the latest trends. We had a couple of patrons from embassies who would sing or whistle tunes currently popular in America, Britain or elsewhere. We'd then write them down, arrange and play them. The audience was always enthusiastic. They were amazed that we were so up to date."

The bar consists of two connected rooms. The bar area proper is done up in the arabesque style that is all the rage in the mid-1930s. There are Egyptian hieroglyphics on the walls, and the ceiling is a golden dome. The restaurant section is located down a couple of steps and decorated in terracotta. There Clara von Gontard and Lillyclaire Berghaus always sit at the same table, drinking nothing but soda water. They don't order anything to eat either, although the food is excellent. The turtle soup à la Ciro, refined with dry sherry and a few drops of cognac, is a must for gourmands, and there are visitors who make their way to Rankestrasse just to try it. But not Clara and Lillyclaire. They stick to water. Having millions in the bank but drinking only sparkling water in an expensive restaurant—can it get any more understated?

Whenever Clara visits the Ciro Bar, Ahmed is never far away. Ahmed is the bar's owner and Clara's lover—or at least he used to be. Ahmed Mustafa Dissouki is his full name: Ahmed is his first name, Mustafa his family name, and Dissouki the name of his grandfather. That's the way people are named in his native Egypt, but in Berlin everybody knows him as just Ahmed. Thirty years of age, he's a fine figure of a man: tall, with dark curly hair and an abundance of charm. Like Leon Henri Dajou and Mustafa El Sherbini, Ahmed began his career in Berlin as a dance partner offering his services to wealthy ladies in the cosmopolitan Femina Bar. One of them was Clara von Gontard, who fell head over heels for him. In January 1932, using Clara's money, Ahmed opened the Ciro Bar and a bit later a summer restaurant in the outlying Kladow district of the city overlooking the River Havel. Both establishments were successes from the moment the first bottles of champagne were uncorked. The only dark spot on Clara's horizon is the fact that Hedda Adlon is financing the Quartier Latin for her favorite gigolo Leon Henri Dajou. Mrs. Adlon and Mrs. von Gontard are mortal enemies, constantly seeking to outdo one another with splendid parties, luxury automobiles, elegant evening dresses and other trappings of being married to millionaires.

The Nazis initially have nothing against the goings-on in the Ciro Bar. On the contrary, they're happy they have such a cosmopolitan bar to show to their international guests during the Olympics. But that will soon change.

DAILY REPORT OF THE STATE POLICE OFFICE, BERLIN:
"Around 7 p.m. on 8 August 1936 at the field hockey stadium, an unknown person smashed a bottle filled with a liquid chemical (pyridine) in the south stands. The smell caused vomiting and coughing. Investigations into the identity of the perpetrator have yielded no results."

*

Glenn Morris takes a blanket and spreads it out on the grass playing surface of the Olympic Stadium. Then he wraps himself in a second blanket and lies down on the first one. Finally, he covers his head with a towel. Morris lies completely still. If you didn't see the towel moving slightly up and down over his mouth, you might think he'd stopped breathing. Perhaps he's asleep. If he's not, perhaps he's thinking about his girlfriend Charlotte, whom he met at college in Colorado. The two are planning to get married next year. The 24-year-old Morris is a decathlete, and in between events he lies on the grass like a mummy, sleeping or dreaming of his fiancée, and gathering his strength for the next discipline. That's what he did yesterday, on the first day of the decathlon competition, and that's what he's doing today. Competing, then resting. And it's hard to argue with Morris's routine. With six events completed, the last one being the 110-meter high hurdles, he's leading the competition. If things continue like that, he'll win the gold medal.

Sometime during the afternoon, after three further events, the German decathlete Erwin Huber goes over to him, bends down, taps him on the shoulder and asks if he can introduce Leni Riefenstahl. Riefenstahl has insisted on meeting Morris: perhaps he'd feel like posing for a few photos for her. Morris takes the towel from his head, frees himself from the blanket and stands up. "How are you?" he asks, almost bashfully, shaking Riefenstahl's hand. "It was an unbelievable moment of the sort I'd never experienced," Riefenstahl will later recall. "I tried to suppress the feelings bubbling up within me and forget what had happened." She's completely blown away by Morris' perfectly toned body, his handsome face and his soulful eyes. As if struck by lightning, she stammers a couple of polite words, but then the start of the next and final discipline is announced. The 1,500-meter race begins at 5:30 p.m. Morris records a time of 4 minutes, 33 seconds, for which he's awarded 595 points. That brings his total to 7,900 points, good enough not just for the gold medal but also for a new world record. Silver goes to Morris's compatriot Bob Clark, and another American, Jack Parker, takes bronze.

"Attention, attention!" the stadium announcer barks out. "*Cérémonie olympique protocolaire…* Medal winners' ceremony." The three Americans mount the podium, and the "Star-Spangled Banner" plays. Morris, Clark and Parker salute, bringing their right hands to their temples. Riefenstahl wants to capture this moment on film, but her cameraman looks at the exposure reader and waves his hands. The sun is setting, and it's too dark to take good footage. Instead of looking through her camera lens, Riefenstahl follows what's going on a few yards away from the playing field. She only has eyes for Morris. After the ceremony, the two approach one another. She congratulates him on his victory, but Morris isn't interested in small talk. "He took me in his arms," Riefenstahl will remember, "ripped open my blouse and kissed me on the breast in the middle of the stadium in front of 100,000 spectators."

*

If diplomacy is the art of keeping your cards close to your chest, then Sir Eric Phipps is a very skilled diplomat. In her memoir *My Years in Germany*, Martha Dodd will write that his face would have remained completely impassive if someone had come up to him and said, "Your grandmother has just been murdered." "As if the words had never made it to his ears," Dodd continues, "he would have said with the somewhat clipped, soft voice of an Englishman with a potato in his mouth: 'You don't say. Very interesting.'" Phipps is almost immune to humor, and for the past three years he's been Britain's ambassador to Germany. Together with his brother-in-law Robert Vansittart, he's one of the Third Reich's biggest detractors among the British diplomatic ranks. But tonight he is once again concealing his antipathy behind a mask of professional British politeness. The British embassy on Wilhelmstrasse is hosting a gala dinner in honor of the German regime, followed by a party for over 1,000 invited guests. "It's all so tiresome," Goebbels complains to his diary. "First a small meal, then a gigantic reception. A thousand people, a thousand bits of chatter."

Henry "Chips" Channon, who's also been invited to the party, doesn't enjoy the evening either, which has to do with the fact that Robert and Sarita Vansittart are there. "The Vansittarts are notoriously pro-French," he writes in his diary, "and I hope their Berlin visit will go some way to neutralize their prejudice." Chips, who never misses out on a Berlin party and keeps a meticulous record of social events, has nothing good to say about Sir Eric's festivities, writing: "The Embassy reception was boring, crowded and inelegant."

Adolf Hitler visits the Olympic Stadium every day. But he doesn't always like what he sees from his VIP box.

Sunday, 9 August 1936

REICH WEATHER SERVICE FORECAST FOR BERLIN: A high pressure system moves in, but skies are still cloudy. Warmer weather during the day, slight circling breeze, isolated thunderstorms. Highs of 23°C.

Peter Joachim Fröhlich is 13 years old and a smart lad. He attends the Goetheschule on Münstersche Strasse in the Wilmersdorf district, a progressive school that places great emphasis on modern languages and the natural sciences. Ten-year-olds begin learning French, and two years later have the option of taking either English or Latin. Peter's parents want him to learn English, but on the advice of his headmaster, Dr. Quandt, he chooses Latin. Peter is a good student, but his true passion is sport. He's a fanatical supporter of the local football club, Hertha Berlin, which in his eyes is the best team in the world. When he goes to the stadium, he chants the club chants and sings the club songs along with all the other fans. So it's no surprise that all Peter has been able to think about for weeks is the Olympics. His father, Moritz, shares his love of sport. The tickets to the Olympic Stadium, which Moritz acquired some time ago on a business trip to Budapest, are displayed like trophies on a sideboard in the family living room. Whenever Peter walks past, he thinks about the upcoming Games, imagining himself sitting next to his father in the stadium and cheering on the athletes.

Moritz Fröhlich earns his living as a salesman and is a supporter of the Social Democratic Party; Peter's mother works in her sister's haberdashery. The family used to be Germans. But since Hitler came to power, they're Jews. "You can become a Jew in three ways," Peter will write years later in a book. "By birth, by conversion and by government decree. At birth, my Jewishness was pretty marginal, but after 30 January 1933, I found myself forced into the third category." Jewishness is a foreign concept to the Fröhlichs. The parents stopped going to the synagogue a long time ago and describe themselves as committed atheists. "Jewish identity" or "Jewish consciousness" means nothing to them. They refuse to be baptised or to convert to Christianity because that would be tantamount to "swapping one superstition for another." Despite his youth, Peter Joachim Fröhlich, who had no bar mitzvah and enjoys going to watch Hertha Berlin on Jewish high holy days, feels he's being forced to play a role that's alien to him. But by September 1935 at the latest, with the promulgation of the Nuremberg Laws, which legally define who's Jewish and enact a whole range of anti-Semitic measures, the Fröhlichs begin to realize that, sooner or later, they will have to leave their homeland. During the Olympic Games, it's as though things have returned to normal for a short time. For sixteen days, the Nazis suspend publication of *Der Stürmer*, the weekly organ of anti-Semitic hatred, and take down the issues displayed in public spaces, which Peter normally has to walk by on his way to school.

Because their tickets come from a Budapest allocation, in the Olympic Stadium Peter and Moritz Fröhlich find themselves sitting in the middle of a group of enthusiastic Hungarian fans. Their section is across from the Führer's box, so that Peter can't help but see what's going on there. He'd like to avert his eyes, but that's impossible. So these are the men, he thinks, who have taken it upon themselves to destroy the lives of so many people? Peter finds the sight of Hitler repulsive and thinks the portly Göring, festooned with medals and pomp, simply looks ridiculous. Goebbels reminds him of an evil dwarf from a fairy tale his mother used to read to him when he was little. Looking at Germany's highest dignitaries, he remembers the popular joke that people used to tell each other surreptitiously: "What does a real Aryan look like? He's blond like Hitler, tall like Goebbels and thin like Göring."

Peter has been looking forward to this Sunday for many weeks. It's shortly after 3 p.m. when the stadium announcer calls out one of Peter's favorite disciplines: the 4 × 100 meter relay. To be precise, Peter's favorite events are those in which the Americans are much better than the Germans. The United States is considered unbeatable in the 4 × 100 relay. They've only lost the event once—at the 1912 Olympics in Stockholm. As the runners take their positions, a hush falls over the arena. The Argentinians have the inside lane, then come the Germans, the Dutch, the Americans, the Italians and all the way to the outside in lane six, the Canadians. Peter is only interested in lane four. He cranes his neck in order to see the other side of the oval track and can make out Jesse Owens, who will run the first leg, followed by Ralph Metcalfe, Foy Draper and Frank Wykoff.

What Peter doesn't know is that there were heated discussions within the American team about who would be allowed to run the relay. Marty Glickmann and Sam Stoller assumed for a long time that they would be running, but coach Lawson Robertson decided against them and in favor of Owens and Metcalfe, breaking his usual habit of using fresh runners for the relays. Glickmann and Stoller, who are both Jewish, suspect an anti-Semitic plot. They think that American sports officials put pressure on Robertson to take them out of the action in an attempt to cozy up to the Nazis. It's understandable that the disappointed athletes might think this, but in reality the logic behind the coach's decision is simple: Robertson wants to prevent a surprise German victory at all costs and doesn't believe he can do this without his strongest runners, Owens and Metcalfe.

Just before the start, the man in the white apron, Franz Miller, inspects his wind gauge one last time. In athletics, world records are not recognized if they are aided by tailwinds of more than 6 feet a second. Miller has reassuring news. The wind is blowing from the side at a speed of 5 feet a second: the conditions are perfect. The start is only seconds away and 100,000 spectators hold their breath. Then the starting gun is fired, and Owens sprints out to an expected lead before handing over the baton. Metcalfe and Draper increase that advantage, and down the home stretch the American team is more than 10 yards ahead of its nearest competitors. Wykoff crosses the finishing line in 39.8

seconds—a new world record! The Italian team comes in second with a time of 41.1 seconds, and one second behind the Germans finish third. Frenetic cheers go up, and many of the spectators rub their eyes. Is it already over? It feels as though the sound of the starting gun has only just died away. The speed of the U.S. team seems supernatural.

Jesse Owens has done it again. With four gold medals, he's become by far and away the biggest star of the Games—and Peter Fröhlich's personal hero. Peter and his father feel safe and protected from prying eyes in the Hungarian supporters' section and can cheer on the Americans with all their hearts. At the medal ceremony, Peter takes to his feet and hums along with the "Star-Spangled Banner." Thanks to Dr. Quandt, he knows Latin but no English, so he doesn't understand the words: "O say, can you see..." But he intuitively understands that the song is a hymn to freedom.

It's the final day of the athletics competitions at the Olympics, and only 15 minutes later, at 3:45 p.m., there's a further highlight: the women's 4 × 100 meter relay. Germany, Britain, America, Canada, the Netherlands and Italy are in the final, but the German women are as highly favored as the American men were earlier on. The result seems to be a foregone conclusion. After the spectacular American victory, Hitler is pacing around in his box, rubbing his hands in anticipation at Germany getting its revenge. Across the arena sits Peter Fröhlich, who doesn't share the Führer's excitement and expects his worst nightmare: a German victory. The referee fires the starting gun, and the first German runner, Emmy Albus, streaks past the competition.

Käthe Krauss takes the baton and increases Germany's lead, before making the hand-off to Marie Dollinger. Peter can't bear to watch. Germany's advantage seems unassailable. Suddenly Moritz Fröhlich jumps up from his seat and cries: "The girl's dropped the baton!" Peter too now realizes what has happened: the Germans have botched the final handover. Anchor Ilse Dörffeldt can't hold on to the baton. The American Helen Stevens crosses the finishing line in first place.

Everyone in the Führer's box is disappointed. Hitler shakes his head in irritation and smacks his knee with his hand. "We've had bad luck," Goebbels writes in his diary. "The girls were all broken up. The Führer consoled them. But the whole stadium was sad." The whole stadium? One 13-year-old boy is beside himself with glee. Even decades later, Peter Fröhlich will describe the misfortune of the German women's relay team as "one of the greatest moments in my life."

DAILY REPORT OF THE STATE POLICE OFFICE, BERLIN: "It has become known that a Hitler Youth patrol brought the Jews Heinrich Frankenstein, born 24 November 1918 and residing in Wörtherstrasse, and Willi Klein, born 12 December 1919 and residing at Wörtherstrasse 30, into the police station after they tried to beg cigarettes from an Argentinian in the Lustgarten. When the patrol approached, the Jews said to the foreigner: 'This is Germany's youth.'"

*

At home in Carwitz, some 62 miles north of Berlin, the writer Hans Fallada is recovering from the latest of his many stays in a detoxification clinic. A few months previously, in mid-May, he was released from Dr. Schauss's Heidenhaus sanatorium in Zepernick near Berlin. Fallada has been suffering from depression and anxiety for years and is addicted to alcohol and morphine. By August 1936, he has got himself together sufficiently to begin work on a new novel. It will be called *Wolf Among Wolves*.

*

Athletics is the most prestigious set of Olympic disciplines, and after the final event, the U.S. team leads the medals table with fourteen gold, seven silver and four bronze. Germany is a distant second with five gold, four silver and seven bronze medals. The Americans have good reason to celebrate their achievements. That evening, the high jumpers Cornelius Johnson and Dave Albritton, together with sprinter Ralph Metcalfe, leave the Olympic Village and head into town. Their destination is the Sherbini Bar on Uhlandstrasse. The three athletes have put on their best attire, but their light-colored suits don't meet the dress code. Mustafa El Sherbini places great emphasis on proper evening wear, and that means dark suits. But for such VIP guests, he's willing to make an exception—unlike in the Quartier Latin, in the Sherbini Bar people aren't more Catholic than the pope—and welcomes the three Americans. No doubt Mustafa's motivations are partly selfish. A visit by world-class athletes has to be good for business.

Johnson, Albritton and Metcalfe's buddy "Mickie" is waiting for them. Mickie's real name is Herb Flemming, and he's American too, although he has lived in Berlin for more than a year. Because he speaks decent German, he's done some translating for the American team in the past few days, which is how he met the three athletes. Flemming is not a professional interpreter, nor does he have anything to do with the Olympic Games. He's what Sherbini and Yvonne Fürstner call a "special attraction"—something out of the ordinary for their customers.

Flemming and his musical combo have had a residency in the Sherbini Bar since the spring. Along with Flemming, who plays trombone and sings, the core of the group consists of Rudi Dumont (trumpet), Franz Thon (clarinet), Fritz Schulz-Reichel (piano), Max Gursch (guitar) and E. Wilkens (bass). As often as his duties in the bar allow it, Sherbini himself sits down behind the drums. This combo is considered by more than a few connoisseurs to be the best swing band in Germany. Evening after evening, they make jazz history. "He was the most unbelievable trombone player I've ever heard," one contemporary remarked of Flemming. "He had a lip vibrato, a tone on the trombone, like a top cellist." On the group's music stands you'll find the latest songs from American film musicals like *Top Hat* and *Broadway Melody of 1936*. Yvonne has her sister purchase the sheet music from a London store. No one in the Sherbini Bar cares that Irving Berlin, the composer of *Top Hat*, and Arthur Freed, the lyricist for *Broadway Melody*, are Jewish. On the contrary, patrons love dancing to catchy songs like "No Strings" and "Cheek to Cheek."

The other special attraction currently in residence are the Mackey Twins, a step-dancing duo. The twins from the United States performed in the bar the preceding year, and business was good. Sherbini no doubt has a nose for this sort of thing. He knows which acts audiences like. But what really makes Herb Flemming and the Mackey Twins into sensations in Nazi Berlin is the fact that they're black. The moral guardians at the Nazi hate rag *Berliner Herold* spew bile at the Sherbini Bar, denigrating it as a venue "where niggers step-dance to hot jazz!" Yet despite such attacks in the press, Flemming and the Mackeys have been able to perform unhindered for quite some time. In early 1936 Flemming had a problem with his work permit, but after intervention from U.S. Ambassador Dodd, he immediately received the necessary documents. Flemming will later claim to have played for Hitler in the Reich Chancellery, although there's not a shred of evidence that this was the case.

Tonight, no one in the Sherbini Bar is wasting a thought on Hitler and the Nazis. The mood is buoyant, and politics are a world away. Johnson, Albritton and Metcalfe celebrate their triumphs, and the booze flows like water. On the face of it, it's business as usual. Flemming and his combo play their red-hot swing music, Sherbini flits through the establishment with a smile on his face, and Aziz de Nasr, watching from the sidelines, pines after Yvonne Fürstner, who stays close to her rubber truncheon. But stormclouds are gathering over Uhlandstrasse. Fürstner has no idea that the Gestapo have her in their sights.

DAILY REPORT OF THE STATE POLICE OFFICE, BERLIN: "In the exhibition halls on Kaiserdamm, various toilet doors have been scrawled with slogans hostile to the state concerning the racial question."

*

Mrs. Volland lives in a respectable building. Her neighbors include the elderly baron and estate owner Michael von Medem, the jeweler Joachim Mersmann and the orthopedist Dr. Gustav Muskat, who specializes in treating flat-footedness. Franz Bannasch owns a fashion boutique, and the worthy Mrs. Aven is a matron at the Erikahaus nursing home. All of these people live at Kurfürstenstrasse 124, on the corner of Courbièrestrasse. Mrs. Volland occupies the largest flat: ten rooms at the front of the building cost her 255 reichsmarks (650 dollars) in rent every month. The lady lives alone. Obviously she likes her space. The owner of the building is a Spanish national named Maurice Gattengo. Señor Gattengo is Jewish, so understandably he prefers to give Germany a wide berth. At present, he's living in Cairo.

The ground floor contains an Italian restaurant called the Taverne, which is run by Willy and Maria Lehmann. The Taverne consists of three connecting rooms and is always full to capacity. Diners sit at small tables, packed close together, so it's easy to strike up a conversation with those around you. There's a piano in the main dining room, but it's rarely played, since people prefer talking. In the lively din any music would hardly be heard anyway. Travel guides tout the Taverne as a restaurant for celebrities. That's because of Willy Lehmann's former job: before he opened the establishment, he was the production manager at Stern-Film. Lehmann knows many actors and actresses, and they've become Taverne regulars. Ever since the tabloids reported that stars like Olga Tschechowa frequent the place in Kurfürstenstrasse, Lehmann no longer needs to advertise. Along with film stars, foreign journalists also like to dine there. William Shirer from the United News Service, Louis B. Lochner of the Associated Press, Sigrid Schulz of the *Chicago Tribune* and others are part of a group that is present almost every evening. Most of the time, the reporters arrive after 10 p.m., once they've cabled their articles to America. Not infrequently, they don't leave until 2 or 3 a.m. Sometimes they are accompanied by friends and acquaintances like Martha Dodd or Mildred and Arvid Harnack. They talk over the news of the day, drink, laugh and dig into Maria Lehmann's spaghetti and excellent *vitello*.

Tonight, when Thomas Wolfe and Mildred Harnack enter the restaurant, there's no one at the journalists' regular table, so they take a seat at a smaller table for two. They can always move if Shirer and some of the others show up. Wolfe has unpleasant memories of the Taverne, he confides to Mildred. During his last visit to Berlin, he went out for a night on the town with Heinz Ledig and some other acquaintances. At an advanced hour, they ended up in the Taverne, where Martha Dodd was drinking a glass of wine with a fellow they didn't recognize. Wolfe, Ledig and the rest of the party sat down at the neighboring table, but Dodd showed no signs of inviting them over. Indeed, she seemed embarrassed by their presence. Wolfe and Ledig were taken aback by Martha's impolite behavior. Later they were told that her companion was Donald S. Klopfer, the founder of the publishing company Random House, a Jew who adamantly refused to sit down at the same table with Germans. Ledig was terribly insulted. How could a foreigner not distinguish between Germans and Nazis, as everyone in Germany did? Ledig couldn't let this rest. He stood up, approached Klopfer, introduced himself and demonstratively extended his hand. Taken off guard, the American returned Ledig's greetings, and the two men briefly made some forced conversation. But the mood was ruined.

Even a good year later, Wolfe still finds Klopfer's treatment of Ledig utterly unacceptable. Wolfe doesn't like Jews, he admits without any sense of shame. Before long he's discussing a topic that has been on his mind for quite some time: freedom of speech. "We say in America that we are free to speak and write and think as we please, but this is not true," he tells Mildred. "We also say that in Germany people cannot speak and write and think as they please. This is also not true. People are free to speak and write and think some things in Germany that they are not free to speak and write in America. For example, in Germany you are free to speak and write that you do not like Jews and that you think Jews are bad, corrupt and unpleasant people. In America, you are not free to say this."

Mildred stares at Wolfe in disbelief. He can't be serious. Surely he doesn't believe that German anti-Semitism is nothing but an expression of free speech? Mildred's face has the same expression she wore a couple of days ago at Rowohlt's party. There's something disapproving in her eyes. She stares at Wolfe like a governess eying a misbehaving child. You must be very careful, she says. What follows is a political eye-opener for Wolfe. Mildred tells him about the state-organized boycott of Jewish businesses shortly after the Nazis came to power, the Law for the Restoration of the Professional Civil Service, which removed Jews from all government posts, and the book burnings. In great detail, Mildred explains the Nuremberg Laws, which were decreed the previous year and completely exclude Jews from society. Mildred has grown visibly agitated. Is Wolfe familiar with *Der Stürmer*? she asks. Does he know about how the newspaper's editor, Julius Streicher, and his cronies constantly incite popular hatred of Jews? Is he aware that there are restaurants and shops with signs in their windows reading "Jews not wanted here"?

Finally, Mildred uses a term that Wolfe hasn't heard until this evening: concentration camp. Does Wolfe know, she asks, that the German government is interning Jews, Social Democrats, Communists, homosexuals and anybody who thinks differently in prison camps? Wolfe shakes his head. Both of them fall silent. Their silence probably lasts only a few seconds, but they seem to Wolfe like half an eternity. As though he's endured a dressing-down for some youthful prank, he looks at Mildred sheepishly. She smiles a bitter smile. "Only the horses are happy in Germany," she says, citing a favorite saying of William Dodd. Wolfe cracks a wan smile. In an age in which most writers are taking a political stand, he is aware of his lack of political commitment, he tells Mildred, who nods understandingly. That evening, cracks begin to appear in Wolfe's idealized image of Germany. Something inside him is beginning to change.

In the popular Residenz Casino, patrons are able to call one another on telephones at the table: "Excuse me, dear lady, would you happen to be ..."

Monday, 10 August 1936

REICH WEATHER SERVICE FORECAST FOR BERLIN: Warm weather continues, with gradually increasing clouds, isolated thunderstorms and moderate easterly winds. Highs of 25°C.

If you exit the Sherbini Bar and walk 300 yards north up Uhlandstrasse, you'll get to Steinplatz, a square built in 1885 that is part of the Charlottenburg district. In the 1920s, waves of Russian émigrés who had fled the revolution in their homeland moved into the luxurious apartment buildings between Kurfürstendamm to the south and Bismarckstrasse to the north, causing Berliners to jokingly rename Charlottenburg "Charlottengrad." The building at Steinplatz 4 is a particularly nice example of Wilhelmine architecture. Designed and built in 1907 by August Endell in art nouveau style, it's home to the Hotel am Steinplatz. In the summer of 1936, Erna Zellermayer runs the establishment. No one calls her Mrs. Zellermayer: guests and employees alike refer to her exclusively as "Mrs. Director."

Zellermayer was only 37 when her husband Max died three years ago. Back then she didn't know the first thing about the hotel business, but from one day to the next, she had to take over the place—and in difficult economic times, to boot. Back in the 1920s, the hotel became a popular place of refuge for Russian aristocrats. Many a grand duke rented a whole floor of the hotel for months at a time for himself and his servants. Among the regulars were also a number of wealthy Jewish ladies who felt unable to keep house on their own and wanted to live out their widowhood on Steinplatz. When business declined after Hitler took power, "Mrs. Director" decided to invest, modernizing the building, installing new bathrooms and redoing the furnishings. That has proven a success. In 1936, the Hotel am Steinplatz is one of the most popular places to stay around Kurfürstendamm. An en suite room costs 9 reichsmarks (23 dollars) a night—only half of what guests in the Adlon have to pay.

Along with the moderate prices and comfortable rooms, guests appreciate the familial atmosphere. "Mrs. Director" and her three children live on the top floor. They mingle easily with the guests, and many of the regulars have come to know the Zellermayer family personally. Erna's older son, Heinz, is 21 and wants to become a restaurateur. His mother knows restaurant owner Otto Horcher and has arranged for her son to do an apprenticeship at Horcher's. His brother Achim, two years younger, is good at drawing and thinks he might like to become an artist. Daughter Ilse is 16. The baby of the family goes to a girls' secondary school and loves music. After finishing school, Miss Zellermayer wants to take singing lessons: she dreams of becoming an opera diva. She's very impressed by all the singers, male and female, who stay at the hotel. Whenever one of them warms up his or her voice before an evening engagement, she eavesdrops outside the door, imagining herself performing the great works of Wagner, Verdi and Puccini someday.

Tonight the Zellermayers aren't attending the opera. They're going to the "Resi" near Jannowitzbrücke in the district of Mitte. The full name of this establishment is Residenz Casino, but that doesn't reveal much about its true nature. The Resi is a famous ballroom and one of the main attractions of Berlin nightlife during the 1936 Olympics. Everything there seems bigger and more lavish than in other comparable dancehalls. Other places have a single band, whereas in the Resi three groups alternate with one another. More than 30,000 lightbulbs create spectacular lighting effects, and in a pond down below, fountains large and small rotate and rock back and forth in time to the music.

People like the Zellermayers who live at elegant addresses like Steinplatz don't usually frequent places near Jannowitzbrücke. But Erna and her children go to the Resi whenever they want to have a bit of fun. Ilse is particularly fascinated by the complex system of telephones and pneumatic message tubes in the establishment. Every table has a phone and a tube for sending sealed capsules with private messages to people at other tables. The pneumatic tube system can also transport small items: cigarettes and cigars, chocolate and perfume, matches for gentlemen and manicure kits for ladies. All you have to do is fill out an order slip, stick it in a capsule along with some money and send it on its way. A short time later, whatever you ordered arrives at your table. This is the only system of its kind in Berlin, and it's a big attraction.

It also provides ideal opportunities for pranksters to get up to all sorts of nonsense. Ilse amuses herself by ordering chocolates for lone women. "Excuse me, dear lady, I'm the gentleman at table 32," she'll write on the greeting card. "May I ask you for a dance?" The woman in question opens the capsule, reads the card with excitement and shoots surreptitious glances at table 32. The gentleman sitting there, of course, has no idea how lucky he is, and the resulting scenes are often quite embarrassing. But because Ilse has to pay up front for the chocolates, she can't always afford this practical joke. A much cheaper variation involves the table telephones. She'll call a man on his own and propose a rendezvous at the bar. At the same time, Heinz or Achim will call a lone woman and make the same proposal, agreeing on a secret signal. "Excuse me, dear lady, would you happen to be..." the man will ask, and that's when the fun commences. Ilse and her brothers observe what's happening from a safe distance, giggling. Tonight, with all the Olympic visitors, the Resi is packed. Ilse, Heinz and Achim have their hands full.

*

Erich Arendt doesn't have fond memories of the Resi. In fact he can barely remember being there around two weeks ago. Now he's sitting in investigative custody in a prison in Eberswalde and doesn't know what to do. The judge, whose name was Krause, told him that he's a man "of inferior character," and the prison guards treat him like a common criminal. That's tough to bear for a proud fellow like Arendt. He's a master bricklayer who runs a thriving business, he says in his defense. He has achieved a modest level of prosperity with his own two hands, and what's more, since January 1932 he has been a member of both the NSDAP and the SA. But that doesn't help either. Erich Arendt has hit rock bottom.

Arendt's fall from grace begins at 9 a.m. on 25 July. Arendt gets in his car in Eberswalde and drives the roughly 30 miles to Berlin, where he's meeting people on business. By the early afternoon he's finished with his appointments, but he doesn't want to return home. His wife, Herta, may be waiting there for him, but here in the capital of the Third Reich, the world is his oyster. The Olympics won't be underway for another week, but Berlin is already at a fever pitch. There are countless tourists in the festively decorated city, and the Games are all anyone can talk about. What is there to do in Eberswalde? he thinks. This is where the party is. He wants to join the celebrations, let his hair down and go a bit mad. He drives to Mitte, parks his car on a side street and goes into Café Welz on Friedrichstrasse. The café is neither as large nor as famous as the elegant Café Kranzler or the legendary Moka Efti, which are both close by, but Arendt likes the Welz. There's always something going on here—and he wants to have a good time.

Arendt orders champagne. After one or two piccolos, he is joined by a fellow who introduces himself as Assistant Secretary Wagner and asks if he may sit down. He may. Arendt is flattered. He has a weakness for titles, offices and dignitaries. He is just a humble bricklayer from Eberswalde, and now here he is talking to a flesh-and-blood assistant to a government minister. "More champagne," Arendt calls out to the waitress, for simplicity's sake ordering a whole bottle and not just piccolos. After the two men have finished it, another one appears to take its place. Arendt never wonders why an assistant government secretary would have the time and inclination to spend the afternoon drinking with a complete stranger. Nor does he get suspicious when a bit later a young woman with the tongue-twisting name Anna Beszezynski joins him and Assistant Secretary Wagner. What did the lady do for a living? Arendt is later asked, but he can't remember. By the time Miss Beszezynski appears, he's already visibly intoxicated. It's gone 10 in the evening. Arendt has been drinking for seven hours, but he still hasn't had enough. "Time for the Resi," he tells the assistant secretary and the young lady. The suggestion is met with great enthusiasm. Arendt takes care of the entire bill. When they leave the café, he gives the waitress a huge tip. All of a sudden, he's no longer Erich Arendt, humble bricklayer. He's a man of the world. He's pleased with himself. The three of them get in Arendt's car, which, despite his inebriation, he manages to pilot to Jannowitzbrücke. The mood is grand. Assistant Wagner tells some dirty jokes, and Miss Beszezynski giggles as only a young woman can.

Once they've settled into the Residenz Casino, the party goes on. Champagne continues to flow, and Arendt is feeling generous. Alcohol makes you hungry, and Arendt pays for his new friends' food, hands the bandleader some bills and buys perfect strangers around him drinks. He enjoys being the center of attention. He puffs out his chest and raises his voice to the point that people at the neighboring tables can hear him too. At some point, the other guests feel that Arendt is becoming a nuisance. The head waiter asks him to be a bit quieter—without success. Arendt starts shouting so loudly that people can hear him throughout the ballroom. The manager, Fritz Sandau, approaches him and asks him to leave. Arendt resists, claiming to be a representative of the government. "My government car with diplomatic plates is parked right outside," he bellows. "I drive to Gibraltar three times a week and earn 54,000 reichsmarks (135,000 dollars) per year from the government." Fritz Sandau laughs. He is used to patrons' drunken boasting. With the help of no fewer than four other men, he succeeds in pushing Arendt out of the ballroom. That's that, he thinks, pleased that he made Arendt pay the bill beforehand. For a moment everything is calm, but then Arendt kicks open the door, walks a couple of yards into the club and shouts a sentence that will change his life: "Adolf Hitler is bankrupt, and I regret joining the party in 1929." Unfortunately for him, the band is taking a break, so his words are clearly audible. Patrons Hugo Brösecke, Willi Kazda, Paul Hirschle and Erich Schulz, in any case, have heard enough. They take to their feet to defend the honor of their Führer.

There's a scuffle, from which Arendt somehow manages to extract himself. He gets into his car and speeds away, but Brösecke and the other three set off in another vehicle in hot pursuit. Arendt knows his way around Berlin. In no time he's made it onto the motorway heading north. He races toward Eberswalde doing 70 miles an hour, but the car with his pursuers is right on his heels. Arendt has to pull over at the outskirts of the city, whereupon the others jump him.

A full-blown fistfight erupts. Blood flows. In the end, the five men go to the local police station to file charges against one another.

It's more than two weeks later, and Arendt is still in investigative custody. The attorney general of Berlin has personally taken over the matter. The case is no longer about the fight and its consequences but something far worse. Arendt is suspected of violating paragraph 2 of the Law against Perfidious Attacks on the State and Party in conjunction with an act of treason, as well as insulting the Führer and the Reich chancellor. If Arendt is found guilty, he'll be sent to prison for years.

Erich Arendt is shaking his head. He can't remember a thing, he keeps telling his solicitor Rudolf Habermann. And anyway, as a party member and an SA man, his true convictions couldn't be further from the things he is being accused of saying. Mantra-like, Arendt repeats that all he wanted was to have a fun day out in Berlin. Assistant Secretary Wagner can confirm that. Has he been interviewed? Arendt wants to know. Habermann shrugs his shoulders. There's no sign of the alleged government official or Miss Beszezynski.

Erich Arendt has come a long way down in the world. The Eberswalde chapter of the NSDAP has kicked him out on 1 August, and some of his party comrades have testified that Arendt is a notorious drunk and a pompous ass. "We all knew that his mouth would get him in trouble one day," one of them has said.

The matter will be adjudicated by the Reich Ministry of Justice, Habermann tells Arendt. In six days, the Olympic Games will be over. There's unlikely to be a decision before then. The authorities will want to wait until the Olympic guests have left Germany. That may be Arendt's salvation—or his great misfortune.

*

In a few days, shooting will begin on the crime comedy *Spiel an Bord* (Game on Board). In the film, Hubert von Meyerinck plays the elegant Marquis de la Tours, who will turn out to be— what else?—a crook. The film is being shot mostly on board the steamship MS *Bremen* on its passage to New York. Before Hupsi heads off to the high seas, he's celebrating one last time in the Quartier Latin.

The club has been especially packed during the Olympic Games. Along with the regular faces, there are lots of international guests, and as is true of Berlin's streets, you can hear a veritable babel of languages. Amidst all the activity, Leon Henri Dajou darts throughout the establishment, welcoming VIP guests and making sure they're shown to good tables. On the face of it it's business as usual, but there's a strange mood in the air. Meyerinck senses that something's not right. "With money and diamonds in my pockets—everything over the border, my dear Hupsi," Dajou confides in his friend in his broken German. It takes a while for him to understand what Dajou is trying to say: that he wants to sell his club and leave Germany as soon as possible. But why? Dajou says that a number of things—trouble with his employees and the jealousy of his competitors—have upset him recently, and that after five years he's sick of the job. An acquaintance named Eugen

Nossek has introduced him to two gentlemen who are willing to pay 60,000 reichsmarks (150,000 dollars) in cash for the Quartier Latin. As far as Dajou is concerned, the quicker the better. With the money, he can resettle in London or Paris.

Now that's surprise news! Meyerinck is dumbfounded. He didn't see this coming. He has no way of knowing that there's little truth in Dajou's explanation for why he suddenly wants to sell his business. What's true is that the bar owner is in deep trouble. He's never told his friend Hupsi that the police are watching him. For years Dajou has played fast and loose with the law, and his police file is correspondingly thick, containing examples of fraud, embezzlement, bribery of government officials, libel and other offenses. One time he was reported for the unhygienic state of the Quartier Latin's kitchen; on another occasion he was caught selling cheap German sparkling wine at champagne prices to a group of Italian diplomats. During a party thrown by Universal Film AG (Ufa), he billed the revelers 12 reichsmarks (30 dollars) a bottle for Mosel wine while serving them his much cheaper house brand. Dajou is not above pouring alcohol into different bottles or swapping labels. It's easy to turn an ordinary German brandy (1.75 marks [4 dollars] a glass) into a French Bisquit Dubouché Napoleon 1811 (6 marks [15 dollars] a glass). He tried to bribe a punctilious official 50 marks (125 dollars) and called a difficult employee a "German pig." It's no wonder that the police, customs officials, the trade office and authorities in charge of resident aliens all keep close tabs on the celebrity bar owner. Countless witnesses have been interviewed, and an equal number of reports written, but none of the cases have been brought to trial. Leon Henri Dajou seems beyond the reach of the law. It's as if someone has been holding a protective hand over him.

But suddenly, and surprisingly, just before the start of the Olympic Games, the Gestapo is ordered to investigate him. The focus is no longer on fraud or bribery, but on Dajou's background. Gestapo officials are convinced that he is not who he claims to be. What's clear is that Dajou arrived in Berlin in 1925, where, after buying a couple of elegant suits, he began working as a gigolo. But where did he come from? What did he do in his days before Berlin? Dajou has Nicaraguan citizenship, which he claims he enjoys as a result of his father having died in South America. Investigations, however, reveal that he purchased his passport for 1,400 reichsmarks (3,500 dollars) in 1927. The Gestapo smells blood and unearths more and more details about Dajou's past. In reality, the charming bar owner was born on 1 September 1903 in Galati, Romania. There's no family by the name of Dajou living there, though. The man the Gestapo are investigating is actually named Leib Moritz Kohn and is the son of Moritz Kohn and his wife, Jeannette (née Cohn). He only adopted the pseudonym Leon Henri Dajou in 1929, four years after moving to Berlin. "With that in mind," writes the Gestapo investigator, "we can certainly assume that Dajou is a Jew."

So that's his big secret. A Romanian Jew is running the most fashionable club in the capital of the Third Reich and has played host to influential Nazi officials, captains of industry and famous artists. For a long time, his disguise worked to a tee. Dajou donated money to the NSDAP and raised the swastika flag on holidays. But now he's been unmasked. He needs to get out of Berlin—and quickly.

Dajou has planned his escape with military precision, running through his flight from Germany over and over in his mind. In under a week's time, on 16 August, the sale of the Quartier Latin will be completed. Together with the notary, the two purchasers—insurance company director Max Apelt and restaurateur Bruno Limburg—will come to the club, and after a bit of small talk, they will all retreat to Dajou's office. The notary will read out the contract of sale in a notary's typical monotone. Dajou, Apelt, Limburg and the notary will sign the document. Dajou will receive a briefcase containing 60,000 reichsmarks (150,000 dollars) in cash, count the money and give the buyers a receipt. In conclusion the men may drink a cognac or a glass of champagne to celebrate the transaction. Dajou will briefly lock the briefcase in his office safe, where he has already stashed 40,000 marks (100,000 dollars) that he managed to siphon off club revenues over the past year. The money has been illegally stashed away, but that's the least of Dajou's worries. He needs every pfennig of the 100,000 marks to start over in life. Before 16 August is over, Dajou will clear out his office, leave the keys with one of his employees and board a train for Paris with two proverbial briefcases full of cash. On the last day of the Olympics, amidst the hustle and bustle of departing international guests—so he thinks—border police and customs officials won't check people too closely. His girlfriend, Charlotte Schmidtke, will take care of the rest—liquidate his flat and sell his Cadillac—and then join him a couple of weeks later. That's the plan, anyway. In six days, he'll find out whether it works.

The roof terrace of the cosmopolitan Eden Hotel is one of Berlin's main attractions in the Olympic summer of 1936.

Tuesday, 11 August 1936

REICH WEATHER SERVICE FORECAST FOR BERLIN: Pleasant
to cloudy, isolated heat thunderstorms in the evening.
Temperatures rising during the day, with winds from the
southwest. Highs of 27°C.

REICH AND PRUSSIAN TRANSPORT MINISTRY ANNOUNCEMENT:
"149 people were killed and 3,793 people injured in road
accidents in the German Reich last week."

Anyone walking up Kantstrasse from the Memorial Church these
days will see one name repeated over and over on advertising
pillars, in display cases and on the sides of buildings: Teddy
Stauffer. The gentleman in question is one Ernst Heinrich
Stauffer, known to his fans as Teddy. Seven years ago he came
to Berlin but ended up a nobody, residing in impoverished
circumstances and living from hand to mouth. Now, in August
1936, the 27-year-old is a star. Stauffer is neither an athlete
nor an actor, nor a fearless Atlantic-crossing pilot like Charles
Lindbergh, nor a race driver like Manfred von Brauchitsch in his
Mercedes Silver Arrow. He's not even German. Teddy Stauffer is
a bandleader and saxophonist from Switzerland.

Elfriede Scheibel is nine years Teddy's senior. She's his boss—a word Teddy doesn't like to hear, although it's true. She manages the Delphi Palast on Kantstrasse and has hired Stauffer and his band, the Original Teddies—named after Berlin's mascot, a bear—for the period from early July to late October. When he enters the Delphi Palast for the first time, Stauffer shrugs his shoulders and says nothing, especially not to Scheibel. But looking around the place, his eyes seem to ask: are you kidding me? Maybe he thinks of the old Berlin joke in which an architect says to the fellow who engaged him: "The frame is finished—what style house would you like?" The builders of the Delphi were fans of Greco-Roman architecture—or more accurately, what was considered Greco-Roman in 1928. There are stylized pillars, meander patterns and *putti* all over the façade. Up on the roof, four stone lions seem to watch over the premises. The building is set back from Kantstrasse, so there's a spacious front garden on the corner with Fasanenstrasse, where patrons can enjoy a summer afternoon tea under palm trees and other exotic plants. The Palast proper is a two-story building. On the ground floor are the cloakroom, a café and the kitchens; the upper floor is home to the actual ballroom, with two dance floors and 530 seats. There's also a gallery with an additional 120 seats and a parquet floor. The interior is a stylistic mishmash of wall paintings, pillars of stucco marble and fake papier mâché accoutrements. The ballroom ceiling is covered with countless tiny lightbulbs that simulate a starry sky. In the Delphi there's not a hint of the New Objectivity that set the architectural tone in the late 1920s. This will be Teddy's place of work for the next four months.

By hiring the band for such a long time, Elfriede Scheibel is putting all her eggs in one basket. Business hasn't been good, and she hopes that the many international Olympic visitors will turn the tide. The gamble pays off. From the very first day of their engagement, Teddy Stauffer and his Original Teddies draw in the crowds like a magnet. The Delphi Palast is always sold out. In the afternoon, when the band performs in the front garden, people cluster on the surrounding streets to listen in; every evening, hundreds of people are turned away at the door because the ballroom is already full. Berlin seems to have been craving the Teddies' sound. "Americans were in the audience," Stauffer will write in his memoirs. "At the Delphi Palast, their presence inspired us to play rhythms previously unheard of. People had already started dancing in the afternoon. The atmosphere in the evening was indescribable. And Berliners were dancing alongside Americans."

Teddy is particularly popular with the ladies of Berlin. He's a tall fellow with combed-back blond hair, which makes him look like a Hollywood film star. The swinging way in which he moves, as he gives his bandmates their cues, plays the saxophone and acknowledges the audience's applause, has a coolness that most German musicians lack. Needless to say, Teddy is an inveterate womanizer. And then there are the songs. The Teddies play an almost exclusively American repertoire, including the hottest swing numbers from Broadway. One of the musicians, Walter Dobschinsky, will later recall: "We played really hot, with no inhibitions, real American jazz, as we musicians say. People wanted to hear it. They really went wild."

The swing music bug is highly contagious, and the Nazis can only stand back and watch as it spreads. "We didn't have any problems because of it," Bob Huber, the Teddies' trumpet player, will remember. "No one said a word. No one told us we shouldn't play American numbers."

National Socialist cultural officials view Stauffer and the public's enthusiasm for swing music, which reaches a high in August 1936, with a mixture of forbearance and indifference. On the one hand, the Nazis are glad to be able to present their international visitors with an internationally known performing artist. On the other hand, the officials don't regard swing as important enough to merit intervention. Reich Radio Broadcasting Director Eugen Hadamovsky may have issued a blanket ban on "nigger jazz" in 1935, but the prohibition has been totally ineffective. The record company Telefunken—"the German brand renowned all over the world," runs its advertising slogan—has been doing everything it can to make swing and jazz more popular in Germany. Two weeks before the start of the Olympics, Teddy Stauffer and his Original Teddies record their first four songs for Telefunken, and they will make many more recordings for the company in the next three years. Stauffer will recall that "They were all, without exception, globally successful songs by Jewish lyricists, composers and music publishers. We recorded them in Hitler's Berlin in 1936."

But Stauffer and Scheibel also have their enemies, of course. One of them is Hans Brückner in Munich. The 39-year-old composer specializes in popular music, writing awkward, kitschy ditties with titles like "Greetings from Faraway," "Dear God, Protect

Your River Rhine" and "What the Old Beach Chair Dreamt." Brückner joined the NSDAP in 1928 and is considered one of the "old street fighters." As the publisher of the polemical magazine *Das Deutsche Podium: Fachblatt für Unterhaltungsmusik und Musik-Gaststätten* (The German Podium: Specialist Journal for Popular Music and Music Clubs), he seeks to whip up hatred for jazz, people of color, Jews and anyone he thinks falls into one of those categories. Brückner's role model is the *Stürmer* editor-in-chief Julius Streicher, whose vulgar turn of phrase greatly resembles his own. But Brückner has few friends within the party. In 1935, when he and the wife of a Düsseldorf dentist, Christa Maria Rock, published a pamphlet entitled "The Jewish Musical ABC," even the Nazi newspaper *Völkischer Beobachter* panned it. The book pretends to be a scholarly encyclopedia, but it is so full of embarrassing mistakes that complaints about it have begun to pile up in the Reich Chamber of Culture. Officials there have little good to say about Hans Brückner, dismissing him as a simple-minded fanatic who only causes trouble and is best avoided. As paradoxical as it might sound, the fact that Brückner is the one who has declared war on jazz protects Teddy Stauffer and his colleagues. Moreover, what Brückner and his lot put forward as a substitute for jazz-inflected dance music elicits yawns even in the highest Nazi Party circles. In November 1935, returning home after a "German dancing" event, Goebbels confided to his diary: "After that, you can only say 'let's go back to jazz.' Terrible, pompous dilettantism. How I suffered!"

Stauffer has no interest in this entire discussion. When he takes to the stage in the Delphi Palast tonight with his Original

Teddies, all he wants is to make good music. He couldn't care less whether the composers and lyricists are Germans, Americans, Jews or Christians. Their music is the reason his audiences love him and celebrate him and his men, day in, day out. One song is a particular favorite of audiences in Berlin: "Goody Goody." The number's fanfare-like introduction has become something of a calling card for the band. "Goody Goody" is the soundtrack to the summer of '36.

*

Elegante Welt magazine announces: "Women with beautiful hair who use Alpecin are invited to send portraits of themselves printed on glossy paper to the 'Permanent Prize Committee of the Dr. A. Wolff Company in Bielefeld.' In 1936, in exchange for the rights to reproduce such images, we will be paying 10 reichsmarks each for up to twelve photos. They will be published, with names and addresses, in these pages. All jurors' decisions are final." The Alpecin model for the month of August is Hilla Kynast from Berlin Tempelhof.

*

The current issue of *Die Dame* magazine has a half-page advertisement for Henkell sparkling wine next to the table of contents. It features a fetching young woman holding a glass and a bottle of Henkell Trocken in an ice bucket. "The high point of a summer night," the ad promises. "Henkell Trocken is pure salubriousness!" The mood in diplomatic circles is rather less than sparkling when it is announced that a member of the Henkell family, Joachim von Ribbentrop, has been named Germany's ambassador to Britain. In 1920 he married the daughter of the company owner Otto Henkell.

The appointment has political observers pulling out their hair. How can Hitler give such an important ambassadorial position to a nitwit like Ribbentrop? The Führer is alone in his high regard for the aristocrat. "He's a man of moderate intelligence and education," writes the French ambassador, André François-Poncet, with tactful understatement. "His ignorance on diplomatic issues is astonishing." Privately François-Poncet terms Ribbentrop a "fool and pretty stupid." Others have quoted the Frenchman telling his American colleague George S. Messersmith that Ribbentrop "spoke English so well and was just the type that would appeal to an English gentleman as a gentleman." Even within leading circles in the Third Reich, Ribbentrop has few friends. Most people consider him an arrogant snob, an unlikable pompous ass and a supercilious lover of clichés who bores others to death with his vacuous monologues. Ribbentrop came by his aristocratic title in 1925 by getting himself adopted by an aunt in return for a lifelong pension of 450 marks (1,116 dollars) a month. For Goebbels, that makes him a charlatan. "He bought his name," the propaganda minister sneers, "married his money and cheated his way into his job."

Ribbentrop is reluctant to go to London. He wants to take over the Foreign Ministry, but the top job there is occupied by the career diplomat Konstantin von Neurath. Hitler isn't about to replace Neurath, and Ribbentrop is slavishly obedient to his Führer, so he complies, although in his eyes, the appointment to the British capital is nothing to celebrate. Unfortunately for him, he and his wife are throwing a party tonight for around 600 guests to celebrate the Olympic Games. When the invitations were issued, Ribbentrop had no idea he'd be heading to the banks of the River Thames.

At short intervals, one limousine after another pulls up with a VIP guest, and as they arrive each one receives a bound copy of the guest list. Flipping through the pages, you find a number of British names, including the Channons. Even Hermann Göring is attending, although perhaps because he wants to see what Ribbentrop and his wife, Annelies, are offering their guests. The day after tomorrow, Göring is throwing his own Olympic party, and he certainly doesn't want to come out second best. It won't be easy to top this, though. The Ribbentrops live in the wealthy Dahlem area of Berlin in an elegant villa with extensive grounds, a swimming pool and a tennis court. Money isn't an issue.

Today the entire estate has been festively illuminated. Singers from the State Opera perform arias, and later there will be dancing. Liveried servants pour endless glasses of Pommery champagne—where's the Henkell Trocken? guests might ask—while a whole ox is being roasted over an open fire. With forced cordiality and a sweet-sour smile, Ribbentrop accepts people's congratulations on his new appointment. But the longer the evening goes on, the more pinched his expression becomes. The new ambassador can hardly conceal his true feelings about his future job. By contrast, Göring is having a marvelous time, going from table to table, whispering jokes about the "sparkling-wine baron" and "Herr von Ribbensnob."

For Sir Henry Channon the evening confirms how tasteless and inelegant the wives of the leading National Socialists are. The Ribbentrops have money to burn and throw parties as wasteful as those in the ancien régime, but the hostess lacks any style whatsoever. "Frau von Ribbentrop is distinguished in the Berlin manner, that is she has intelligent eyes, appalling khaki-colored clothes and an un-powdered, un-painted face," Chips wrote in his diary on 29 May. Joachim von Ribbentrop is described as looking like "the captain of someone's yacht." Rather ironically, given his own leanings, Channon asks: "How can Germans be so silly about things that don't matter, or is it because their women are so unattractive that the race is largely homosexual?" Nonetheless, that doesn't prevent Chips from having a good time at the Ribbentrops' do. "We stayed at the party until three, and I enjoyed myself quite wildly," he writes after the festivities. "The lovely evening, the fantastic collection of notabilities, the strangeness of the situation, the excellence of the Ambassador's (or more correctly Frau von Ribbentrop's) champagne, all went somewhat to my head."

*

While Ribbentrop is holding court in Dahlem, the Berlin Philharmonic Orchestra is expected for a concert in the Olympic Village. The event is part of an entertainment series intended to introduce the athletes to musicians, dancers, acrobats and other more or less well-known contemporaries. The aviator Charles Lindbergh, the boxer Max Schmeling and the tenor Jan Kiepura have already visited the Village. Now it's the turn of Germany's most famous orchestra. To be precise, it's the second time the Philharmonic have appeared here. In late July, shortly before the Games began, they gave a concert that was originally planned as an open-air event but had to be moved into the Sporthalle because of rain. Tonight the weather is much better, and the performance can go ahead outdoors. The orchestra is large, and the program is first rate, including works by Wagner, Carl Maria von Weber and Georges Bizet. Only the conductor, Alois Melichar, is less than top standard. The Philharmonic's usual leader, Wilhelm Furtwängler, apparently couldn't find the time or simply had no desire to pick up his baton.

The musicians take their seats on the "Birkenring," a central square in the Village, and listeners fan out onto the surrounding open spaces. The sun is already setting when Melichar kicks off the overture to Wagner's *Tannhäuser*. One hour later, by the time the orchestra plays excerpts from Bizet's *Carmen*, it's completely dark. Torches bathe the musicians in a yellow-and-reddish light. Looking down from the Village's bastion, you'd almost think there was glowing lava in the Birkenring. It's an enchanting sight.

One of those listening is Wolfgang Fürstner, a Wehrmacht captain who's been in charge of the Olympic Village, which was built by the military, for two years. Up until the spring of 1936, the facility was under his command, and although as planned a higher-ranking officer officially took over as the Games approached, he's still something like the Village's unofficial mayor. By rights, the 40-year-old should be enjoying the evening. After all, the Olympic Village, which has been praised by everyone, is partly his work. But Fürstner is in a grumpy mood. He can't even appreciate the fireworks that light up the heavens over Berlin once the concert is over.

Fürstner's superior officer, Baron Werner von und zu Gilsa, is worried about his deputy. In his experience, Fürstner's behavior has always been beyond reproach, but he's heard from others that the captain has lost control of himself on occasions, that his reactions to things have been surly and erratic, and that his heart is no longer in this project. The truth is that Fürstner is in deep trouble. He's recently learned that his wife, Leonie, is having an affair with his very own adjutant and wants to get divorced. And in addition to his private life, he's got problems at work. Rumors about Fürstner's non-Aryan background are circulating within the Village. Someone has hung up posters reading "Down with the Jew Fürstner!" and there are murmurings that he's become the subject of an official investigation. Fürstner's paternal grandfather is in fact Jewish, and one of his cousins is the Jewish music publisher Otto Fürstner. He is also distantly related to Yvonne Fürstner, the owner of the Sherbini Bar.

Under Nazi law, Fürstner is one-quarter Jewish, making him a so-called hybrid of the second degree. The Olympic Games have offered him a measure of protection. While tens of thousands of tourists are in Berlin, neither the NSDAP, of which he is a member, nor the Wehrmacht are going to take any action against him. The Nazis don't want any scandals. But what will happen once the Games are over? What does the future hold once the international visitors are gone and the world's attention is no longer focused on Berlin? It's no wonder that Wolfgang Fürstner can't enjoy the Berlin Philharmonic's performance. He is consumed with fear. And a week from now he'll be dead.

DAILY REPORT OF THE STATE POLICE OFFICE, BERLIN: "The Latvian national Olga Schwabe from Riga has reported via an SA section leader on the behavior of the alleged journalist Dr. Wilhelm Lindner. She says that while he was showing her some of Berlin's sights, he remarked that he didn't think it was right to have a swastika flag on Frederick the Great's grave. In the course of their conversation, Lindner is supposed to have said that Hitler was a perilous adventurer, an Austrian only interested in waging war and building military barracks. Dr. Goebbels is a Jesuit, he said, who constantly repeats himself and has a club foot, as do all his children. Moreover, Lindner allegedly boasted that he has never uttered the words *'Heil Hitler!'* in his life."

Director Leni Riefenstahl makes the official film about the 1936 Olympics and often puts herself at the center of attention.

Wednesday, 12 August 1936

REICH WEATHER SERVICE FORECAST FOR BERLIN: Bright skies early in the day with increasing clouds and thunderstorms as temperatures cool. Slight wind from the south and then the west. Highs of 24°C.

It's the dawn of 12 August, and the provincial Rhineland city of Bonn is still asleep when Hans Eduard Giese is led into the interior yard of the court prison. The 32-year-old's life is nearly over: in a few minutes he'll be executed. Giese is no murderer. He's been convicted of theft and embezzlement, and he recently did two years in jail for counterfeiting. Last June, Giese had a really bad idea. He kidnapped the 11-year-old son of a Bonn merchant, tied him to a tree in a forest, where he fed him apple juice, oranges and chocolate, and demanded 1,800 reichsmarks (4,500 dollars) in ransom. Giese's plan went badly wrong. The boy was discovered after a mere six hours, and Giese was arrested. According to paragraph 239 of the Reich criminal code, kidnapping is an offense punishable by up to five years' imprisonment. But the Reich government learned of the case and hastily pushed through a new law concerning the ransoming of kidnapped children. Hans Eduard Giese is to be made an example of, so that the government can win points with the general public. On 22 June, only six days after the kidnapping, the Reich legal gazette published paragraph 239a. It reads: "Whosoever kidnaps someone else's child, using deception, threats or violence, for the purpose of obtaining ransom shall be put to death." The law was backdated to 1 June 1936 so that it applied to Giese. On 1 July, after a trial that attracted a great amount of public attention throughout Germany, the judge handed down the death sentence. In his verdict he thanked the Reich government in the name of all German mothers and fathers for the new law.

Giese's hands are bound behind his back as he stands in the yard of the court. A Catholic priest approaches, murmurs a short prayer and administers absolution. Then an officer of the court reads out the judge's verdict and issues the command: "Executioner, do your duty!" Everything else happens swiftly. The executioner's assistants seize Giese by the arms and shoulders, march him to the chopping block and strap him to it. A few seconds later, the executioner's ax falls and severs Giese's head from his body. In Berlin, day 12 of the Olympics is getting underway, and Hans Eduard Giese is dead.

EXCERPT FROM THE DAILY INSTRUCTIONS OF THE REICH PRESS CONFERENCE: "Today in Bonn, the child kidnapper Giese has been executed. In light of the Olympics, the German press service report about this incident should not be blown into something big. Commentary is to be avoided."

*

Hannes Trautloft, Max von Hoyos and the other German legionnaires have left Cádiz and have arrived in Seville, where, at the nearby Tablada Airport, they reassemble the airplanes they've brought with them. Temperatures reach 40°C (104°F) or more in the shade at this time of year in Andalusia, so it's not surprising that the reassembly procedure takes longer than anticipated. During the day, you can hardly move outside. Only when the sun begins to set do things get somewhat more pleasant. Unsuitable tools also slow down the work, and to make things worse, many of the German soldiers aren't used to Mediterranean food and spend more time on the toilet than in the airplane hangars. The Spaniards take it easy in the midday heat, which their guests from *Alemania* interpret as a lack of work ethic. The two groups have trouble communicating, and the mood is constantly threatening to turn sour.

"We've learned more about our mission and aren't very pleased," writes Trautloft in his diary. "We are to instruct Spanish pilots on how to fly our warplanes." Trautloft is very disappointed—he was hoping to fly the planes himself. But Hitler has given the Germans strict orders not to actively participate in any fighting. Not yet at least. Goebbels confides in his diary: "The Führer would like to intervene in Spain. But the situation's not ripe. Maybe the time will come. First we need to bring the Olympics to a happy conclusion."

In the meantime, both the Spanish putschists and the Republicans have launched brutal attacks on one another.

Thousands of people have been tortured and murdered. At first the German press restrained itself, but as the Olympics approach their conclusion, the newspapers publish more and more articles about real and purported Republican atrocities. The reporting is completely biased. General Franco isn't exactly treating his adversaries with kid gloves, but German readers don't learn anything about that. Instead, they're given copious accounts of the "bestial horrors" meted out by the Spanish government in the name of promoting Bolshevism. "Every morning more executions," reads one headline. "Seventy soldiers executed in a bullfighting arena." The reports are often based on nothing more than word of mouth and cannot be confirmed, but that doesn't stop Goebbels from passing on hearsay as fact. Many of the atrocities are described as taking place in churches and monasteries. There are reports of nuns being raped in public or having their breasts cut off by the "Reds," while monks are made to dance until they collapse from exhaustion. Furthermore, there are accounts of men, women and children being crucified in places of worship, and priests being burned alive on pyres made of wooden pews.

True or not, such horror stories are very useful to the propaganda minister. Goebbels has no love for priests, monks and nuns, but he knows only too well how a mixture of sex and violence can influence popular opinion. Sadistic treatment of innocent members of the clergy represents a level of moral depravity with which Goebbels hopes to whip up fear of Bolshevists in his own country. What he's really interested in is gradually preparing the German people for a war against the Soviet Union.

EXCERPT FROM THE DAILY INSTRUCTIONS OF THE REICH PRESS CONFERENCE: "Once again a magazine has published an inappropriate article on the race problem, an excerpt from a book entitled *Sport and Race*, which effectively argues that only Teutons have a chance to win the decathlon. Racial science has certainly not been enriched by this publication, but it has irritated some of our Olympic guests. Thus the publication was highly inappropriate and should be censured...By the way, it is also inappropriate to call peoples 'exotic' in the context of the Olympic Games. The word is to be avoided, particularly as we are hosting the Games under the motto of Olympic equality for all nations."

*

Germans drink too much alcohol—at least that's what Dr. Theo Gläss thinks. Every day Gläss travels from his home in the suburb of Britz to Linienstrasse in the city center to renew his battle against intoxicants. The 40-year-old is the chief executive of the German Order of Good Templars, a self-help organization originally from the United States that preaches abstinence. With some 32,000 members in 1,150 local chapters, the Good Templars are the largest but not the only group of their kind. In 1936 there are more than twenty anti-alcohol groups, including the German Association for the Fight against the African Brandy Trade, the German League of Abstinent Pastors and the Evangelical Reich Working Community for the Fight against Alcohol Affliction.

Alcoholism in the Third Reich is considered neither a disease nor a personal weakness: as Gläss called it in one of his pamphlets, dependence on alcohol is nothing short of "a crime against national health" and "terrible enemy of our race." It's no wonder that Gläss approves of the compulsory sterilization of alcoholics under the Law for the Protection against Genetically Ill Descendants.

How much do Germans really drink during the Olympic year of 1936? The fact is that, after hitting a low in 1930, alcohol consumption is on the rise. In 1933, 6 million bottles of sparkling wine were consumed. By 1936 that figure is 14.2 million bottles. Brandy consumption rose over this period from 15 to 20 million gallons, while beer drinking went up from 898 million to 1 billion gallons. Is the Third Reich a nation of drunks? In isolation, the figures might support that notion, but on closer examination, the amounts drunk in 1936 don't measure up to those further in the past. In 1908, Germans drank 68.7 million gallons of brandy, while in 1919 almost 16 million bottles of sparkling wine were sold in German shops. German beer consumption was highest in 1901, when 1.8 billion gallons were drunk. In other words, more alcohol was consumed in the Wilhelmine Empire and the Weimar Republic than in Nazi Germany.

Nonetheless, it's also true that Germans' increasing consumption of alcohol is an expression of a deep-seated unease. In a summer issue of the monthly *Germany Reports*, a magazine published by the Social Democratic Party in exile in Prague, one author mentions for the first time a "particular mood of the moment" in Germany. "There's more beer being drunk than in the Weimar

Republic," reports an observer from Bavaria. "In small pubs, you encounter more and more little groups of workers drinking." The worst thing, the anonymous observer writes, is that young people are being systematically depoliticized by ritualized celebrations and drinking. "And the older people?" the observer asks. "You see many of them sitting in pubs buying young people beer, and then trotting out all of their tired old war stories. All the suffering of war has been forgotten, and they bask in the enthusiasm for their heroic deeds of yesteryear in the glowing eyes of adventure-seeking youngsters." The author's prognosis for the future is bleak. "The basic mood of today's youth, both in the country and the city, is that there's nothing like being a soldier."

*

The post office at Lietzenburger Strasse 235. It's early afternoon when Mascha Kaléko arrives to pick up her daily love letter. The sender is Chemjo Vinaver. He's twelve years older than Kaléko and works as a musicologist and a conductor. The two of them have crossed paths a number of times in the past few years: in the theater, in the Romanisches Café, which Kaléko frequents, at evening lectures or simply on the street. Once they met in front of Kaléko's house. It was raining cats and dogs, and she was on her way to an appointment. What terrible weather, Vinaver was about to say, trying to start a conversation, but Kaléko had no time and hopped away through the puddles. Years later, Vinaver will recall that this and other chance meetings weren't as accidental as they may have seemed. In fact he followed Kaléko sometimes just to get a glimpse of her, although he didn't dare confess his feelings because Kaléko was married. But at some point in 1935, a spark must have been ignited between the two of them. Mrs. Kaléko and Mr. Vinaver became lovers.

Kaléko suffers from the situation, from all the hiding, the keeping of secrets and her betrayal of her husband, Saul. The two have a relatively modern, open relationship, but Mascha doesn't want to cheat on him. Once Saul wrote her the lines

> I don't care if you are true
> But I don't want to lose you.
> Be as untrue as you want to be.
> But don't you ever tell me.

Mascha answered with a poem entitled "For Someone," which read:

> The others are the deep blue sea
> But you are the port.
> Believe me, you can be at peace.
> It's you I steer toward.

But such mutual declarations of affection are ringing ever hollower. Less than two weeks ago, on 31 July 1936, Mascha and Saul Kaléko celebrated their eighth wedding anniversary, and Mascha feels very sad. The more she visits the post office, the more clearly she realizes that she doesn't love Saul anymore, and probably never did. And as if that weren't enough, something she's suspected has recently been confirmed: she's pregnant with Vinaver's child. Mascha doesn't have the strength to tell Saul the truth. Instead, she prefers to keep living a double life, with the post office on Lietzenburger Strasse as a relay station. Saul believes he's the father. He's understandably thrilled and begins making plans for the future. The flat is too small for a child, he decides. It would be best to move before the birth. No sooner has the decision been made than he finds a place—a larger flat on nearby Bleibtreustrasse in the Charlottenburg district. He rents it for Mascha and himself from October.

Mascha sits in the post office, holding Vinaver's latest letter in her hands and staring at the linoleum. Her eyes seem to fix on a single point in the gray floor covering, motionless, but in truth Mascha is staring into nothingness. Her future is as devoid of color as the ground beneath her feet. She knows that she doesn't want to live with Saul and is afraid that as a Jew she soon won't be able to live in Germany anymore. "I have suffered more than humanly possible in the last two years," she will recall in 1938. While Mascha sits there, lost to the world, a number of people enter and leave the post office. When the door opens, the noise from the street fills the room. In front of the building a newspaper boy calls out the headlines of the official Olympic paper. Snatches can be made out. "Great day for Japan's swimmers," the boy cries. "Two gold medals." Etcetera, etcetera. The Olympic Games? Mascha Kaléko doesn't care a whit about them. She has much bigger things to worry about.

DAILY REPORT OF THE STATE POLICE OFFICE, BERLIN: "A division director of the German Labor Front reported that in the Siechen Bar on Behrenstrasse a German woman from a white-collar background made a disparaging remark to an Olympics guest about the Führer and the state."

*

At the Schauspielhaus theater on Gendarmenmarkt square tonight, they are putting on Shakespeare's *Hamlet*. The cast is first-rate: Gustaf Gründgens is playing Hamlet, Hermine Körner, Queen Gertrude, and Käthe Gold, Ophelia. The performance is part of the cultural program accompanying the Olympic Games, and many international guests are expected. The play has naturally been sold out for weeks, and Gründgens is nervous. It's by no means a given that the 36-year-old actor will be allowed to take the stage tonight. Until recently, he seemed to be headed for disaster. Gründgens, who's considered politically unreliable and is also homosexual, is a thorn in the side of influential circles around the Nazi Party's chief ideologue, Alfred Rosenberg. It's no secret among elevated party members that Thomas Mann's unloved former son-in-law is drawn to the same sex. "The Führer doesn't like Gustaf Gründgens," notes Goebbels. "He's too unmasculine for him." Hitler knows best. But Gründgens has a powerful patron in Hermann Göring, who is in charge of the Prussian State Theater. As different as Göring and Gründgens are, they share a personal affinity. "His relationship to Göring was one of genuine admiration, even friendship," recalled one contemporary of the actor. "Toward all other leading Nazis he had a skeptical and ironic attitude, which in the case of Streicher, Ley and most definitely Himmler, turned into disregard, even hatred." In the autumn of 1934, Göring appointed his protégé the director of the State Theater and granted him numerous privileges. That sticks in the craw of Rosenberg and his clique.

In the months before the Olympics, Gründgens' detractors sensed that their chance was at hand. In early May the *Völkischer Beobachter* ran a malicious attack on the actor's homosexuality. It's scarcely credible that this journalistic assault could have been printed without Rosenberg's approval. After all, he's the editor-in-chief of the Nazi daily. Waldemar Hartmann, the author of the article, was very clever in any case, jabbing at Gründgens's weak spot without actually naming it. With false guilelessness, Hartmann warned his readers against seeing Hamlet as a sixteenth-century Dorian Gray. The implications were obvious, and the attack hit its mark. Gründgens felt directly threatened by the reference to the homosexual dandy Oscar Wilde and his most famous novelistic hero.

Without doubt, Gründgens' situation is perilous. In 1934, his fellow actor Kurt von Ruffin was found guilty of homosexuality and sentenced to nine months in the Lichtenburg concentration camp in Saxony, where he suffered terribly. The fate of Bruno Balz, the well-known poet and popular music lyricist, who was confined for eight months in the Plötzensee concentration camp, was no better. After he was released, Balz quickly had to marry a blond peasant woman from Pomerania. Untold thousands of homosexuals are being sent to camps, mistreated and murdered. What if the regime doesn't shy away from arresting the great Gustaf Gründgens?

Gründgens immediately flees to friends of his in Basel. At the same time, Göring receives a letter from the actor, informing him in no uncertain terms that he has emigrated. Most probably, Gründgens has no intention of leaving Germany forever: he's just creating some drama. The writer Carl Zuckmayer considers the actor an inveterate gambler with an intrinsic desire to take risks. "His relationship to power is thoroughly cynical," Zuckmayer writes, "and he thus always puts himself in danger." Just before the start of the Olympic Games, Gründgens's tactics pay off. Göring calls his favorite actor in Switzerland to assure him of his safety, promising him a dizzying rise in salary and the arrest of Waldemar Hartmann. Once Gründgens returns to Berlin, Göring appoints him a Prussian state councilor—a politically empty title that does, however, carry immunity from legal prose-cution. Gründgens has won his own personal test of strength.

Just to be on the safe side, Gründgens proposes marriage to his fellow actress Marianne Hoppe, who is ten years his junior. It's unclear whether the proposal comes at Göring's insistence, but Gründgens and Hoppe truly do feel a deep personal affection for one another. "There was something about Gustaf," Hoppe will later recall. "He was really a friend you could rely upon." The wedding takes place in late July 1936. Berliners joke: "Hoppe and Gründgens / Won't have any children / And if Hoppe has some children / They sure won't be from Gründgens."

Having overcome the threat to his own person, you'd have thought that Gründgens would play it safe and avoid provoking his adversaries. But he can't resist playing with fire. During tonight's performance of *Hamlet*, he takes center stage, faces the audience and starts the famous sentence: "Man delights not me…" He suddenly pauses, and the audience holds its breath. You can hear a pin drop. What is he trying to do? Gründgens scans the rows of seats as if he is trying to look each audience member directly in the eye. After a few seconds, he continues: "… no, nor Woman neither." The effect is huge. When the curtain comes down shortly after 11 p.m., the actors receive wave upon wave of ovations.

In the audience is 16-year-old student Marcel Reich, who under the name Marcel Reich-Ranicki will go on to become West Germany's most influential literary critic. As he will remember Gründgens' performance: "He particularly stressed Hamlet's words 'the time is out of joint' and 'Denmark is a prison'—or at least it seemed that way to me. Could the Nazis' cultural leaders and journalists fail to notice that this *Hamlet* could also be understood as a political manifesto, as a protest against tyranny in Germany? No, of course not."

Aenne Maenz's bar on Augsburger Strasse is a favorite among intellectuals and artists: "*Maenz agitat molem!*"

Thursday, 13 August 1936

REICH WEATHER SERVICE FORECAST FOR BERLIN: Mostly cloudy, isolated showers and somewhat cool, with westerly breezes. Highs of 20°C.

In Dresden, some 110 miles away from the Olympic Village, Victor Klemperer shakes his head in irritation. The morning papers revolt him. For weeks, the only topic has been the Olympic Games. The Nazified press in the Third Reich lies without compunction, but Klemperer finds the situation particularly awful in August 1936. Everywhere he looks, he reads about how peaceful and friendly things are in Berlin, about how the German people and their sport-loving Führer are one, and how marvelous life in Nazi Germany is. The Berlin Games are the greatest success story and the best Olympics the world has ever known, says the regime, praising itself. One newspaper reaches for the superlatives and gushes about an imminent "Hitler-inspired German Renaissance."

Language like this makes Klemperer see red. He was a respected professor of Romance languages who held a chair at Dresden's Technical University from 1920 to 1935, when he was fired for being Jewish. Now without income, he often doesn't know how to pay his bills. He has every reason to view what's going on in Berlin with disgust. "The honor of a whole people depends on whether a single ethnic comrade can jump ten centimeters higher than anyone else," he scoffs in his diary. Thinking back to Helene Mayer, who won a silver medal for Germany last week and performed the Hitler salute at the awards ceremony, he's dumbfounded: "I don't know which is more shameless: the fact that she competed as a German for the Third Reich or the fact that the Third Reich laid claim to her achievement." Klemperer sums up the real tragedy of the champion fencer. It is precisely because of her Jewish background, not despite it, that Mayer is part of Nazi Germany's Olympic team. Mayer, an athlete with no interest in politics, who just wants to compete in her sport, has become party to a nasty game whose dimensions she herself cannot comprehend. Her story is that of a boycotted boycott.

Shortly after Hitler assumed power in 1933, protest movements formed in Britain and the United States began to press the Nazi regime about whether it would allow Jewish athletes from Germany to take part in the 1936 Olympics. Should that not be guaranteed, the protestors proposed, the international community must boycott the Games. The conflict was most unwelcome to the International Olympic Committee. Henri de Baillet-Latour absolved himself of any responsibility. No one was allowed to intervene in the internal affairs of another country, the count argued. If Germany didn't want to put forward any Jewish athletes, that was Germany's business. It was a facile argument, and Baillet-Latour underestimated public opinion in the United States, which refused to be mollified by clichés about national sovereignty. The IOC and its president had a lot to lose. The United States was the greatest sporting nation on earth. The Games would dramatically lose athletic and political importance if the Americans stayed at home. Moreover, an American boycott would have sent a powerful signal and perhaps would have led other countries to skip the Games as well.

In the autumn of 1934, with public pressure increasing, the American Olympic Committee visited Berlin to check out the status of Jewish athletes in the Third Reich. The investigation was carried out by a lone man: Avery Brundage, a former decathlete who had made billions as a construction magnate and now served as the president of the AOC. Brundage stayed in the capital of the Third Reich for six days, inspecting construction on the Olympic Stadium and other facilities, visiting a number of museums and generally enjoying life. He had little time left over for meeting representatives of Jewish athletics. When they told him that Jews were no longer allowed to join German sports clubs, he replied, "In my club in Chicago Jews are not permitted either." For Brundage, that was that. Upon returning to the United States, America's most powerful athletics official reported, against all evidence, that German Jews were happy with their sporting status and recommended that his colleagues from the AOC accept Germany's invitation to attend the 1936 Olympics. But the public outcry continued, so that in the summer of 1935, the IOC felt compelled to send a delegation of its own to Berlin.

Charles Hitchcock Sherrill was already retired when he was asked to lead this sensitive diplomatic mission. The 68-year-old was a longtime member of the IOC and an experienced sports official, who was as uninterested in the situation of Jews in Germany as Avery Brundage was. His main qualification for this task was something completely different: a conspicuous personal fascination with Adolf Hitler. As long ago as June 1933, in a letter to the *New York Times*, Sherrill had praised the newly elected German chancellor as the strongest man in Europe. On 24 August 1935, when Sherrill was received by Hitler for an hour-long conversation, it was a dream come true. The retired army general seemed to feel he'd been called to something higher. Perhaps he saw himself as the new U.S. ambassador in Berlin. In any case, he wrote up a report on his meeting with Hitler and sent it to none other than Franklin D. Roosevelt. Sherrill raved about Hitler's personal modesty, his impressive physical condition and his upstanding character. We can only imagine what Roosevelt thought about this missive. Be that as it may, Sherrill also had a copy of his report delivered via the German embassy in Washington to Goebbels's Propaganda Ministry, just so no one in Berlin could have any doubts as to his warm feelings for the Nazi leader.

In his conversation with Sherrill, Hitler made no concessions. Jews were not being discriminated against, he lied. They were merely being treated as separate from the German people and thus could not be members of the German Olympic team. Sherrill pressed the Führer on the issue. He was Germany's friend, he said, and wanted only the best for the country. But if the Führer insisted on this position, the IOC would take the Games away from Berlin. Hitler snarled that, in that case, the Third Reich would stage a purely German Olympic Games, but that was just a bluff. In reality,

Hitler had a vested interest in the Americans taking part in "his" Games. Sherrill knew that too, and proposed a diplomatic escape route. The regime should call upon the Jewish sports federations in Germany to nominate a representative for the German team. Sherrill only made his suggestion obliquely, but the idea of "token Jews" was born. Hitler promised to review the idea and, as a sign of his regard, invited Sherrill to be a guest of honor at that year's Nuremberg Party Rally. Sherrill gratefully accepted.

During his four-day stay in that city later in 1935 the former general had further talks with Reich Sports Leader von Tschammer und Osten, who warmed more and more to Sherrill's idea. Of course Jewish athletes would be accepted into the German team, so ran the new line of the regime, as long as they would "measure up to the Olympic standard." By the time Sherrill departed Nuremberg, one candidate seemed to have been chosen: Helene Mayer. On 21 September 1935, Tschammer und Osten invited her to join the German team. Sherrill advised the Reich sports leader to send his invitation via registered mail. That way, whether the athlete accepted the invitation or not, Tschammer und Osten could show that he respected the IOC's principles.

Back in the United States, Sherrill gave the regime in Berlin the expected clean bill of health, saying that the treatment of Jews in Germany was as little his business as the "lynching of Negroes in the American South" was. He even directed a veiled threat toward Jews in the United States. In a communiqué to Berlin, the German news agency quoted Sherrill as saying: "In the United States we have half a million U.S. athletes preparing for the Olympics and a trip to Germany. If these athletes suddenly see that around 5 million Jews out of an American population of 120 million try, and even succeed, in robbing them of a once-in-a-lifetime opportunity, we'll surely experience anti-Semitic difficulties that will last for many years." In other words, Sherrill implied, Jews should beware of spoiling the party. No doubt, Sherrill's views made him quite popular in Berlin.

And Helene Mayer? She was under pressure from all sides not to accept the German invitation. The fact that she did in the end was, she said, down to homesickness and wanting to see her family. In her answer to Tschammer und Osten, she stressed that it was important for her to compete for Germany as a German citizen. As a "half-Jew," Mayer was a more acceptable alternative than Gretel Bergmann, whose name had also been mentioned in conjunction with the German team. The high jumper was in excellent form, well up to the Olympic standard, but two weeks before the Games, Tschammer und Osten informed her that her performances weren't good enough. Bergmann's real problem was that she's a "full Jew."

Including Helene Mayer in the German team took the wind out of the sails of the international movement to boycott the Olympics. The American team accepted the invitation to go to Germany, and now nothing could prevent the XI Olympic Games from taking place. Would things have been different if Mayer had declined the Nazis' invitation? The United States and other countries might possibly have refused to travel to Berlin. Perhaps Hitler's Games would have never happened at all.

In any case, that's what George S. Messersmith, America's ambassador to Austria, thinks. He doesn't trust the Nazis as far as he could throw one, and in his dispatches to Washington he tirelessly warns against the German regime. In mid-November 1935, he wrote to Secretary of State Cordell Hull: "There are many wise and well-informed observers in Europe who believe that the holding or the non-holding of the Olympic Games in Berlin in 1936 will play an important part in determining political developments in Europe. I believe that this view of the importance of the Olympic Games being held in Berlin is not exaggerated...I believe that our dignity and prestige and our adherence to the ideals of fair-play and the non-political character of sport make it necessary and imperative that the American Olympic Committee revise its attitude and make it clear what the real position is in Germany." But no one heeded Messersmith's words.

*

In exile in London, the writer and former star journalist for the liberal *Berliner Tageblatt* newspaper Alfred Kerr writes his poem "Nazi Olympics":

A racist storm of outrage
Runs through the brown-shirt hordes
Three Negroes took center stage
And set the world records.
The Nazis came up short
(Olympic laughter—snort!)

The keeper of the racial faith
Holds his hands before his face.
Three Negroes—what a disgrace.
What will "mein Führer" say?
Silent the German fencers and their swords
(Olympic laughter—snort!)

The Führer groans: "These Olympic Games
(so much has gotten outside)
Are, just like the French state,
Thoroughly Jew- and Negrified."
The Führer sighs: God, He who's just in deed and word
(Olympic laughter—snort!).

*

Hermann Göring is the last of the Renaissance men—at least in his own estimation. It's not clear precisely what he means when he uses the phrase, although if we equate that period in human history with brutality, excess boastfulness, gluttony, greed and corruption, then, yes, Göring is indeed the last Renaissance man. And that self-conferred appellation is only one of his titles. The others include Prussian Interior Minister, Prussian State Premier, Deputy Reich Representative in Prussia, President of the Prussian State Council, President of the Reichstag, Reich Forestry Minister, Reich Hunting Minister, Reich Aviation Minister, Reich Commissioner for Air Travel, President of the Reich Aerial Defense Association, Colonel General, Supreme

Commander of the Luftwaffe and many, many more. For every one of his offices, Göring draws a separate salary, and for each of his functions he has a special uniform designed by himself. Sometimes he appears attired entirely in white, sometimes in light blue, sometimes in a reddish-brown doublet with baggy sleeves, green boots and a spear in his hand. In private, he prefers kimonos of violet silk that flatteringly conceal his considerable bulk. Göring loves accessories. He wears gemstone rings and golden daggers and swords. Meetings with tailors, hairdressers, jewelers, perfumiers and art dealers are all part of the Renaissance man's regular duties.

Tonight, Göring is throwing a gigantic Olympics party in the garden of the Reich Aviation Ministry, playing the lord of the manor in the massive square building on the corner of Leipziger Strasse and Wilhelmstrasse, which was only recently finished after a record construction time of eighteen months. Money is no object here, and international visitors are once again being pampered. Along with the diplomatic corps and foreign government officials, the guest list includes members of the national and international Olympic committees, ministers from the German regime, representatives of the NSDAP and the Wehrmacht, artists, athletes and aristocrats from home and abroad.

Heralds and fanfare-playing musicians clad in medieval garb announce the opening of the festivities. Ballet artists from the State Opera perform a dance, then the master of the house opens up the previously sealed-off rear portion of the garden, revealing the miniature reconstruction of a village, replete with a hotel, a post office, a bakery, a shooting range, a mill, a Rhine river steamboat sailing by the famous Drachenfels cliff, fairground stands and a carousel. The French ambassador, François-Poncet, can't believe his eyes when the portly Göring—clad in a white fantasy uniform and wearing diamond rings—climbs upon a little white horse and rides the merry-go-round. How repulsive!

Of course, such extravagance comes at a price. The food alone, which has been ordered from Horcher's, costs a small fortune. The American ambassador, William E. Dodd, estimates the total cost of the evening at around 40,000 reichsmarks (100,000 dollars), but that's probably an underestimate. Göring is pulling out all the stops to live up to his larger-than-life reputation. "Max Reinhardt could not have done it better," a bowled-over Chips Channon notes in his diary. "'There's never been anything like this since the days of Louis Quatorze.' 'Not since Nero,' I retorted, but actually it was more like the Fetes of Claudius, but with the cruelty left out." The only one who's at pains not to be impressed is Goebbels. "Göring's garden party," the propaganda minister notes in his diary. "A lot of people. Somewhat stiff and cold. I conversed with the German female runners who were so unlucky on Sunday. Otherwise only there for a short time." Goebbels's big day is still ahead.

EXCERPT FROM THE DAILY INSTRUCTIONS OF THE REICH PRESS CONFERENCE: "With regard to Saturday's football final between Austria and Italy, the Italians should be made more the focus than previously."

*

When Eleanor Holm Jarrett boarded the USS *Manhattan* in New York and set sail with over 300 other male and female athletes on 15 July 1936, she was one of the heroines of American sport. In seven years of competition, the swimmer is undefeated. Now she was taking part in her third Olympics, after Amsterdam in 1928 and Los Angeles in 1932. That alone could be a record. Everything Jarrett touches seems to turn to gold, even in show business, where she also wins over the public's hearts and their dollars. She takes the stage with her husband, the bandleader Art Jarrett, and wearing a white bathing suit, a Stetson and high heels sings the song "I'm an Old Cowhand from the Rio Grande." But by the time the week's passage was over and Jarrett set foot on German soil in Hamburg, her sports career was history, and her reputation ruined. So what happened out at sea?

During the Atlantic crossing Jarrett regularly had a drink or two too many, spent her nights playing cards with journalists, smoked and generally ignored onboard decorum. During the night before the ship was due to land in Germany, she went particularly wild. After another drinking session, she was too disoriented to find her own cabin and stumbled into the quarters of the female team's chaperone. Jarrett slurred her words and joked that she was training with the help of some champagne and a few cigarettes, but the governess didn't find it funny. When Jarrett tried to get into bed with her, she called the team doctor, who diagnosed acute alcohol abuse. She only took a few sips of champagne, Jarrett said in her defense, but Avery Brundage had had enough. Jarrett had gone too far, the AOC president declared, and threw her off the U.S. Olympic team.

But if Brundage hoped that he'd got shot of the capricious swimmer, he was wrong. Jarrett's dishonorable discharge from the team put her on the front pages of the tabloids, and the sports star became a glamour girl. Americans love such dramatic twists of fate. Before she even left Hamburg, Jarrett received a $5,000 offer to cover the Olympics for a press agency. She agreed and immediately felt she was in her element. The newly made journalist resided at a luxury Berlin hotel and got a press pass, granting her free access to all the sports events and major festivities in the city. She also got to meet Hitler. "Hitler was fascinated by what happened to me," she will recall many years later. "He told me the Americans were not very bright to dismiss me, a sure gold-medal winner. Especially for something like drinking champagne…Hitler also told me that if I had been a German, any punishment like that would have come after the Olympics, not before." Was she drunk, Hitler wanted to know? "Of course not," Jarrett replied.

When Göring learns that Eleanor Holm Jarrett is in attendance at his garden party, he has the young woman summoned over and chats to her extensively. He senses a chance to put one over on the Americans. He'd like to award her a medal, Göring says in his pompous stage voice, whereupon he takes a silver swastika— one of the many pins and medals he habitually wears in public— from his lapel and pins it to Jarrett's collar. "I had such fun!" she will later remember. "I enjoyed the parties, the 'Heil Hitlers!,' the uniforms, the flags…Göring was fun. He had a good personality. So did the one with the club foot."

*

Unlike Jarrett, Thomas Wolfe isn't invited to Göring's garden party, and even if he were, he probably wouldn't go. His conversation with Mildred Harnack in the Taverne has given him food for thought. Again and again he asks himself: has he deceived himself about the Germans? Wolfe can't confirm any of the ugly information Mildred whispered in his ear that night. He's never witnessed anyone being arrested, mistreated or murdered, and he's only ever heard the words "concentration camps" from Mildred's own mouth. Since arriving in Berlin, Wolfe has never seen any public evidence of the tyranny she described. But what if Germany is putting on a show to fool him and the other Olympic visitors? What if the Games are just a gigantic piece of propaganda? And what if the Germans Wolfe meets every day are just extras in an exceedingly horrible play? Well then, he and all the other visitors from around the world are being fooled. Wolfe shies away from pursuing these thoughts to their logical conclusion. From that moment on, he avoids Nazis and their pompous daily festivities. As if to convince himself that some Germans aren't part of the Olympic hocus-pocus, Wolfe spends tonight at Mother Maenz's place.

*

Augsburger Strasse is one of Berlin's many streets dedicated to nightlife. Restaurants, pubs and bars line its approximately 1-mile length. At the top of the street, where it gives out onto Joachimthaler Strasse, a stone's throw from Wolfe's hotel, is Aenne Maenz's watering hole. The owner's full name is Anna

Maria Maenz (née Schneider), but patrons just call her Mother Maenz. Her other nickname is Maria Theresa because some of the regulars think that, with her oval face, towering hairstyle and corpulent physique, she's the spitting imagine of the Austrian empress.

Mother Maenz alias Maria Theresa's place has been around for quite a while—since April 1913, to be exact. Back then there were very few automobiles on the streets and a correspondingly large number of horse-drawn carriages. Today it's the other way round. All you see are cars, and very rarely a carriage. But if the outside world has changed dramatically, inside Augsburger Strasse 36 life is much as it was twenty-three years ago. There are no tablecloths. At Mother Maenz's, people sit at plain wooden tables as they would in their own kitchens. Maenz serves fresh draft beer, various sorts of schnapps and liqueur, and decent wines as well as a small assortment of hearty foods: chicken soup, rollmops and fried herring, ham, sour gherkins and pickled eggs.

The pub is the antithesis of the chic world of Kurfürstendamm just down the street, but it's precisely the simplicity that has drawn in generations of artists and intellectuals. Over the years, film director Ernst Lubitsch, actors Emil Jannings, Conrad Veidt, Alexander Granach, Werner Krauss, Jakob Tiedtke and the legendary Fritzi Massary, the writers Bertolt Brecht and Kurt Pinthus, and the painter Emil Orlik have all been regulars here. The unofficial motto of the pub is *"Maenz agitat molem,"* a variation on Virgil's *"mens agitat molem"*— the spirit moves the material.

People like Mother Maenz are beloved figures in the earthy parts of Berlin. For her patrons Aenne Maenz is bartender, adviser, psychologist, consoler and confidante all rolled into one. Three weeks ago, on 21 July, she celebrated her 57th birthday. Business is pretty good. Actually she doesn't need to work behind the bar everyday anymore, but Maenz won't hear of taking it easy. A mother doesn't leave her family in the lurch, she says, any time anyone suggests anything of the sort.

Since his Berlin visit last year, Thomas Wolfe has been part of her family. It doesn't matter that the two can barely communicate. For Maenz, Wolfe is the giant guy from America, and whenever he comes into the bar, as he does tonight, she automatically pours him a beer. Wolfe has become interested in Maenz's serving girl Elly, a buxom blonde who is barely contained by her blouse, a fact Wolfe finds very erotic. To him the waitress looks like a large, delicious ham on two legs. As he once remarked to Heinz Ledig, gesticulating with his knife and fork: "She is a fine piece, I'll cut a slice of her."

Whatever Mildred Harnack may have told him about life in the Third Reich, in Wolfe's eyes it can't apply to Mother Maenz's. For the American writer, it's as if he's entered a world where National Socialism doesn't exist. But tonight Wolfe will be proven wrong. The great actress Fritzi Massary used to come here a lot, a fellow customer tells him, but now, like her colleague Alexander Granach, she lives abroad. For Jews, the man says, noticeably lowering his voice, Hitler's state is a dangerous place. Another customer tells Wolfe about all the pubs and bars that had to shut after Hitler took power—the Auluka-Diele, for example, or the Geisha Bar on August Strasse, not far from Mother Maenz's. Those were places for women only, he says, but Germany's new masters don't like lesbians. In Nazi doctrine, women are potential mothers whose duty is to deliver children for the Führer. Wolfe shakes his head in disbelief. Only a few years ago, Berlin had an extensive homosexual subculture, with around a hundred gay and lesbian bars. Some legendary establishments like the Eldorado on Motzstrasse in the Schöneberg district even made it into the tourist guides. The writer Emil Szittya remembers going to the transvestite bar Mikado: "At the piano sat Baron Sattlergrün, who referred to himself as 'the baroness.' He played pieces by Count Eulenburg." Another famous location was Silhouette on nearby Geisbergstrasse. It was a small, smoky place that stayed open until the wee hours. If Wolfe had come to Berlin a few years earlier, he's told tonight, he'd have been able to meet Marlene Dietrich and Friedrich Hollaender. But those days are long gone. Where once a pale young boy in women's clothing sang melancholy songs to the accompaniment of a blind pianist, while customers ate chicken soup, there's now a health-food shop.

Wolfe is silent and pensive, not because he's such a great fan of gays and lesbians, but because he intuitively senses that something has been lost forever. "Then something happened," he'll remember. "It didn't happen suddenly. It just happened as a cloud gathers, as fog settles, as rain begins to fall." Wolfe realizes that the National Socialists hate everyone who's not like them, and he sees that the Nazis want to poison and destroy the country he loves so much. "The poisonous emanations of suppression, persecution, and fear permeated the air like miasmic and pestilential vapors, tainting, sickening, and blighting the lives of everyone..." he'll write. "It was a plague of the spirit—invisible, but as unmistakable as death."

The gourmet restaurant Horcher on Lutherstrasse is a culinary institution and is considered one of the leading places to eat in Europe. "Where is the footstool for the countess?"

Friday, 14 August 1936

REICH WEATHER SERVICE FORECAST FOR BERLIN: Mostly cloudy, with scattered rain showers. Westerly winds. Temperatures constant. Highs of 20°C.

The weather forecast was wrong when it predicted scattered showers. It's positively pouring today. The heavens have opened, and there's no let-up. Berlin's drainage system can barely cope with the deluge, and huge puddles form everywhere on the city's streets and squares. Artistic leaps are necessary if you want to get from point A to point B without getting your feet wet. The sheer mass of water is a headache for Joseph Goebbels. He has invited 2,700 guests to an Olympic party on his own private island tomorrow evening. Can the festivities take place as planned? Or will he have to cancel them?

*

André François-Poncet stands in front of the mirror inspecting his mustache, whose curled ends have been primped so that they point straight upward. He clicks his tongue: tsk, tsk, tsk. That's what he does when he's not satisfied with something. François-Poncet still isn't happy with his looks. He takes both ends of his mustache in his fingers and twirls them briefly between his thumb and index finger. *"Bon!"* he now says to his reflection. To an outside observer there's no difference, but the French ambassador is utterly uncompromising when it comes to his appearance.

François-Poncet is always perfectly attired—his elegance is only exceeded by his vanity. The look on his face is usually friendly, if a tad haughty. *De haut en bas,* as the French say. Once, when an underling accompanied his boss outside, bareheaded, François-Poncet asked with a sweet smile: "Where is your hat?" The man said he didn't have one. "Then how do you know when you're outside?" the ambassador retorted.

François-Poncet and his wife, Jacqueline, regularly host afternoon teas, elaborate dinners, concerts and other genteel events in the French embassy on Pariser Platz. In high society, these are considered top invitations. In any case, as the French ambassador, François-Poncet represents the undisputed diplomatic center of the Third Reich's capital—no festivity is complete without France's highest foreign representative in attendance. On many occasions he's seated directly next to Adolf Hitler. The Führer is crazy about the French diplomat, whom he calls simply Poncet, perhaps because he's unable to pronounce the first half of the ambassador's surname. The two men have formed a good, many-layered relationship. Hitler likes the fact that he can converse without an interpreter with François-Poncet, who has perfect German. As a parvenu, it also flatters him to be treated with respect by a grand seigneur of the French old school.

François-Poncet behaves with ironic subservience toward Hitler. On one occasion, the dictator shows the ambassador around an exhibition of Nazi art, and the two stop to admire a rather stout female nude, painted from the rear, by the artist Adolf Ziegler. Before Hitler can say a word, François-Poncet purrs: "Oh, my Führer, I see. It's Madame de Berlichingen." Hitler is amused by the reference to the portly German knight of yore and subject of an early play by Goethe.

*

Sauerkraut with pork belly and a glass of beer—the very thought of it makes Ernst Rowohlt's mouth water. It's shortly after noon, and Rowohlt takes his umbrella and leaves the publishing house. He walks through the rainy streets to Olivaer Platz, where Ludwig Mehlgarten runs his eponymous restaurant. Rowohlt could have taken the number 12 bus, which stops directly in front of Mehlgarten's place, but he'd rather stretch his legs, even though it's pouring. Rowohlt covers the short distance in around ten minutes. Once he's arrived, he takes off his thin summer coat, puts his umbrella in the stand and sits down at one of the rustic wooden tables. Ludwig Mehlgarten welcomes him and takes his order. It's a quarter of an hour until the food arrives. In the meantime, Rowohlt removes his jacket, hangs it over the back of his chair and rolls up his sleeves. All in all, it's around thirty minutes from when he left Eislebener Strasse to the time when he starts eating his lunch. Today, as he hoped, sauerkraut with pork belly is on the menu. He'll also drink a glass or two of beer.

This has been Rowohlt's lunchtime routine for several weeks now. He recently discovered Mehlgarten's when his wife was out of town and he didn't know what to do with himself on his own. Rowohlt was delighted to learn that the Mehlgartens are originally from the town of Vegesack near the northern German city of Bremen, just as he is. Mrs. Mehlgarten, who is in charge of the kitchen, does good, old-fashioned Bremen homecooking: corned-beef hash, broad beans with bacon, baked smelt, Madeira cake, pears and bacon, and eel soup. Naturally Rowohlt can also appreciate a filet steak with Béarnaise sauce and *pommes soufflés*, but simple dishes remain his favorites. He especially likes *Pluckte Finken*, a stew made of white beans, beef, carrots, potatoes, apples and pears. It needs to be served directly from the stove to the table—only then does it develop its special aroma. Mrs. Mehlgarten is a good cook and serves her *Pluckte Finken* piping hot, the way it should be. On occasions, Rowohlt enjoys taking unsuspecting authors to Mehlgarten's and watching them struggle with the unfamiliar names of the dishes—as well as Mrs. Mehlgarten's more than filling creations.

For people who enjoy well-prepared heavy food in great quantities, Mehlgarten's is paradise. Along with literary types, and the bus and taxi drivers who take their breaks here or stop in after work on Olivaer Platz, a stout young blond woman of around 20 has also begun frequenting the restaurant. She always sits alone, and once she's placed her order, she only opens her mouth to shovel food in. The writer Ernst von Salomon, another regular, is astonished by the sheer amount the woman can eat. "She devoured a bowl of *Pluckte Finken*," he writes, "then kale with smoked sausage, then a knuckle of pork with sauerkraut and pease pudding, and finally a butcher's plate with tongue, heart, blood and liver sausage." She also drank five steins of beer. The woman's name is Ellinor Hamsun. She's the daughter of the Norwegian writer, Nobel laureate and Hitler admirer Knut Hamsun, and she's recently moved to Berlin. After her extensive lunch, she leaves Mehlgarten's without a word and proceeds next door to Robert Heil's confectionery. It's said that there Ellinor Hamsun has an extra-large piece of pyramid cake for dessert.

*

Someone like André François-Poncet would never be caught dead in a place like Mehlgarten's. The mere idea of *Pluckte Finken* or a plate of fatty pork belly would no doubt draw a disapproving "tsk, tsk." His Excellency prefers the haute cuisine of his native land, and the place to go for that in Berlin is Horcher. Those who want to dine in the gourmet restaurant at Lutherstrasse 21 need bulging wallets. Horcher is very, very expensive, but it's a real experience. The cuisine is superb. Many connoisseurs consider it the finest restaurant in Europe.

The establishment takes up the entire ground floor of a block of flats and consists of a main dining room with twelve tables and a number of small salons, where four to ten people can be served. The interiors of the rooms are first-rate. One of the private rooms, for example, has walls covered entirely in fine green silk, while the main dining room is all done up in leather. Thick Persian carpets muffle every sound. There's a lot of space between the tables, but on request wood and glass dividers can be put up so that diners enjoy additional privacy. Naturally, only silver cutlery and handblown glasses are allowed to grace the damask tablecloths.

At Horcher, one speaks and dines *en français*. A brigade consisting of a *chef de rang*, three *demi-chefs de rang* and four *commis de rang* waits on tables. Otto Horcher, the maître d'hôtel, obsequiously pampers every individual guest, personally welcoming VIPs and showing them to their tables. One of the restaurant's trademarks are the small footstools covered in pink silk that are discreetly positioned under female diners' feet. If one is forgotten, the boss will hiss: "Where is the footstool for the countess?" The forgetful waiter then has to pay Horcher a fine of one mark. When François-Poncet reserves a table, the master of the house brings out silver candlesticks and twelve figurines of Meissner porcelain depicting Napoleon's twelve marshals. Horcher has elevated subservience into an art form.

Otto Horcher knows the culinary likes and dislikes of all his regular guests and unobtrusively tries to honor them, be they for turtle parfait, Rhine salmon, rolled veal on a bed of artichokes, flambéed kidneys or chamois venison steaks. Horcher is famous for its beef tournedos. A 1-inch-thick piece of meat is cut from the middle of the fillet, sautéed in butter until pink and then placed on a bed of heated pastry filled with liver mousse. The chef smothers the whole thing in Béarnaise sauce and tops it with a mushroom cap. Horcher's *canard à la rouennaise* is also world famous. It involves strangling a duck so that the blood stays in the body, making the meat redder and more tender than usual. The bones are crushed in a silver poultry press, and the juice is mixed with puréed raw duck liver, pepper, salt, herbs, a little lemon juice, a glass of port wine, some Madeira and a splash of champagne, and then reduced to form a dark-brown sauce. The lightly seared duck meat is cooked in the sauce until ready. Almost all the dishes are prepared at the table. There's not a poulard, pheasant or back of venison that isn't carved in front of the diners' eyes. Even the side dishes like spinach *à la crème* are whipped up *sur place* in a chafing dish.

Along with actors like Heinz Rühmann and Gustaf Gründgens, Horcher's regular clientele includes politicians, diplomats and captains of industry. Otto Horcher doesn't care much about the political views of his customers, invariably siding with whoever is in power at the moment. In the Weimar Republic, his restaurant was visited by Jewish artists and intellectuals like Charlie Chaplin, Franz Werfel and Max Reinhardt, and former German chancellors Gustav Stresemann and Heinrich Brüning. Nowadays it's frequented by high-ranking Nazis like Göring, NSDAP Reich Director Robert Ley and Luftwaffe General Quartermaster Ernst Udet. Rumors swirl around the restaurant. People whisper that the Gestapo has bugged several of the tables so that they can listen in on diplomats' conversations. It's difficult to say whether there's any truth to this. According to another anecdote, Otto's father, Gustav Horcher, once showed German President Paul von Hindenburg the door after an argument about wine. But it's doubtful that the former general, who was socialized in military mess tents, ever set foot in Berlin's number-one temple of gourmet food. And anyway, the Horchers don't distinguish between good and bad customers. Anyone with enough cash to spare is welcome. The restaurant is booked out for the duration of the Olympic Games.

DAILY REPORT OF THE STATE POLICE OFFICE, BERLIN: "Yesterday an American woman, who is visiting the city for the Olympics, noticed during a train trip from Munich to Berlin that foreign passengers were repeatedly asked about their impressions of Germany by German-speaking persons. While the foreign visitors praised the new Germany in every respect, the Germans (apparently provocateurs) sought to denigrate Germany and present it in a negative light. The American woman, who can be reached via City Inspector Meier, has declared herself willing to provide more details about the incident."

*

Today is a difficult day for Eleanor Holm Jarrett. This afternoon will see the final of the women's 4 × 100 meter relay. Jarrett was supposed to be swimming in the race, and she would probably have won a medal, had Avery Brundage not thrown her off the team. Jarrett feels as though one of her own countrymen has cheated her of a near-certain triumph. Didn't Adolf Hitler himself say how stupid Brundage's decision was? And all because of a trifle—a couple of glasses of champagne and a few cigarettes. To put it mildly: Jarrett doesn't have too many kind words for Brundage. Yet she tries not to let it show how much she hates him. Her revenge is much more subtle and effective. Wherever possible, she steals his limelight. At Göring's garden party yesterday, she was the center of attention, whereas no one paid any mind to America's top Olympic official. Today as well, Jarrett cuts a good figure in the stands of the swimming arena and does her best to be recognized by the spectators. But the real focus on this rain-drenched Friday afternoon is someone else.

If Jesse Owens is the king of track and field, then Hendrika Wilhelmina "Rie" Mastenbroek is the queen of the swimming events. The 17-year-old Dutch girl has been a tour de force in recent days, winning gold in the 100-meter freestyle and silver in the 100-meter backstroke. She's also performed well in the preliminaries of the 400-meter freestyle and the relay. All in all she's swum nine races by 4:45 p.m., when the gun fires to start the final of the women's relay. Mastenbroek is the Dutch team's anchor and has a lead over the German swimmer Gisela Arendt. Then, a few yards before the finish, she accidentally inhales some water. Usually a swimmer would abandon the race, but Mastenbroek manages to finish and touches the side of the pool before Arendt, winning her another gold medal. "That's the physical condition a top-class athlete needs," the commentators say. "That's the toughness we admire."

Mastenbroek's teammates haul her out of the pool, and while she's painfully coughing the water out of her lungs, a tall woman in an ostentatious polka dot dress bends down beside her. It's Mastenbroek's coach Maria Johanna Braun, whose fondness for extravagant hats, necklaces and brooches has made her something of a celebrity poolside. "Mother Braun," as the

German press has nicknamed the 45-year-old, demands a lot from her athletes. Along with training hard, her swimmers are expected to live ascetic lives with no time for the usual youthful diversions. When asked what sort of nutrition is best for young female swimmers, she gives a surprising answer: white beans with bacon.

*

Throughout the Third Reich there are around 700 so-called *Stürmer* boxes, public display cases in which people can read the virulently anti-Semitic newspaper. They are located in small villages and big cities, in the countryside and in the capital, on the walls of houses, in marketplaces and in underground stations. In Berlin, for example, there is one in front of the Theater am Schiffbauerdamm, the stage where, only eight years ago, in August 1928, Bertolt Brecht and Kurt Weill premiered the *Threepenny Opera*. The theater's glory days are long gone: Brecht, Weill and the former house director Ernst Josef Aufricht fled Germany in 1933, and the plays performed nowadays at the Theater am Schiffbauerdamm are insipid comedies. Anyone approaching the theater from Friedrichstrasse has to make his way around the *Stürmer* box.

The newspaper is the brainchild of the editor-in-chief, Julius Streicher. The 51-year-old has been a Nazi ever since the inception of the party. In the autumn of 1922 he formed the Nuremberg chapter of the NSDAP; in April 1923 he established *Der Stürmer*; in November 1923 he took part in Hitler's attempted putsch in Munich; and since 1925 he's been the regional leader, or *Gauleiter*, of Franconia. "Anyone who wants National Socialism gets Streicher with it," Adolf Hitler once declared. The Führer has nicknamed the former schoolteacher his "Franconian bull," and indeed there's something very bullish about the hulking man with the shaved head who delights in verbally goring and trampling his adversaries. Hitler likes cold-blooded, unscrupulous fanatics of Streicher's ilk. He's one of the few people allowed to address the Führer with the familiar *du*. Hitler considers Streicher the personification of National Socialism. Many others consider him a dangerous psychopath.

Streicher's view of the world can be summed up in a single sentence: "The Jews are our misfortune." The German historian Heinrich von Treitschke's words are quoted on the front page of every edition of *Der Stürmer* and run through the newspaper like a *basso continuo*. Every article or piece that has ever appeared in the thirteen-year history of the paper has been a variation of this one theme. Streicher's anti-Semitism is shot through with sexual obsession: he is constantly printing pornographic stories of young "Aryan" girls being violated by old Jewish men. "Starving German maidens in the claws of horny Jewish goats," reads one of the more lurid headlines. *Der Stürmer* also runs frequent stories about alleged ritual murders. "Who is the child butcher of Breslau?" screams one headline. Another reads: "The bloodhound. Terrible deeds committed by Jewish murder organizations. The carved-up Polish girl."

Even hard-core Nazis often shake their heads at this sort of excess. Goebbels considers *Der Stürmer* nothing more than a pornographic scandal sheet. In August 1935, after Streicher held a *Stürmer*-style speech in Berlin's Sportpalast arena, Goebbels noted in his diary: "Well intentioned, but primitive. Parts of his speech made me laugh." Streicher may be as ridiculous as he is repulsive, but his newspaper sells and has made him a millionaire. By the mid-1930s, it has a circulation of 486,000.

But in the Olympic summer, *Der Stürmer* is a liability. With *Stürmer* boxes all over Berlin, it's inevitable that many international visitors would happen upon one and read what it contained. For example, if they walked from Friedrichstrasse to the Theater am Schiffbauerdamm, they might see an illustration of a buxom, naked women being seduced by a tongue-flicking "Poisonous Snake Juda," topped by the headline "The Blood Sin." Tourists might also learn that the Hessian spa town Bad Orb has been declared "Jew-free." If Jesse Owens got hold of a copy of the paper, he might ask his friend Herb Flemming to translate for him and hear the words: "This is how racially conscious men in America act: they lynch any Negro who even attempts to defile girls of the white race."

Foreigners need to be kept innocent of Streicher's unappetizing scribbles. During the Olympics, issues of *Der Stürmer* continue to be published, but it's forbidden to sell the paper on the streets of Berlin. *Stürmer* boxes are hastily taken down or filled with harmless sports news. For a couple of weeks in the summer of 1936, Berlin is Streicher-free.

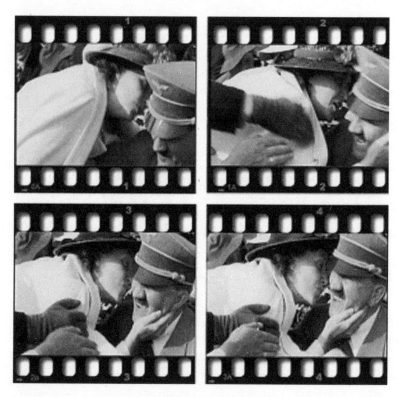

The American tourist Carla de Vries gets noticeably close to Hitler and makes history with her "kiss attack" on the Führer.

Saturday, 15 August 1936

REICH WEATHER SERVICE FORECAST FOR BERLIN: Cloudy and cool in the morning, with occasional showers. In the afternoon sunny and warmer. Highs of 23°C.

"The weather is clearing," Goebbels writes in his diary. "The sun is shining. [The party on] Pfaueninsel has been rescued. This sort of garden party is a test for your nerves."

*

The penultimate day of the Olympic Games and the final day of the aquatics competition. Four gold medals are up for grabs in the afternoon: in the men's 200-meter breaststroke, the women's 400-meter freestyle, the men's 1,500-meter freestyle and the men's water polo. Among the approximately 18,000 spectators following the day's action are 43-year-old Carla de Vries and her husband, George. The couple comes from Norwalk, California, where George had made a considerable fortune as one of the state's largest milk producers, and they're using the Olympics as a welcome excuse to finally

221

fulfill their dream of traveling to Europe. In addition, George will be celebrating his 43rd birthday in exactly two weeks, on 29 August, on the Continent. But today Carla isn't thinking about the future, about the visits they've planned to Rome, Paris, London and other European cities, or her husband's upcoming birthday. Carla is completely focused on one goal. She simply must get a closer look at Adolf Hitler.

She's in luck. The first two events have been concluded when the Führer suddenly appears in the swimming arena. As always, his arrival at one of the sites of competition is stylized into a compelling performance. Terse announcements via the loudspeakers ensure that the spectators—willingly or not—are all aware that Hitler is coming. Carla has learned a few bits of German, so she understands when the stadium announcer says: "The Führer and Reich chancellor is entering the arena."

Hitler is surrounded by the customary crowd of SS men, who accompany him to his seat, where Hans von Tschammer und Osten and Reich Interior Minister Wilhelm Frick are already waiting. Sitting directly next to Hitler is August von Mackensen, the 86-year-old general field marshal who, since the death of Paul von Hindenburg almost two years ago, has been the highest-ranking officer of the venerable Imperial German Army. If Hindenburg was a kind of ersatz Kaiser, then Mackensen is an ersatz Hindenburg. Like Hindenburg, Mackensen serves the Führer as a figurehead of "Old Prussia" and is one of the many archconservative military leaders who eagerly allow themselves to be hitched to the Nazi wagon. The ever-sarcastic residents of Berlin refer to officers like Mackensen as "silver centerpieces," since their function is to lend major state functions in the Third Reich some Prussian elegance and patina.

Carla de Vries, however, isn't interested in Mackensen. She only has eyes for Hitler, sighing over and over "I'm so excited" like a teenager. George couldn't care less and simply shrugs his shoulders at his wife's schoolgirl excitement. Suddenly, Carla leaves her seat and heads in the Führer's direction. No one stops her, even as she gets closer and closer. When there are only a few yards between her and the German leader, she opens her handbag, removes a miniature camera and takes an image of Hitler giving a young man an autograph. No one gets in her way. Carla approaches Hitler and asks him to sign her admission ticket. She's so excited she hops from one foot to the other.

By this time, Hitler's entourage has taken note of the breathless American woman, but no one perceives her as a threat, perhaps because Carla is very well dressed. She's wearing a white skirt and blouse with a shawl and a fashionable red hat. Then, the unthinkable happens. Carla leans over the balustrade behind which Hitler is seated, grabs his head and pulls it toward her, and gives him a kiss. Actually she's trying to kiss him on the lips but Hitler turns away slightly so she only hits his cheek. Only now do the SS men intervene and lead the woman away. The entire stadium is laughing and applauds Carla as she makes her way back to her seat. Hitler, too, seems to take this "kiss attack" in good humor, laughing and joining in the applause.

George de Vries is less amused. What if the SS men had mistaken his wife for an assassin? Carla's foolishness could have been very dangerous. But none of Hitler's bodyguards seems to have considered it possible that Carla might be attacking the Führer with a knife instead of her lips.

The German media, which otherwise cover the Führer's every movement, don't report on this little amorous intermezzo—probably because it represents a lapse in security. A 14-second film sequence that documents the "kiss attack" is confiscated and kept under lock and key. But several articles about Carla de Vries' *coup de main* appear in the United States. She even makes headlines as far away as Sydney, Australia, where the *Morning Herald*, reporting from Norwalk, writes: "Admitting surprise at comment caused by her stolen kiss from Chancellor Hitler during the Olympic games in Berlin, Mrs. Carla de Vries returned to her home here today. 'Why I simply embraced him because he appeared so friendly and gracious…I don't know why I did it, I hadn't planned such a thing. It's just that I'm a woman of impulses, I guess.'"

*

"Gruesome Discovery in Express Train," says the headline in the 16 August edition of the *B.Z. am Mittag* newspaper in Berlin. The article reads: "Shortly after Pressburg, when a passenger opened the door to the toilet, a decapitated, bloody corpse fell out. The passenger passed out in shock. The authorities determined that the deceased had his head completely severed with a cut-throat razor." The train was en route from Berlin to Budapest. The *B.Z.* contains no information on the identity of the deceased, reporting only that he was from Peru. Perhaps it was someone who had been at the Olympics?

DAILY REPORT OF THE STATE POLICE OFFICE, BERLIN: "As previously reported, a man has been causing a commotion in restaurants by launching inflammatory tirades in front of foreigners. Whenever the foreigners reply and voice their enthusiasm about their experiences in Berlin, he tells them to have a look in the north and the east, and they will get a different impression. He himself knows that things are different since he has done time in a concentration camp. Investigations into the perpetrator's identity were initially difficult since his alleged name turned out to be false, and his physical description was not completely accurate. But Criminal Secretary Kümmel, who was charged with the case, has now positively identified him as a certain Herr Selle, and he has confessed to the crime. The man has never been interned in a concentration camp. But he is recorded as having made statements hostile to the state in 1934. The Reichsführer SS has ordered that he be confined to a concentration camp for five years."

*

In Germany, even children are overcome by the mania for titles and offices that is an extension of the so-called Führer principle. In the Hitler Youth, for example, there are squad leaders, superior squad leaders, cadre leaders, superior cadre leaders, group leaders, superior group leaders and primary group leaders. These cumbersome designations are the result of the omnipresence of hierarchies in everyday German life. It's not enough just to have leaders. Wherever there's a leader, there has to be a superior or a primary leader as well—although for some reason, there's no such thing as a superior primary leader.

Another title invented by the Nazis is that of "Reich culture administrator." The German word for this position, *Reichskulturwalter*, was created on 15 November 1935 by official edict, the German language having had no need for it throughout all the preceding centuries. The position, which is largely symbolic, is occupied by Hans Hinkel, a powerful party official whose main job is as one of three directors of the Reich Culture Chamber. The chamber itself was only established by Goebbels in the autumn of 1933 and is charged with monitoring and Nazifying German culture. Anyone who wants to work culturally in the Third Reich must be a member of one of the chamber's seven subdivisions. At the inception of this new organization, all "creators of culture," including Jews, were automatically accepted as members. Then came Hinkel. Born in 1901, he's a card-carrying National Socialist from the party's earliest days, having joined the NSDAP (membership number 287) as a university student in 1921. Two years later, he took part in Hitler's dilettantish, failed putsch in Munich. Now, in the summer of 1936, Hinkel is Goebbels's "special representative for the monitoring of intellectually and culturally active Jews and non-Aryans." The wordiness of this designation conceals the true nature of Hinkel's remit. In reality, he's in charge of "cleansing" the chamber of Jews.

Hinkel is proud of his work. "In terms of creating culture, non-Aryans are no longer involved at all in German intellectual life," he boasts today in an article in the *12-Uhr-Blatt* newspaper. "In the area of artistic reproduction, with the exception of perhaps 1 percent, Jewry has been eliminated." Hinkel adds: "The minute we push a Jewish citizen off his desk chair, we have to address the question: 'What should become of this man?'" Chapters of the so-called Jewish Cultural Association all across the Third Reich are supposed to accommodate unemployed Jewish artists by allowing them to produce Jewish culture for a Jewish audience. Yet even high-ranking Nazi officials often attend association events, in particular musical ones, where they can enjoy the works of banned composers like Felix Mendelssohn and Gustav Mahler. "We saw how they applauded," a Jewish culture association veteran recalled. "They couldn't attend events like ours anywhere else. They were particularly taken with our operas."

But it would be a massive distortion to conclude that the association truly promoted Jewish culture and Jewish artists. What may have looked like the positive assertion of a Jewish cultural identity entailed the acceptance of Nazi restrictions on and discrimination against those they defined as Jews— they were two sides of the same coin. And the former served to mask the latter. "You can't say that things are only done *against* the Jews in Germany," Hinkel cynically says in his newspaper article, claiming to have received letters of gratitude from Jewish representatives for his efforts. "The Zionistic leaders of the

Jewish Cultural Association freely admit that Jewry forgot and denied itself when it tried to take over a cultural sphere that was not appropriate to its nature."

What might the Olympic visitors think, sitting in a café or restaurant on the penultimate day of the Games, if they happen to flip through the *12-Uhr-Blatt* and read Hinkel's article?

GESTAPO TO CUSTOMS INVESTIGATIONS: "Very urgent! We have learned from a confidential source that the Jew Dajou, known until 1929 under the name Leib Kohn, intends to sell his establishment for 60,000–80,000 reichsmarks in cash to a buyer from Zoppot on 16 August 1936 (or at the latest 17 August 1936) and leave the territory of the Reich."

*

For Carl Diem, the penultimate day of the Olympics is chock-full of appointments. At 8 a.m. he's already at the riding events at the military parade grounds in Döberitz just outside the city limits, although he has to leave before the end so that he can make it to the high-diving competition in the swimming arena. The secretary general of the German Olympic Committee also has a number of meetings in his office. At 8:30 p.m. the gold-medal bouts in boxing are taking place, but Diem can't attend because at the same time, the Olympic Concert is being played at the Dietrich Eckart Open-Air Stage, today known as the Berlin Waldbühne.

Adopting an idea by the IOC about how to connect art and athletics, the organizers of the 1936 Olympics are staging a cultural competition. Gold, silver and bronze medals are being awarded in five disciplines: architecture, painting and graphic arts, sculpture, poetry and music. Each genre is divided into sub-disciplines. Poetry, for instance, is broken down into lyric, dramatic and epic works, while music includes orchestral, chamber and vocal categories. Artists from all the Olympic countries are eligible to participate—the only condition is that their works have to deal in artistic form with the Olympics. Individual countries have made preliminary selections, and an international jury will determine the prize winners from the entries submitted. As promising as this idea might sound, the reality is disappointing. The quality of some of the works submitted is so poor that in some disciplines no medals at all are awarded.

At the Olympic Concert, the Berlin Philharmonic is premiering the musical medalists. The concert begins with Strauss's "Olympic Hymn," performed, so to speak, out of competition. The 20,000 members of the audience won't find any other such famous names on their concert programs. The majority of reputable contemporary composers are boycotting the Olympics for political reasons; other refuse to write works for mass spectacles. Thus only nine of the forty-nine Olympic nations have even taken part in the music competition. The international jury consists largely of Nazi flunkies, augmented by the Finnish composer Yrjö Kilpinen and his Italian counterpart Francesco Malipiero, and their preferences are hardly surprising. All three medals for vocal works are given to German composers. In the symphonic category, the Bavarian Werner Egk takes gold, while silver and bronze go to Italy's Lino Liviabella and the Czech Jaroslav Křička. No medals are awarded for chamber music. That simplifies things. There's little foreign presence to disrupt this festival of German self-congratulation.

The concert concludes with Paul Höffer's choral piece "Olympic Oath." The final note has hardly faded when Carl Diem leaves his seat and hurries off. His chauffeur is waiting, with the engine running. They race at near-record speed down the Avus motorway to Pfaueninsel island, where Joseph Goebbels's Olympic party is already in full swing.

*

The figure of the day is 320,000 or, to be more precise, 320,000 reichsmarks (800,000 dollars). That's the cost of the party Goebbels is throwing in the name of the Reich government on Pfaueninsel island. Two comparisons suffice to illustrate the value of that sum in 1936. Two-thirds of all German taxpayers earn 1,500 marks or less this year, making 320,000 marks the equivalent of 213 annual incomes. Or in different terms, Goebbels is spending the average monthly worker's wage of 118 marks on each of his 2,700 guests. No official figure will ever be released for how much Germany is spending on hosting the 1936 Summer Games. As the American ambassador William E. Dodd and others note, the overall sum must be enormous. But nobody dares ask that question publicly.

Goebbels's go-to man for festivities is Benno von Arent, a trained costume designer, self-educated architect and hard-core Nazi. Hitler too appreciates Arent's work and regularly contracts him for special projects such as the design of new diplomatic uniforms, which are covered in so much kitschy gold ornamentation that they are also being used in operettas like *Zar und Zimmermann* and *Die Fledermaus*. Hitler loves them. Since early 1936, Arent has enjoyed the pompous title "Reich Set Designer," an appellation gleefully mocked by salt-of-the-earth Berliners.

For Goebbels's festive finale to the Olympic Games, Arent has come up with a superlative party backdrop intended to transform a small island in the River Havel southwest of Berlin into an exotic, fairy-tale realm. To allow guests to reach their destination without getting their feet wet, a company of engineers have built a pontoon bridge across the Havel. Once they set foot on the island, invitees are welcomed by pages entirely dressed in white who show them the way to the party. The first views are lovely. Thousands of butterfly-shaped lamps decorate the treetops, bathing the tree trunks in muted green. In the center of the island is a clearing, where the party proper is being held. Martha Dodd will later recall festively decorated tables, rivers of wine and a menu with never-ending courses of expensive delicacies. An orchestra plays classical music melodies, and dancers perform atop a raised platform, one of several stages. For later in the evening, Goebbels has engaged the popular bandleader Oscar Joost and his swing orchestra who usually play in the luxurious Eden Hotel.

Joseph and Magda Goebbels personally welcome their many guests of honor, including Martha Dodd and her father William, who is revolted at having to shake Goebbels's hand and relieved not to be seated at the hosts' table. The guests also include the young actress Lída Baarová and her boyfriend, the actor Gustav Fröhlich. Goebbels has met Baarová briefly once or twice in his capacity as propaganda minister, which includes responsibility for films. Tonight the two will become better acquainted, and Goebbels will shower Baarová with compliments. Within a few weeks, he'll be head over heels in love with her.

Chips Channon calls Goebbels's party "the last of the fantastic entertainments, and in a way the most impressive, though it lacked the elegance and chic of Ribbentrop's and the extravagance of Göring's." By this point in the Olympic festivities, it's no longer easy to wow one's guests. The high point of the evening is a gigantic midnight fireworks display. At first the guests marvel at the pyrotechnicians' skill and admire the spectrum of colors in the nighttime sky. But as the spectacle goes on and on—Dodd and Channon both put its duration at a half an hour—the crowd grows uneasy. The endless massive explosions remind many of the guests of artillery fire. Finally, the din comes to an end with a gigantic concluding boom that turns the nocturnal heavens blood-red. It's hard to image a clearer statement by the German government that after the end of the Olympics the period of political moderation will be over.

EXCERPT FROM THE DAILY INSTRUCTIONS OF THE REICH PRESS CONFERENCE: "From the individual local state offices, newspapers will receive guidelines about their concluding commentaries on the Olympic Games. As a general principle, it is announced today that there should be neither any hysterical exclamations of triumph nor any diminishment of German successes. The achievements of all countries are to be honored equitably. If Germany leads the final medals table ahead of the United States, it should be pointed out that Germany will do everything possible to maintain the success it has achieved without the medals being used as a way of displaying German arrogance. Comparisons to German achievements at previous Olympic Games are permitted."

During the closing ceremony of the Olympic Games a cathedral of light is projected into the evening sky. "Never have I seen a show so minutely planned into the very last detail."

Sunday, 16 August 1936

REICH WEATHER SERVICE FORECAST FOR BERLIN: Partly cloudy skies, warmer weather continues. Dry with slight, swirling breezes and some early morning fog. Highs of 25°C.

Bad news for Leon Henri Dajou. The sale of the Quartier Latin has fallen through at the last minute. Actually the two parties had agreed on all the details, and the deal was supposed to be completed today, but the two buyers, Max Apelt and Bruno Limburg, got cold feet. All the notary can do is to communicate the withdrawal of their offer. It's possible that Apelt and Limburg have been tipped off about the investigation of Dajou for various cases of money smuggling. Perhaps they were unsettled by Dajou's insistence that the not inconsiderable purchase price of 60,000 reichsmarks (150,000 dollars) be paid in cash. Whatever the reason, Dajou's situation has taken a dramatic turn for the worse. His plan to flee Germany has failed—so what will become of him and his establishment? It is imperative that he keep his nerve. Dajou decides, for the time being, to continue running his business. As a Nicaraguan citizen, he tells himself, he's safe, and he'll be able to handle Customs Secretary Schulz, who has summoned him for questioning on 20 August. If the worst comes to the worst, he can ask one of his regular customers, Berlin Police President Wolf-Heinrich von Helldorff, to come to the rescue. What Leib Moritz Kohn alias Leon Henri Dajou doesn't realize is that the money-smuggling suspicions are no longer his main worry. The Gestapo is hot on the trail of his Jewish past.

DAILY REPORT OF THE STATE POLICE OFFICE, BERLIN: "The 241st Police Precinct reports that at 10 a.m. on 16 August 1936, civilians found 250 Communist hate pamphlets in Forestry Sections 12, 13 and 17."

*

Thomas Wolfe has just finished breakfast when there's a knock at his door and Heinz Ledig comes in. Wolfe is in a hurry. He doesn't want to miss the start of competition at the Olympic Stadium, and he should already be on his way. He goes to the sink, which is installed in his room's wardrobe, opens the doors and turns on a light. While he brushes his teeth and shaves, Ledig stands at the window, staring down at Kurfürstendamm.

He will be heading to Tyrol with Thea Voelcker for a few days, Wolfe tells his friend while energetically scrubbing his teeth. Tyrol? Ledig looks at Wolfe incredulously, as if to say: why would you take a person like that to northern Italy? The accusing glare reminds Wolfe of the unbearable looks his mother used to give him as a child. He's met up repeatedly with Thea in the past few days, Wolfe adds with a hint of rebelliousness. She's really very nice, and he's looking forward to the trip with her to the Alps. "So you've forgotten your irritation at the 'pig's face'?" Ledig wants to ask, but he holds his tongue. Wolfe is impulsive and quick-tempered, and such a remark is bound to make him flare up. So he doesn't say anything at all. He senses that Wolfe is trying to come up with a harmless excuse for the trip, but that there's really another reason why his friend wants to get out of Berlin.

Ledig puffs on his cigarette and blows the smoke up toward the ceiling. He's trying to get away from the bloody Nazis, Wolfe suddenly exclaims. He's had so many beautiful and fascinating experiences in the past two weeks and at the same time heard so many terrible stories that he needs time to process his thoughts. He has to sort things out, work them through, Wolfe says. Maybe he'll put his experiences of Berlin into one of his books.

Ledig is electrified by the idea. "You must tell zese dret-ful people vhat zey are ..." he urges Wolfe. "I haf a little fantasy ... Ven I feel bad—ven I see all zese dret-ful people valking up and down in ze Kurfürstendamm and sitting at ze tables and putting food into zeir faces—zen I imagine zat I haf a little ma-chine gun. So I take zis little ma-chine gun and go up and down, and ven I see one of zese dret-ful people I go—ping-ping-ping-ping-ping!" Wolfe has to laugh at the idea of his haggard little mate Ledig carrying out a bloody massacre on Kurfürstendamm. But Ledig is deadly serious. He can't write books, and the machine gun only exists in his imagination. As a writer, Wolfe himself possesses a more effective weapon of self-defense, Ledig continues. But he must be careful. Ledig warns him not to say anything that will anger the Nazis.

Wolfe stares at his friend in disbelief. It's now his turn to be disapproving, since for him resistance and appeasement are mutually exclusive. "A man must write what he must write," he says portentously. "A man must do what he must do." Ledig lights his umpteenth cigarette of the day and takes several deep drags before declaring, "You are one big fool." Ledig crosses the room, sits down, stands back up again. He stubs out his cigarette in an ashtray, only to immediately fish the next one from the packet. "You can write everysing you need to write wizout zese Party people coming down on you," he says. "You do not need to mention zem. And if you do mention zem, and do not say nice sings, zen ve can no longer read you, and you cannot come back." Ledig asks Wolfe if he wants the Reich Writers Chamber to ban his works. Of course not, the writer answers. He loves Berlin and wants to come back again, often. "You and I and all the friends we know…" he promises, "we'll sit together drinking, we'll stay up all night and dance around the trees and go to Aenne Maenz at three o'clock in the morning for chicken soup. All of it will be the same." But Ledig knows that he has failed to convince his friend to censor himself—and that nothing will ever be the same again. He looks at the clock and tells Wolfe that he needs to leave now if he wants to get to the Olympic Stadium in time. Then he stubs out his latest cigarette and say to Wolfe with a sad smile: "Vell, zen, you must do vhat you must do. But you are one big fool."

*

William Edward Dodd has had enough of the Olympics. The U.S. ambassador may have only returned to Germany a week ago, having missed the first seven days of the spectacle, but ever since he's been back, his life has consisted of nothing but appointments and receptions. Professor Dodd would much prefer to be poring over his history books. The social and diplomatic duties attending the Games are a nightmare. Unlike André François-Poncet, he feels revolted whenever he has anything to do personally with the Nazi leadership. The antipathy is mutual. Whereas Hitler has nothing bad to say about the French ambassador, he considers "old Dodd" nothing short of an "idiot." Dodd would like nothing better than to avoid the Nazis entirely, but that's impossible for a diplomat—to say nothing of the American ambassador to Germany. So Dodd has gritted his teeth and gone to various Olympic festivities, called upon Ribbentrop and Göring, and yesterday attended Goebbels's party. The memory of the fireworks still makes him feel queasy.

The Olympic closing ceremony today is another diplomatic chore. Around 1 p.m., Dodd gets in a limousine waiting in front of his villa with his wife and his daughter, Martha. In his diary, he describes seeing countless flags of Germany and other nations as the car makes the 7-mile-journey from Tiergarten park in central Berlin to the Olympic Stadium. Dodd estimates that 100,000 SS and SA men line the route in tightly packed rows. After arriving at the Olympic Stadium, the Dodds take their seats at the front of the diplomatic box. Other ambassadors and foreign VIPs like Sir Henry Channon and his wife Lady Honor Guinness are already there. Hitler is expected to appear shortly in the "Führer's box" overhead.

Although Hitler has no official function on the final day of the Olympic Games, he's still the center of attention. As he enters the arena, the so-called Führer pennant is raised. Dodd is chilled at the sight of over 100,000 people taking to their feet to salute one individual. After Hitler sits down, the last athletic chapter of the XI Summer Olympic Games commences: the finals of the equestrian events.

The German team is leading the competition, thanks in no small measure to First Lieutenant Konrad von Wangenheim. Yesterday, the 26-year-old and his horse Kurfürst fell during the eventing, and Wangenheim broke his left collar bone. Despite the painful injury, he got back in the saddle and finished his ride. Understandably, doctors have advised Wangenheim not to compete in today's jumping, but he's having none of their advice. A gasp goes through the stadium when the spectators see him with his shoulder in a sling sitting atop his horse and riding out into the course. At first everything goes smoothly, but just after the halfway point, the scene takes a dramatic turn. Kurfürst falls while going around a sharp bend and lies on the ground, motionless. Many of the spectators fear that the horse has died. But suddenly the gelding regains its feet, and in accordance with the rules Wangenheim gets back in the saddle without help and completes his ride. This coup de main wins the hearts of the crowd and seals the gold medal for Germany.

There's only one person in the stands who refuses to join in the admiring applause. "For hours we watched the competitors, saw the humiliation of England, in a field where she surely ought to excel, and witnessed the German and other countries' 'victories,'" Chips Channon confides in his diary. It's not Britain's day, with the equestrian team earning only a meager team bronze in the eventing. Disgusted, Chips begins paying more attention to the athletes' interactions with the Führer than to the action down below. "As each horseman rode into the arena, he smartly saluted Hitler, who always lifted his hand in return. We saw him all the time in the distance and he seemed amiable and enjoying himself."

Konrad von Wangenheim's heroism is a gift to the Nazi propaganda machine. Newspaper writers immediately begin composing paeans to the young man's "willingness to sacrifice," "comradely spirit" and "courageousness." These are all qualities that Hitler expects to find in Germany's soldiers. By this point, he is already determined to go to war.

*

12-Uhr-Blatt newspaper announces the setting of a new record: Berlin's public transport system, the BVG, has serviced almost 62.6 million passengers in the past twenty days.

*

Werner Finck is an actor and a cabaret artist, but for Joseph Goebbels he's tantamount to an enemy of the state. For years Finck's plays on words have infuriated the propaganda minister, even though Finck avoids voicing open resistance to the Nazi regime. His gift for seemingly accidental, passing remarks makes Goebbels see red. Earlier in his career, with his face the very picture of innocence, Finck regularly took to the stage of the Katakombe, the cabaret theater he himself founded, to poke fun at the Third Reich and its representatives. Humor can be a particularly effective weapon.

"As far as proof of Aryan identity is concerned, I've always—knock on wood—had good luck," ran one of Finck's routines. "The only exception was a family member of mine from medieval times, a squire named Lewinski. Fortunately the church in his parish burned down, and no disadvantageous information survived." In another routine, he told the audience that he had planted an oak tree in honor of Hitler and was very satisfied at how it had grown. "A couple of months ago, it was very small," Finck said. "A bit later is was knee-height, and now I'm up to my neck in it."

Jokes like this went too far for Goebbels, who in 1934 had the Katakombe closed and Finck arrested and sent to the Esterwagen concentration camp, where he was confined along with the left-wing journalist Carl von Ossietsky and the Social Democrat Julius Leber. But fortune smiled on Finck. In early July 1935 he was released at the behest of Hermann Göring, although he was prohibited from working for a year. "Back then, I involuntarily had a lot of free time," Finck later recalled. "What was I to do? I got married." Finck's ban on working elapsed just as the Olympic Games started. The cabaret artist is enormously popular in Berlin, and the Nazis want to profit from that. Finck is allowed to write a daily column entitled "Short Olympic Conference" about everyday life in Berlin for the *Berliner Tageblatt* newspaper.

Finck, however, cannot curb his tongue, taking risks with allusions and wordplay. In the final instalment of his column, he writes: "The visitors from all over the world are leaving. Never have they been so spectacularly welcomed. The question is: how have Leni's cameras recorded it all?" Finck imagines Leni Riefenstahl inspecting the negatives of footage of Jesse Owens's spectacular triumphs. "Suddenly she sees in reverse how positively the Negro ran. In the negatives, we get our revenge. The white man is at the head of the pack. Meters in front of the others, while the black fellows bring up the rear!"

*

"Endless awards ceremonies," Goebbels writes in his diary. Up in the stands, the propaganda minister is slowly but surely losing patience. The equestrian events, in which he's never been able to take an interest, go on for hours, and the awarding of the medals takes far too long for his taste. "All that needs to be more concise and effective," Goebbels huffs. He probably isn't the only one with itchy feet. Most of the other spectators too are probably eagerly awaiting the closing ceremony.

The sun is slowly setting behind the Marathon Gate, when Paul Winter's "Olympic Fanfare" heralds the start of the Olympics' final act. All eyes are on the tunnel underneath the gate, where the Olympic countries march in, carrying their national flags. Leading the way is Greece, the Olympic homeland, and the parade is concluded with the German team bearing the swastika. As the athletes strut along, the Olympic Symphony Orchestra plays Julius Möllendorf's "Parade March 1." As its last notes fade, after a few seconds' silence Henri de Baillet-Latour steps up to the microphone, thanks Hitler and the German people for their hospitality and declares the end of the Games. The count's concluding words are shown on a giant display: "May the Olympic flame shine through all generations for the benefit of an ever higher striving, courageous and pure humanity."

After some more music, Beethoven's "Opferlied," the Olympic flag is taken down to a volley of salutatory gunfire. Then the orchestra plays "Fahnenabschied" (Departure of Flags) by Paul Höffer, one of the winners of the Olympic music competition, as the national teams exit the stadium. The Olympic flame is extinguished, and the Olympic flag is handed over to the city of Berlin for safekeeping until the next Games, scheduled for 1940 in Tokyo. Finally a further Paul Höffer composition, "Olympia-Ausklang" (Olympic Finale), is played. Massive spotlights mounted all around the stadium beam columns of light into the evening sky, slowly moving toward one another and eventually crossing paths 325 feet above the arena. The result is a gigantic cathedral of light—an effect the National Socialists use for their party rallies in Nuremberg. "Never have I seen a show so minutely planned into the very last detail," William Dodd writes in his diary. The final item on the program is the song "Die Spiele sind aus" (The Games are Over), with the spectators singing along. With that the ceremony is over. Adolf Hitler hasn't said a word the entire time. But in the end the pretense of international Olympic harmony collapses as tens of thousands of people leave their seats to bellow "*Heil Hitler!*" and sing "Deutschland, Deutschland über alles."

In Zurich, Thomas Mann sits by his radio listening to the Olympics' concluding ceremony, which is being broadcast live throughout Europe. In his diary he writes: "Great theater, fanfares, choruses and ceremonial flag-waving. A voice from above summoned the youth of the world to Tokyo. Everyone pronounced the name of the city correctly except the mayor of Berlin, who said Tock-EE-o. He also talked about peace on earth."

*

On the evening of 16 August, Reich Sports Leader Hans von Tschammer und Osten prepares a party for the Olympic participants in the Deutschlandhalle arena. But many of the athletes went home after their events were over, and others departed Berlin earlier today, so that only about 1,000 people are left in the Olympic Village. "We're all deeply moved and somewhat melancholy," Goebbels writes. "Went with the Führer through the cheering crowds. At the Reich Chancellery." Thousands and perhaps tens of thousands have assembled on neighboring Wilhelmplatz, chanting, "Dear Führer, be a good fellow and make an appearance at your window." Hitler is happy to oblige.

Hitler and Goebbels have every reason to be satisfied with the past sixteen days. The XI Olympic Games will go down in the history books for a variety of reasons. Almost 4,000 athletes from 49 countries took part in 129 competitions—more than ever before. Forty-one new Olympic records were set, as well as 15 world records. With 89 medals (33 gold, 26 silver, 30 bronze),

Germany is far and away the most successful country, followed by the United States (24 gold, 20 silver, 12 bronze) and Hungary (10 gold, 1 silver, 5 bronze). Bringing up the rear in the medals table are Portugal, the Philippines and Australia, which only took one bronze medal each. All in all, the competitions were conducted fairly, there was no hostility toward any particular nations, and no instances of cheating emerged. Jesse Owens was the most successful athlete, with four gold medals, while Konrad Frey was the best German one, taking gold three times.

At least 380,000 tourists registered in Berlin in July and August 1936, of which 115,000 came from abroad. The largest groups, with around 15,000 apiece, were the Czechs and the Americans. The authorities will count 1.3 million nights spent by tourists in the German capital. Hitler later claims that the Olympic Games brought half a billion reichsmarks (1.25 billion dollars) to Berlin. It's hard to say whether this figure is correct. But we can safely assume that hosting the Games has been worthwhile.

Any potential earnings are only a pleasant by-product in the eyes of the National Socialists. The value of the 1936 Olympic Games cannot be measured in marks and pfennigs. Most of the foreign visitors enjoyed their trips and came away overwhelmed by what Nazi Berlin had to offer. Hitler and his regime were able to present themselves as peace-loving, reliable members of the family of nations. These sixteen days of August give many people new hope that things will change and Hitler can be trusted to keep his promises of peace. The sporting spectacle has helped pull the wool over their eyes. Few of the Olympic tourists were able, as Thomas Wolfe ultimately was, to see through the masquerade.

The Olympic Games mark the end of the era in which the Nazis consolidated power. But André François-Poncet will later take issue with the idea that the 1936 Games were *only* a propaganda triumph. "In the history of the Nazi regime," the French ambassador will write, "the ceremonies of the Olympic Games in Berlin in August 1936 were a high point, a summit and maybe an apotheosis for Hitler and the Third Reich."

Late in the evening of 16 August, Hitler and Goebbels take leave of one another. A few hours later, the Führer departs for his retreat in Berchtesgaden, while Goebbels withdraws for a short holiday in his villa on the Havel River island of Schwanenwerder. In three weeks, on 8 September, the next mass spectacle will get underway—the Nazi Party rally in Nuremberg. Goebbels has urged Hitler to cancel that rally this year so that he can recover from the stress of the Olympics, but the Führer has refused. The "Rally of Honor," as it's known, must go ahead. The restoration of Germany's "honor" and sovereignty must be celebrated. What Hitler means is the remilitarization of the Rhineland in violation of international treaties.

Victor Klemperer views the upcoming Nazi self-congratulation with alarm. He fears that many Nazis will be feeling pent-up aggression after having to conceal their true nature from the foreign visitors for the past weeks. "The Olympics will be over next Sunday," Klemperer writes while the Games are still in full swing. "The NSDAP Party Rally is approaching, an explosion is imminent, and of course people will take out their frustrations first on the Jews."

In the summer of 1964 Jesse Owens returns to the scene of his triumphs. Time has left its marks on both the athlete and Berlin's Olympic Stadium.

What became of…?

In November 1936, Leni Riefenstahl begins editing more than 1.3 million feet of film—an endeavor that takes eighteen months. The end result is a two-part documentary using 20,000 feet of film that premieres on 20 April 1938, Hitler's 49th birthday. *Olympia* is a huge hit in Nazi Germany, earning more than 4 million reichsmarks (10 million dollars) within the space of a few weeks. Riefenstahl also makes English, French and Italian versions of her work and tours Europe showing it. The director is Nazi Germany's most famous artist. By the end of the Second World War, Riefenstahl is only 43 years old. She'll live for another 58 years, but she never makes another film. Instead, she reinvents herself and starts a second career as a photographer.

In the early 1980s, Riefenstahl writes her memoirs, 900 pages' worth, often playing fast and loose with the truth. She dies in September 2003 without ever critically examining her role in the Third Reich. On the contrary, she spends considerable time and energy legally pursuing people who claim that she had an affair with Adolf Hitler. In fact there's nothing to the rumors to that effect. As early as 1943/4, the German writer Carl Zuckmayer told the American secret service: "[She's] supposed to have slept with Hitler, which the author doubts. (We can assume mutual impotence.)"

*

Henri de Baillet-Latour remains the president of the International Olympic Committee until his death in January 1942. After the Berlin Games, Theodor Lewald is forced to resign from all his offices. He dies in April 1947. In 1938, Walter von Reichenau, a military officer, is named as Lewald's replacement. Two years later, toward the end of May 1940, Baillet-Latour will get to experience Reichenau in a wholly different capacity: as the Wehrmacht colonel general who accepts the capitulation of Baillet-Latour's home country, Belgium.

*

After departing from Berlin, Eleanor Holm Jarrett lives up to her glamour-girl reputation. In 1938, she acts alongside her former Olympic teammate and gold-medal-winning decathlete Glenn Morris in the film *Tarzan's Revenge*. That year, she divorces Art Jarrett to marry the enormously wealthy impresario William "Billy" Rose. Rose is Jewish. As a wedding present, Holm gives him Hermann Göring's swastika, which she has had embellished with a Star of David made of diamonds. Holm dies in January 2004.

*

Leon Henri Dajou may not have succeeded in selling the Quartier Latin to the highest bidder, but in the months following the Olympics he is able to siphon off large sums of money from the business. After his misfortune, he enjoys some luck. The Nazis still have him under investigation, but they don't notice his embezzlement. By February 1937, the Quartier Latin is deep in debt, and Dajou absconds to Paris, taking along his girlfriend Charlotte Schmidtke. At the end of March, Dajou opens the Cotton Club on rue Pigalle. The concept—high prices, elegant atmosphere and beautiful women—is the same as in the Quartier Latin, but Dajou fails to re-create his success in Paris and goes bankrupt by the end of the year. He whiles away his time in the cafés of Montmartre, as the Parisian immigration police note, and his relationship to Schmidtke falls apart. In the chaos of the Second World War, he tempo-rarily disappears from view. Schmidtke moves to Portofino in Italy, where she gets a letter from a Berlin lawyer who asks, probably at the behest of the Gestapo, whether she knew Dajou was Jewish. "At the time I never suspected that Dajou could be from a Jewish background," she replies. "The people who frequented his establishment were always very respectable, and without doubt, they would have had to avoid him and would have done so." It's a sly dig at the many high-ranking Nazis who patronized the Quartier Latin. The Gestapo doesn't ask any more questions.

Suddenly, in the early 1940s, Dajou turns up in England. In September 1942, he marries his new girlfriend, Rosalie, and four years later he adopts both British citizenship and another new identity. Leon Henri becomes Rico Dajou, passing himself off as two years younger than he is. Rico is a fixture of London nightlife in the 1950s and '60s. He opens the Don Juan club in Mayfair and, a few doors down, the Casanova Club. Both establishments cater to high society. The Queen's rambunctious younger sister, Princess Margaret, is a regular. Dajou tells a regional American newspaper that he's going to write his memoirs, but he never gets around to it. In 1984, Leib Moritz Kohn alias Leon Henri Dajou alias Rico Dajou dies in his adopted homeland of England. The building where the Quartier Latin was located in Berlin doesn't survive the bombardment of the city during the war. Today the site is occupied by a bank.

*

Leon Henri Dajou's friend Hubert von Meyerinck completes around twenty films by the end of the Third Reich. But "Hupsi" despises the system of which he is a part. "He never bragged about it," the film director Billy Wilder will tell the German news magazine *Der Spiegel* many years later, "but during the Kristallnacht pogrom he walked down Kurfürstendamm and called out, 'Anyone who's Jewish, follow me.' He hid people in his apartment. Yes, they did exist, upstanding people whose word you could trust, because it was very difficult to practice resistance in a time like that. People like Meyerinck were tremendous, wonderful." The postwar years are the high point of the actor's career. In countless films and TV shows, he jokes and puns his way through the Federal Republic of Germany's cinemas and living rooms. In 1967, more than thirty years after the Berlin Games, he writes in his autobiography: "How I'd like to go to Dajou's place again!" Hubert von Meyerinck dies in Hamburg in May 1971.

*

At some point, Mascha Kaléko admits the truth to her husband, Saul, telling him that little Evjatar Alexander Michael, who sees the light of day on 28 December 1936 in Berlin, is not his son. To mark the birth of her only child she writes the following poem:

> You whom I loved before he lived
> Born of unreason and of love
> The light of pale hours and heaven's reward
> My little son.
>
> You, my child, fully owned my heart
> When you were still nothing, a far-off glimmer
> From your father's dark eyes
> In that year.

Mascha and Saul divorce in early 1938 and never lay eyes on one another again. In the autumn of 1938, with Chemjo Vinaver, whom she marries while still in Berlin, and her son, Kaléko emigrates to the United States. After the fall of National Socialism, Kaléko visits Berlin and Germany a number of times. She dies in Zurich in 1975.

*

After the Berlin Games, Tilly Fleischer ends her track-and-field career. She leads a quiet life, marrying a dentist and opening two leather goods shops in the Black Forest in southern Germany. Then, in 1966, a book is published in France with the trashy title *Adolf Hitler mon père*. The author is Philippe Mervyn, whose real name is Philipp Krischer. He comes from Vienna and is engaged to Fleischer's daughter Gisela. The book alleges that Tilly Fleischer and Hitler had an affair a short time after the 1936 Olympic Games, and that Gisela is the offspring of the Führer and not the daughter of a dentist. Gisela Hitler? The book's introduction reads: "The daughter of the bloodiest dictator of all time addresses coming generations and dedicates to them this unsettling human document, which is more genuine than any other historical memoirs by any other authors." Krischer alias Mervyn claims to have heard the story from Gisela herself, but she denies telling him anything of the sort. The case goes to the courts, and Gisela's true parents win. The judge orders all copies of the "memoirs" to be confiscated. Tilly Fleischer dies in July 2005 in the Black Forest.

*

Peter Joachim Fröhlich, the little boy from the Olympic Stadium, flees Germany with his parents in April 1939, initially landing in Cuba. Two years later, the family emigrates to the United States. In 1946, Peter becomes an American citizen and changes his name. Peter Fröhlich becomes Peter Gay, one of the most respected historians, authors and experts on Germany. Peter Gay dies in May 2015 in New York.

*

Teddy Stauffer and his Original Teddies play regular gigs in Berlin and Hamburg for the next three years. By late March 1939, the band has recorded more than fifty records for the Telefunken label, including their smash hit "Jeepers Creepers." They are booked to play a residency in Berlin's Femina Bar, but the Second World War intervenes. Stauffer stays in Switzerland, while the German band members are forced to leave the Alpine country, and the group breaks up. Stauffer tries to go to Hollywood to work as a film composer, but he lacks a residence permit and ends up in Mexico. He makes his way to Acapulco, where he starts a nightclub and works as a hotel manager. Within a few years, "Mister Acapulco," as Stauffer soon becomes known, helps turn a fishing village into a hot spot for the international jet set. Clark Gable, Josephine Baker, Errol Flynn and the Kennedys are all friends and regular customers. Stauffer marries and divorces five times. He dies in Acapulco in 1991.

*

Helene Mayer returns to the United States, where she wins eight national fencing championships. She earns a living teaching German and sport. But she feels homesick, and in 1952 she moves back to Germany. She marries the aeronautical engineer

Erwin Falkner von Sonnenburg, nine years her senior, and moves to Heidelberg. There she intends to start a new life, but she is diagnosed with breast cancer. Helene Falkner von Sonnenburg dies in October 1953 at the age of only 43.

*

Two days after the end of the Olympic Games, the commandant of the Olympic Village, Baron Werner von und zu Gilsa, invites his fellow members of the organizing committee to the Berlin Guards' casino. The colonel wants to take stock of the Olympics over a meal and a glass of wine and express his gratitude to everyone who made the event happen. His predecessor Wolfgang Fürstner doesn't show up. While the others are celebrating, Fürstner dons his best uniform, replete with medals, and marches through the Olympic Village toward the lake in the woods. By the sauna building, he draws his pistol, puts the barrel to his forehead and pulls the trigger.

*

On the evening of 10 November 1936, Yvonne Fürstner gets a visit from two gentlemen named Scherer and Franke. They're neither friends nor acquaintances, nor customers from the Sherbini Bar. In fact, Yvonne can't recall seeing them ever before in her life. But here they are at the door to her apartment, demanding to be let in. Scherer and Franke are customs officials. "Search warrant," one of them says, and hands Yvonne an official notification, while the other one gets down to work. The two men don't go about their job gently. They fish through her closets and drawers, look behind her books and peer underneath her bed. In the course of their search, the officials find some cash, various bank statements and several personal letters. That's enough for them. Two days later, Fürstner is arrested and taken into investigative custody at Moabit prison. She's accused of money smuggling. The officials suspect that with the help of her sister, who lives in England, Fürstner has transferred considerable sums abroad to hide them from the German tax authorities. The papers found in her apartment are cause for "considerable suspicion," Scherer writes in his report, although no convincing evidence is ever located. Fürstner is released on 19 December.

The game of cat and mouse continues. In the summer of 1937, Fürstner tells the authorities that she has married the Egyptian diplomat Aziz de Nasr and is now living with him in the quiet Berlin suburb of Lichterfelde. "Your husband isn't registered there," Scherer objects. "And the Foreign Ministry has no knowledge of a trade attaché named de Nasr at the Egyptian embassy." How could they? The purported trade attaché is none other than Fürstner's 23-year-old admirer from the Sherbini Bar, who is still living as a lodger with Frau Oppenheim. The marriage, if indeed there ever was one, is for appearances only. Perhaps Fürstner thinks that she'll be safe from the Nazis if they think she's the wife of an Egyptian diplomat. It's unclear whether she is still seeing Mustafa El Sherbini at this juncture.

The bar on Uhlandstrasse exists until 1938, after which there's no trace of Sherbini and Fürstner. In March 1941, Sherbini's name appears in a book of wanted persons in Germany, but he seems to have already left the country. Fürstner also succeeds in fleeing Germany, but destiny isn't on her side. Exactly ten years after the Berlin Games, in August 1946, Yvonne de Nasr dies in Cairo. She is only 45 years old. After the war, Mustafa El Sherbini also settles in Cairo, opening a hotel there. Later he moves to London, where he dies in 1975. Herb Flemming, the Sherbini Bar's great attraction, stays on for a year in Berlin before returning to the United States in 1937. After the war, Flemming resumes performing in Europe. In 1969, when he revisits Berlin, he can't recognize Uhlandstrasse. There's not a brick left in place at the location where he played the hottest of jazz thirty years earlier. Flemming dies in New York in 1976.

*

Carla and George de Vries return to the United States after their European trip. The excitement about Carla's "kiss attack" soon dies down, but in November 1936, Mrs. de Vries is once again back in the public eye, thanks to a drama in front of a high-rise building in Los Angeles. A deranged woman has climbed out of an upper-story window onto the ledge and is threatening to jump. The police arrive, but officers find it difficult to communicate with the woman, who speaks a mishmash of German and English. Her name is Emma Neumann. She comes from a German family and is confined to a suburban mental asylum from which she has escaped. Carla, who happens to be passing by, sees the commotion, pushes her way through the crowd of gawkers and gets involved. She speaks a little German, she tells a police officer. Maybe she can talk the woman out of jumping. The officer in charge assents—he doesn't know what else to do. Carla climbs out of the window and begins talking to Neumann. On the street below, hundreds of people are staring up at the spectacle. The police begin to spread rescue nets. Doctors and paramedics are at the scene. Unfortunately we don't know what Carla says to the unhappy woman. Perhaps she tells her about the trip to Europe she just took with her husband, George, and what the two of them had experienced in Berlin. In any case, at some point Emma Neumann nods her head. Carla climbs back inside the building, extends her hand and pulls the would-be suicide from the ledge. Carla is a heroine, and the newspapers go berserk. The woman who kissed Hitler has saved some crazy lady's life. Carla de Vries outlives her husband by thirty-five years, passing away in June 1985 in California.

*

Reich Cultural Administrator and Reich Director of Film Hans Hinkel is one of the many former Nazis who never have to answer for their crimes in the Federal Republic of Germany. Hinkel is, however, interned at the end of the Second World War, and in 1947 he is extradited to Poland and convicted of looting Polish cultural treasures. After serving five years in prison, he returns to Germany in 1952. He dies in Göttingen in 1960.

*

The fate of Ahmed Mustafa Dissouki is largely unclear. What we know is that he runs the Ciro Bar until the spring of 1939, although the establishment has long been on the decline. Dissouki stops paying his bills and social insurance contributions for his employees and keeps racking up fresh debts. At some point, he loses track of his finances, and with insolvency looming, legal action is taken against him. In July 1939, he is scheduled to be deported to Egypt. But suddenly, Heinrich Himmler intervenes and countermands the deportation order. We don't know why. The Foreign Ministry files on the case are destroyed in the Second World War.

The next trace of Dissouki comes in October 1941, when Himmler issues a prohibition upon him residing in Germany. Nonetheless, three years later he is still in Berlin. In September 1944, he's taken into investigative custody for a couple of weeks in Moabit prison. The last we see of him is in April 1945. "He approached me on Adolf-Hitler-Platz with a lady on his arm," Hubert von Meyerinck will later recall. "I wanted to say hello, but he waved me off fearfully."

Dissouki's lover Clara von Gontard is visiting relatives in the United States with her husband and daughter when the Second World War begins in 1939. The Gontards stay in St. Louis, where Paul von Gontard dies in December 1941. Bernhard Berghaus, on the other hand, remains in Germany and continues to do brisk business with the Nazis. Exploiting his excellent connections, he succeeds in transferring a large portion of his wealth to his parents-in-law in Switzerland. After the war, the family villa in the Tiergarten district is restored to Clara von Gontard. She dies in 1959, and four years later her heirs sell the mansion to the city of Berlin. The Villa Gontard, once the revolving-door playground of the rich and beautiful, is now home to the general directorship of Berlin's state museums.

The Ciro Bar survives the war and experiences a miniature renaissance in the 1950s. Today, there is still an establishment by the name of Ciro at Rankestrasse 31–32—a lap-dance bar.

*

Elisabeth L.'s family is taken from the camp in Marzahn to the Sachsenhausen concentration camp and then deported to the so-called gypsy camp at Auschwitz in 1943. Of the approximately 22,600 people imprisoned there, more than 19,000 die. Elisabeth herself survives the Third Reich.

*

In mid-July 1945, Heinz Zellermayer opens the Restaurant Zellermayer in the provisionally repaired remains of the bombed-out Hotel am Steinplatz. It's the beginning of a unique career that over the years will see Zellermayer become Berlin's leading restaurateur. He goes down in city history in June 1949 when he convinces the American military commander in Berlin, Frank L. Howley, to revoke mandatory closing hours for bars and restaurants at the next meeting of the Allied Control Council. From now on, people in Berlin can enjoy themselves throughout the night. In 1950, Heinz's brother Achim opens the Volle Pulle Bar on the ground floor of the family hotel. The smoky place soon becomes a favorite haunt of postwar West German intellectuals. Their sister, Ilse, fulfils her lifelong dream of studying singing. However, she becomes famous running an agency for opera performers that represents none other than the great Luciano Pavarotti.

*

Mildred and Arvid Harnack are arrested in September 1942 and accused of being members of the anti-Nazi resistance organization Rote Kapelle. The Reich War Court wastes no time in sentencing Arvid to death for high treason that December. Mildred receives a six-year term of imprisonment, but Hitler refuses to approve the sentence. He orders a new trial, which concludes in mid-January 1943 with a death sentence. Arvid is hanged in Berlin's Plötzensee prison on 22 December 1942. Mildred is put to death there by guillotine on 16 February 1943. Shortly before the blade is dropped at 6:57 on that Tuesday evening, Mildred's last words are recorded as: "And I loved Germany so very much."

*

Jesse Owens, the undisputed hero of the Berlin Olympics, hangs up his running shoes upon returning to the United States. The 23-year-old athlete simply doesn't earn enough money from sport to feed his family. He's also disappointed at the reception he's given in America. In September, his achievements are honored with a parade in New York, but because of his skin color he's forced to use the service elevator to get to the ceremonial banquet at the Waldorf Astoria hotel. "Hitler didn't snub me," Owens once famously says. "It was our president who snubbed me. The president didn't even send me a telegram."

Owens opens up a dry cleaner's and appears at vaudeville shows and nightclubs. That earns him a tidy little income, which he unfortunately squanders on the stock market. Three years after the Olympic Games, the hero of Berlin is bankrupt. Owens tries to exploit his reputation as the fastest man in the world by racing against motorcycles, greyhounds and horses at country fairs. That's not a long-term solution to his problems. He only begins to receive the appreciation he deserves in the 1950s. In the summer of 1964, he visits West Berlin and returns to the Olympic Stadium to appear in a documentary film. He dies of lung cancer in March 1980. By that point, his friend and competitor Luz Long has been dead for thirty-seven years. Having been drafted into the Wehrmacht, Long is killed in battle in Sicily in July 1943.

*

Miraculously, Victor Klemperer survives both the Third Reich and the firebombing of Dresden in February 1945. Two years after the end of the Second World War, he takes his revenge on his persecutors. In his book *The Language of the Third Reich*, Klemperer details how National Socialism degraded the German language into a *"lingua tertii imperii."* In the 1950s, he is involved in the reconstruction of East Germany. He dies in 1960 in Dresden. His diaries are published posthumously in 1995 and become a worldwide literary sensation.

*

André François-Poncet stays in Berlin for two years before being made French ambassador to Italy. In 1940, he returns to France and becomes an adviser to the collaborationist Vichy government. In late August 1943, after the German occupation of France, he is arrested by the Gestapo and interned along with two dozen other prominent French personalities as "guests of honor of the Reich government" at Itter Castle in Austria and the Ifer Hotel in western Germany. Even years later, François-Poncet remains outraged at the privations he was forced to endure, recalling, "I had to eat stews!" In August 1949, he is named French High Commissioner in the newly formed Federal Republic of Germany. He holds that office until 1955. François-Poncet dies in January 1978 in Paris.

*

Otto Horcher continues to make good money servicing the needs of Hermann Göring. As the gastronomic rearguard of the Wehrmacht, Horcher takes over restaurants in Vienna (Zu den drei Husaren) and Paris (Maxim's). But as the course of the war turns against Germany in early 1943, Joseph Goebbels increasingly trains his animosity on Horcher. After the battle of Stalingrad, the propaganda minister wants to shut down all of Berlin's gourmet eateries. The conflict with Horcher's regular Göring is inevitable, and a nasty feud breaks out, in which Goebbels enlists Hitler on his side. One night, when SA men smash his restaurant windows, Otto Horcher acknowledges that the tide is turning against him. Göring provides the restaurateur with the necessary papers and an entire Reichsbahn train to transport his restaurant: the kitchen appliances, stoves, tables, chairs, porcelain, silverware and the famous poultry presses. Horcher leaves nothing behind in Berlin. He's off to Madrid. As unbelievable as it may sound, while Europe is engulfed in flames, Horcher has his gourmet restaurant carted all the way across the Continent. By mid-November 1943, he celebrates his reopening in the Spanish capital. Today the restaurant is still family-owned and considered one of the top gourmet addresses in Madrid.

The site in Berlin where André François-Poncet used to savor the *canard à la rouennaise* is now occupied by an ugly postwar building. On the ground floor there's a kebab shop.

*

In January 1937, six months after his night of drunken excess ended so badly, the master bricklayer Erich Arendt learns his fate from the judge. The Reich Ministry of Justice has decided not to prosecute him for violating "Paragraph 2 of the Law against Perfidious Attacks on the State and Party in conjunction with an act of treason, as well as insulting the Führer and the Reich Chancellor." The Berlin court does, however, decide that there is enough evidence to convict him on another charge. Still, Arendt is a lucky man. The verdict reads: "The defendant is sentenced to six weeks in prison for violating the Law on Title, Medals and Honors of 15 May 1934 and is responsible for bearing all costs. The sentence is deemed to have already been served thanks to the time the defendant has spent in investigative custody."

*

As he announced to his friend Heinz Ledig, Thomas Wolfe takes a trip with Thea Voelcker to the village of Alpbach near Kufstein in Tyrol, where they take a room at a small inn. During the day, Wolfe works on a manuscript. At night he visits the local restaurant with Voelcker. The first few days are enjoyable, but then he starts to feel increasingly uneasy. Voelcker's melancholy disposition, the smallness of their room and the rural environs get on his nerves. "He was irritated and disappointed," Ledig will recall. "Although not in so many words, he let me know that he had abandoned his blond traveling companion up in the mountains and left."

In early September, Wolfe returns to Berlin via Munich. As though he suspects that he will never see the city that is so close to his heart ever again, he plunges into its nightlife, visiting the Scala and the Delphi Palast, having dinner at Schlichter and drinking at Aenne Maenz's place. But he is suddenly no longer enjoying the capital. He's feeling restless, and makes plans to head to Paris and then back to the United States. On his last evening in Berlin, he meets up with Ledig. "We kept drinking and drinking, and he picked a fight with me on the street so that

I parted from him in drunken anger," Ledig will recall. "This time I didn't shed any tears. Our farewell seemed just as absurd as everything going on around me. Some sort of creeping poison had destroyed our friendship. I stumbled into bed, dead tired, and slept until the middle of the next day. That afternoon in the office, I found a note from him: 'Never mind our trouble. Love to both of you. Tom.'"

By the time Ledig discovers the note, Wolfe is already sitting on a train that will take him via Aachen to France. It's Tuesday, 8 September 1936. Wolfe shares his compartment with four others, including a woman, a fellow American and a little man who's visibly nervous. The train journey is long and tedious, so Tom and his fellow countryman go to the dining car for an extended lunch. When they return to the compartment, he begins conversing with the others. Wolfe is American, is that right? asks the small man. Would he mind doing him a favor? Wolfe agrees. The train will soon be arriving in Aachen, the small man tells him, which is near the border. The passengers will be checked— there are strict rules against taking more than 10 reichsmarks (25 dollars) out of the country. He has some cash...The man doesn't finish his sentence, showing the coins in his hand. Wolfe understands immediately and takes the money from him. When they're safely across the border, Wolfe will return the coins.

When they arrive at Aachen, German border police get on the train and proceed from compartment to compartment. Wolfe takes the opportunity to stretch his legs. When he returns to his seat, there's a big commotion, and he sees the police leading the small man away. What's the matter? Wolfe asks the woman in his compartment. The man seems to have had a larger sum of money on him, she whispers, and that's not allowed. Plus, he's apparently a Jew. Wolfe looks at his fellow passengers with querying eyes. It's his own fault, the woman says, gradually working herself into an anti-Semitic rage. Everyone knows that exporting larger sums of money is forbidden. "But the ten marks!..." the woman jeers. "Since he had all this other money, why, in God's name, did he give ten marks to you? It was so stupid! There was no reason for it!"

The arrest of the Jewish man and the woman's coldhearted reaction to it leave a deeply disturbing impression on Wolfe, who is filled with hatred and anger at the people responsible for such injustice. He then remembers the promise he made to Heinz Ledig on the final day of the Olympic Games: someday he'll write a book about his experiences in the Third Reich.

As soon as he's back in New York, he immediately sits down to work. Before long he has published an autobiographical short story entitled "I Have a Thing to Tell You." On the one hand, the story is a love letter to Berlin; on the other it's a vivid final reckoning with the Nazis and their regime. Ernst Rowohlt, Heinz Ledig, Thea Voelcker and his fellow passengers from the train all feature in the text in barely fictionalized guise. When Ledig reads a prepublication excerpt from the story in an American newspaper in the spring of 1937, he can't believe his eyes. Wolfe has remembered conversations with him, Rowohlt and other Berlin friends with amazing accuracy. What will happen if officials from the Propaganda Ministry read it and figure out who the thinly veiled inspirations for the fictional characters are? It wouldn't be difficult to put two and two together and draw a connection with the Rowohlt publishing house. In a hastily convened emergency meeting, Ledig, Rowohlt, Ernst von Salomon, Martha Dodd and other friends of Wolfe discuss the danger they potentially face because of the story's publication. Dodd bursts into tears and advises the others to leave Germany as soon as possible, but the others never seriously consider it. "After rocking his upper body back and forth the whole time like a polar bear," Salomon will later recall, "Rowohlt suddenly beamed with relief and bellowed, 'Ho, ho…nothing can happen to me! All I ever said was: Cheers!'" After some further discussion, Wolfe's friends decide that they shouldn't panic. They should just wait and see how things develop. But the fear remains.

Thomas Clayton Wolfe dies of tuberculosis on 15 September 1938 at the age of 37. Disappointed and tired of life, Thea Voelcker overdoses on sleeping pills in August 1941. Ernst Rowohlt lives to drink countless further bottles of Mosel. After the Second World War, he resumes publishing, first in Stuttgart, then in Hamburg, and becomes one of the most important cultural figures in the young Federal Republic of Germany. One of his biggest hits is Ernst von Salomon's autobiography *Der Fragebogen* (The Questionnaire). After Rowohlt dies in 1960, his illegitimate son Heinz Ledig takes over the publishing house. Salomon dies in August 1972, Martha Dodd in August 1990, and Heinrich-Maria (Heinz) Ledig-Rowohlt in February 1992.

The very Thursday that the world learns of the death of the American writer Thomas Wolfe, the British prime minister, Neville Chamberlain, boards a plane to southern Germany. His destination is the Obersalzberg near Berchtesgaden. At Hitler's Alpine retreat, he will negotiate with the German dictator about the Sudetenland in an attempt to stop Germany's expansionism and fend off a new world war. But his efforts will only delay, not prevent that catastrophe.

Acknowledgments

I received a lot of help in my work, and I would particularly like to express my heartfelt gratitude to all the employees of the archives and collections I consulted, especially Annette Thomas and Gisela Erler at the Landesarchiv Berlin, who were always willing to guide me through their institution's holdings.

I would also like to thank Thomas Rathnow and Jens Dehning at my German publisher, Siedler Verlag; my Munich editor Karen Guddas; and Ditta Ahmadi, who did her usual excellent job in the aesthetic presentation of words and photographs. My agent Barbara Wenner was my constant support in word and deed. I'm very grateful to her.

For various reasons, I also want to thank Christian Becker, Shareen Blair Brysac, Christine Casapicola, Dr. Elke Fröhlich, Armin Fuhrer, Dr. Heike Görtemaker, Professor Dr. Manfred Görtemaker, Professor Ulrich Gröner, Andrea Hofmann, Dr. Florian Huber, Dr. Emanuel Hübner, Dorothea Hütte, Dr. Hans Kitzmüller, Dr. Jürgen May, Dr. Steven B. Rogers, Jutta Rosenkranz, Dr. Claus W. Schäfer, Michael Töteberg, Professor Dr. Michael Tsokos, Beatrice Vierneisel, Annegret Wilke, Ilse Zellermayer and Gisela Zoch-Westphal.

Finally I offer huge thanks to my parents Ilona and Wilfried Hilmes and—last, but not least—to Peter Franzek.

Notes

Saturday, 1 August 1936

2   "directors of a flea circus": Elke Fröhlich (ed.), *Die Tagebücher von Joseph Goebbels*, Part I, Vol. 3/II, Munich, 2001, p. 146.

4   "first man who crosses my path": Harry Graf Kessler, *Das Tagebuch: Vierter Band 1906–1914*, Stuttgart, 2005, pp. 590f.

5   "beggars rampant in Garmisch": Richard Strauss to Municipal Council Garmisch, 1 Feb. 1933, copy in BAB, R 8076/236.

6   "makes work for idle hands": Willi Schuh (ed.), *Richard Strauss— Stefan Zweig: Briefwechsel*, Frankfurt/Main, 1957, p. 90.

6   "important that he like it": Richard Strauss to Hans Heinrich Lammers, 20 Dec. 1934, copy in BAB, R 43II/729.

7   "I'm starving!": Hannes Trautloft, *Als Jagdflieger in Spanien: Aus dem Tagebuch eines deutschen Legionärs*, Berlin, 1940, p. 15.

9   "It's raining slightly": Fröhlich (ed.), *Die Tagebücher von Joseph Goebbels*, Part I, Vol. 3/II, p. 146.

11   "radio proposals, photographers, etc....": Richard S. Kennedy and Paschal Reeves (eds.), *The Notebooks of Thomas Wolfe*, Vol. 2, Chapel Hill, 1970, p. 748.

11   "people I've met in Europe": Thomas Wolfe to Maxwell Perkins, 23 May 1935, in Elizabeth Nowell (ed.), *The Letters of Thomas Wolfe*, New York, 1956, p. 460.

12 "sound of music in the air": Thomas Wolfe, *You Can't Go Home Again*, New York, 2011, p. 528.

13 "such as the Buddha or Messiahs use": ibid, p. 533.

15 "learn this sentence by heart": "Alle Welt ist begeistert. Die Boykott-Bewegung gegen Hitlers Olympiade 1936 in Berlin scheiterte," in *Der Spiegel*, No. 5/1980, p. 123.

16 "That fellow really can compose": Fröhlich (ed.), *Die Tagebücher von Joseph Goebbels*, Part I, Vol. 3/II, p. 112.

16 "Handshake with Hitler": Franz Trenner (ed.), *Richard Strauss: Chronik zu Leben und Werk*, Vienna, 2003, p. 573.

17 "just as smoothly for war": cited from "Alle Welt ist begeistert," p. 116.

17 "his eyes were filled with tears": Stephan Tauschitz to Guido Schmidt, 5 Aug. 1936, ÖSTA/ADR, Neues Politisches Archiv, Politische Berichte Berlin, No. 176/1936.

18 "can be found for this accusation": BAB, NS 10/51.

Sunday, 2 August 1936

23 "daily reports as ordered": BAB, R 58/2322.

24 "That's the terrible thing!": Fröhlich (ed.), *Die Tagebücher von Joseph Goebbels*, Part I, Vol. 3/II, p. 147.

26 "in front of the Führer": "Olympiasiegerin Tilly Fleischer grüsst die Leser der Nachtausgabe," in *Berliner illustrierte Nachtausgabe*, 2 Aug. 1936.

27 "Adolf + I with oak": Reinhard Rürup (ed.), *1936: Die Olympischen Spiele und der Nationalsozialismus*, Berlin, 1996, p. 182.

30 "have got over it somehow": Horst Winter, *Dreh dich noch einmal um: Erinnerungen des Kapellmeisters der Hoch- und Deutschmeister*, Vienna, 1989, p. 26.

32 "gestures stimulating intercourse": Vernehmung Hanns Curth, LAB, A Pr.Br.Rep. 030–02–05 No. 20.

Monday, 3 August 1936

36 "'I think it's time to go'": Mascha Kaléko, "Der nächste Morgen," from *idem, Das lyrische Stenogrammheft: Kleines Lesebuch für Grosse,* © Rowohlt Taschenbuch Verlag GmbH, Reinbek bei Hamburg 1978; digital rights © dtv Verlagsgesellschaft, Munich 2015.

38 "And that's for the best": Fröhlich (ed.), *Die Tagebücher von Joseph Goebbels,* Part I, Vol. 3/II, p. 148.

38 "Now she's inconsolable": Elke Fröhlich (ed.), *Die Tagebücher von Joseph Goebbels,* Part I, Vol. 2/II, Munich, 2004, p. 133.

39 "a woman born as a Jew": "Wir gratulieren, Herr Goebbels!" *Die Rote Fahne,* 18 Dec. 1931.

39 "gruesome person": Elke Fröhlich (ed.), *Die Tagebücher von Joseph Goebbels,* Part I, Vol. 2/III, Munich, 2004, p. 115.

39 "nauseous": ibid., p. 150.

40 "wretched hypocrite": Fröhlich (ed.), *Die Tagebücher von Joseph Goebbels,* Part I, Vol. 2/II, p. 63.

40 "We've separated internally": Elke Fröhlich (ed.), *Die Tagebücher von Joseph Goebbels,* Part I, Vol. 3/I, Munich, 2005, p. 67.

40 "recover from this": Fröhlich (ed.), *Die Tagebücher von Joseph Goebbels,* Part I, Vol. 3/II, p. 147.

40 "two-day visits": Hans Bohrmann and Gabriele Toepser-Ziegert (eds.), *NS-Presseanweisungen der Vorkriegszeit: Edition und Dokumentation,* Vol. 4/1936, Munich, 1993, p. 830.

42 "make it to the top three?": "Borchmeyer im Endlauf," *Olympia-Zeitung,* 4 Aug. 1936.

43 "shaking hands with this Negro": Baldur von Schirach, *Ich glaubte an Hitler,* Hamburg, 1967, p. 217.

43 "and other sporting competitions": Albert Speer, *Erinnerungen,* Berlin, 2007, p. 86.

43 "which preaches racial hatred": BAB, R 58/2320.

44   "should be mentioned occasionally": Bohrmann and Toepser-Ziegert (eds.), *NS-Presseanweisungen der Vorkriegszeit*, pp. 831f.

45   "in Montparnasse and not in Berlin": "Tumult im Luxusrestaurant," *Berliner Herold*, 11 Nov. 1934.

47   "by different standards": Yvonne Fürstner to Lieselotte Meigs, 15 Nov. 1935, in LAB, A Rep. 358–02 No. 118497.

47   "of Bornemannstrasse 3": BAB, NS 10/51.

48   "Very nice!": Thomas Mann, *Tagebücher. 1935–1936*, ed. Peter de Mendelssohn, Frankfurt/Main, 1978, p. 344f.

50   "my large intestine": ibid, p. 350.

Tuesday, 4 August 1936

55   "splendid Rüdesheimer Riesling": Thomas Wolfe, "Brooklyn, Europa und ich," *Die Dame, Illustrierte Mode-Zeitschrift*, Issue 3/1939, pp. 41f.

55   "arrived at Tempelhof shunting yard": BAB, NS 10/51.

55   "Will Owens win a second gold?": *B.Z. am Mittag*, 4 Aug. 1936, p. 1.

56   "who he's up against?": Jeremy Schaap, *Triumph: The Untold Story of Jesse Owens and Hitler's Olympics*, Boston, 2007, p. 200.

56   the sort of story: "Jesses Märchen," *Der Spiegel*, No. 1/2015, p. 105.

57   " 'to give my best!' ": Luz Long, "Mein Kampf mit Owens," in Kai-Heinrich Long, *Luz Long—eine Sportlerkarriere im Dritten Reich: Sein Leben in Dokumenten und Bildern*, Hildesheim, 2015, pp. 101f.

58   "without any culture over there?": Fröhlich (ed.), *Die Tagebücher von Joseph Goebbels*, Part I, Vol. 3/II, p. 149.

58   "embrace a Negro": Long, *Luz Long—eine Sportlerkarriere im Dritten Reich*, p. 208.

58   "during the Olympic Games": BAB, R 58/2320.

59   "spaghetti and macaroni": "Speisekarte für Olympia-Gäste," *Berliner Lokal-Anzeiger*, 17 July 1936.

59   "the English and the Dutch": "Speisekarte für Olympia-Gäste,"
     Berliner Lokal-Anzeiger, 14 July 1936.

60   "the glory of their history and art": "Wir sprachen Thomas Wolfe,"
     Berliner Tageblatt, 5 Aug. 1936.

61   "as a woman could be": Wolfe, *You Can't Go Home Again*, p. 530.

61   "here is a friend": Thea Voelcker to Thomas Wolfe, 20 Oct. 1936, HLB.

62   "the women seen there": *Die Dame*, Issue 16/1936, pp. 33f.

64   "at Monbijoustrasse 2": BAB, NS 10/51.

65   "as best they could": *Die Olympischen Spiele 1936*, Vol. 2, Berlin 1936,
     p. 120.

Wednesday, 5 August 1936

68   "'they all know the truth'": Ernst von Salomon, *Der Fragebogen*,
     Reinbek, 2003, pp. 273f.

69   "read from their faces": Stephan Tauschitz to Guido Schmidt, 5 Aug.
     1936, ÖSTA/ADR, Neues Politisches Archiv, Politische Berichte Berlin,
     No. 175/1936.

71   "s'ink it str-a-a-nge?": cited in Kennedy, *The Notebooks of Thomas
     Wolfe*, Vol. 2, p. 834.

72   "turn your nose up at": H. P. Tillenburg, "Klirrender Stahl im Kuppelsaal:
     Wir besuchen die olympischen Amazonen," *Olympia-Zeitung*, 7 Aug.
     1936.

77   "inflammatory pamphlets were found": BAB, R 58/2320.

77   "that's for sure": Fröhlich (ed.), *Die Tagebücher von Joseph Goebbels*,
     Part I, Vol. 3/II, p. 150.

79   "a halo of importance": Bella Fromm, *Als Hitler mir die Hand küsste*,
     Berlin, 1993, p. 250.

79   "you old cow": Jürgen Trimborn, *Riefenstahl: Eine deutsche Karriere*,
     Berlin, 2002, p. 256.

80   "make his exit": Carl Zuckmayer, *Geheimreport*, Munich, 2007, pp. 93f.

81 "pre-1870, that is": Salomon, *Der Fragebogen*, p. 277.

81 "you are that woman!": Martha Dodd, *Meine Jahre in Deutschland 1933–1938: Nice to meet you, Mr. Hitler!*, Frankfurt/Main, 2005, p. 74.

81 fluttered around his groin like a butterfly: Shareen Blair Brysac, *Mildred Harnack und die Rote Kapelle: Die Geschichte einer ungewöhnlichen Frau und einer Widerstandsbewegung*, Berlin, 2003, p. 229.

83 "so I yelled": cited in David Herbert Donald, *Look Homeward: A Life of Thomas Wolfe*, Boston, 1987, p. 386.

Thursday, 6 August 1936

86 "velvety as Oxford sward": Wolfe, *You Can't Go Home Again*, p. 540.

88 "austere royal Prussian pomp": Heinrich Maria Ledig-Rowohlt, "Thomas Wolfe in Berlin," in *Der Monat. Eine internationale Zeitschrift für Politik und geistiges Leben*, Oct. 1948, p. 74.

91 "I enlightened him": Fröhlich (ed.), *Die Tagebücher von Joseph Goebbels*, Part I, Vol. 3/II, p. 151.

92 "'You're right'": Alfred Rosenberg, *Die Tagebücher von 1934 bis 1944*, ed. Jürgen Matthäus and Frank Bajohr, Frankfurt/Main, 2015, pp. 186f.

92 "liked him and his wife at once": *Documents on British Foreign Policy 1919–1939*, Second Series, Vol. 17, London, 1979, p. 768.

93 "what he meant by it": ibid., pp. 767f.

93 "with racial perspectives": Bohrmann and Toepser-Ziegert (eds.), *NS-Presseanweisungen der Vorkriegszeit*, p. 853.

93 "I could find anywhere": Fröhlich (ed.), *Die Tagebücher von Joseph Goebbels*, Part I, Vol. 3/II, p. 151.

94 "it won't cloud our friendship": Fröhlich (ed.), *Die Tagebücher von Joseph Goebbels*, Part I, Vol. 2/II, p. 98.

94 "good to one another": ibid., p. 100.

94 "the way I like him best": Fröhlich (ed.), *Die Tagebücher von Joseph Goebbels*, Part I, Vol. 3/II, p. 151.

95 "particularly transparent": "Deutsch—nicht Schachteldeutsch!" *Berliner Lokal-Anzeiger*, 6 Aug. 1936.

96 "the Olympics as camouflage": Fromm, *Als Hitler mir die Hand küsste*, p. 250.

97 "Every sentence hit its mark": Fröhlich (ed.), *Die Tagebücher von Joseph Goebbels*, Part I, Vol. 3/II, p. 151f.

97 "unite the peoples of Europe": "Festlicher Abend in der Staatsoper," *Berliner Lokal-Anzeiger*, 7 Aug. 1936.

97 "major feat of propaganda": Fröhlich (ed.), *Die Tagebücher von Joseph Goebbels*, Part I, Vol. 3/II, p. 151f.

98 "are impressed?": Willy Brandt, *Erinnerungen*, Frankfurt/Main, 1989, p. 110.

99 "even moderate resistance": Paul Schmidt, *Statist auf diplomatischer Bühne 1923–45: Erlebnisse des Chefdolmetschers im Auswärtigen Amt mit den Staatsmännern Europas*, Bonn, 1953, p. 325.

100 "within four years": Wilhelm Treue, "Hitlers Denkschrift zum Vierjahresplan 1936," *Vierteljahrshefte für Zeitgeschichte* 3/2 (1955), p. 210.

100 "No culprit located": BAB, R 58/2320.

100 "his mother's opinion": Ledig-Rowohlt, "Thomas Wolfe in Berlin," p. 74.

101 "personal answers only": *Berliner Lokal-Anzeiger*, 6 Aug. 1936.

Friday, 7 August 1936

105 "Long live the maidens of Germany!": "Sven Hedin besucht ein Arbeitsdienstlager," *Berliner Lokal-Anzeiger*, 7 Aug. 1936.

106 "no one did voluntarily": Jewish prisoner Alfred Lomnitz, cited in Günter Morsch (ed.), *Sachsenhausen: Das "Konzentrationslager bei der Reichshauptstadt,"* Berlin, 2014, p. 27.

107 "They are too many in number": *Lernen Sie das schöne Deutschland kennen: Ein Reiseführer, unentbehrlich für jeden Besucher der Olympischen Spiele zu Berlin*, copy in BAB, R 58/2320.

107 "from the Olympic Games in Berlin": Trautloft, *Als Jagdflieger in Spanien*, pp. 20f.

108 "Then there will be some shooting": Fröhlich (ed.), *Die Tagebücher von Joseph Goebbels*, Part I, Vol. 3/II, p. 152.

110 233,748 oranges: all statistics from *Amtlicher Bericht 11. Olympiade Berlin 1936*, Berlin, 1937, Vol. 1, pp. 234–45.

110 "agreement on basic questions": "Unterrichtung über Rassengesetze," *Nationalsozialistische Parteikorrespondenz*, 7 Aug. 1936.

111 "a piece of mass suggestion": Fröhlich (ed.), *Die Tagebücher von Joseph Goebbels*, Part I, Vol. 3/II, p. 152.

111 "athletes' first names": Bohrmann and Toepser-Ziegert (eds), *NS-Presseanweisungen der Vorkriegszeit*, p. 860.

113 "speed that was astounding": Wolfe, *You Can't Go Home Again*, p. 531.

114 "lasted a lifetime": Salomon, *Der Fragebogen*, pp. 265f.

115 "be over soon": Fröhlich (ed.), *Die Tagebücher von Joseph Goebbels*, Part I, Vol. 3/II, p. 153.

Saturday, 8 August 1936

117 "extraordinarily bad": Bohrmann and Toepser-Ziegert (eds.), *NS-Presseanweisungen der Vorkriegszeit*, p. 864.

119 "There was nothing": cited in Rürup, *1936*, p. 141.

119 "anyone and everyone": Oskar Böhmer, cited in Patricia Pientka, *Das Zwangslager für Sinti und Roma in Berlin-Marzahn: Alltag, Verfolgung und Deportation*, Berlin, 2013, p. 77.

121 "even a pistol": www.theguardian.com/sport/blog/2011/now/24/forgotten -story-football-1936-olympics.

121 "But Germany is completely innocent": Fröhlich (ed.), *Die Tagebücher von Joseph Goebbels*, Part I, Vol. 3/II, p. 156.

122 "but spectators too": "Schwarze Kunst Basketball," *Der Angriff*, 8 Aug. 1936.

123 "Marvelous World of Illusions": *Berliner Lokal-Anzeiger*, 6 Aug. 1936.

124 "swank magazines": Carl von Ossietzky, "Gontard," in *Die Weltbühne*, 16 Dec. 1930.

125 "we were so up to date": Fritz Schulz-Reichel, cited in Knud Wolffram, *Tanzdielen und Vergnügungspaläste: Berliner Nachtleben in den dreissiger und vierziger Jahren*, Berlin, 2001, p. 189.

127 "have yielded no results": BAB, R 58/2320.

129 "in front of 100,000 spectators": Leni Riefenstahl, *Memoiren*, Munich, 1987, p. 272.

129 "'Very interesting'": Dodd, *Meine Jahre in Deutschland*, p. 360.

129 "a thousand bits of chatter": Fröhlich (ed.), *Die Tagebücher von Joseph Goebbels*, Part I, Vol. 3/II, p. 153.

130 "crowded and inelegant": Robert Rhodes James (ed.), *Chips: The Diaries of Sir Henry Channon*, London, 1993, p. 108.

Sunday, 9 August 1936

134 "forced into the third category": Peter Gay, *Meine deutsche Frage: Jugend in Berlin 1933–1939*, Munich, 1999, p. 63.

134 "swapping one superstition for another": ibid., p. 67.

138 "the whole stadium was sad": Fröhlich (ed.), *Die Tagebücher von Joseph Goebbels*, Part I, Vol. 3/II, p. 154.

138 "one of the greatest moments in my life": Gay, *Meine deutsche Frage*, p. 100.

138 "This is Germany's youth": BAB, NS 10/51.

140 "like a top cellist": drummer Jonny Heling, cited in Wolffram, *Tanzdielen und Vergnügungspaläste*, p. 187.

141 "step-dance to hot jazz!": "Sherbini will verkaufen," *Berliner Herold*, 20 Jan. 1935.

141 that this was the case: see Egino Biagioni, *Herb Flemming: A Jazz Pioneer around the World*, Alphen, 1977, p. 51.

142 "concerning the racial question": BAB, NS 10/51.

144 as everyone in Germany did?: Ledig-Rowohlt, "Thomas Wolfe in Berlin," p. 71.

144 "you are not free to say this": Kennedy, *The Notebooks of Thomas Wolfe*, Vol. 2, p. 829.

145 "Only the horses are happy in Germany": ibid., p. 822.

Monday, 10 August 1936

154 "would get him in trouble one day": Craftsmen's Guild Eberswalde-Oberbarnim to Chief Prosecutor, Regional Court, 12 Aug. 1936, LAB, A Rep. 358–02 No. 18117.

155 "my dear Hupsi": Hubert von Meyerinck, *Meine berühmten Freundinnen: Erinnerungen*, Düsseldorf, 1967, p. 114.

157 "that Dajou is a Jew": Berlin's Police President to Gestapo, 2 March 1938, LAB, B Rep. 202 No. 4258.

Tuesday, 11 August 1936

161 "last week": *Berliner Tageblatt*, 11 Aug. 1936.

163 "dancing alongside Americans": Teddy Stauffer, *Es war und ist ein herrliches Leben*, Berlin, 1968, pp. 115ff.

163 "They really went wild": interview with Walter Dobschinsky, in Bernd Polster (ed.), *Swing Heil: Jazz im Nationalsozialismus*, Berlin, 1989, p. 69.

164 "play American numbers": interview with Bob Huber, in Wolffram, *Tanzdielen und Vergnügungspaläste*, p. 143.

164 "Hitler's Berlin in 1936": Stauffer, *Es war und ist ein herrliches Leben*, p. 117.

165 "How I suffered!": Fröhlich (ed.), *Die Tagebücher von Joseph Goebbels*, Part I, Vol. 3/I, p. 334.

166 "decisions are final": "Foto-Wettbewerb," *Elegante Welt*, Nr. 15, 1936, p. 64.

167 "is astonishing": André François-Poncet, *Als Botschafter in Berlin 1931–1938*, Mainz, 1949, p. 296.

167 "as a gentleman": George S. Messersmith to Cordell Hull, 21 March 1935, UOD, MSS 109.

167 "cheated his way into his job": Goebbels, cited in Joachim C. Fest, *Das Gesicht des Dritten Reiches: Profile einer totalitären Herrschaft*, Munich, 1988, p. 246.

169 "un-painted face": James (ed.), *Chips: The Diaries of Sir Henry Channon*, p. 62.

169 "went somewhat to my head": ibid., p. 110.

172 "in his life": BAB, NS 10/51.

Wednesday, 12 August 1936

176 "shall be put to death": *Reichsgesetzblatt* Nr. 56/1936, 22 June 1936, p. 493.

176 "Commentary is to be avoided": Bohrmann and Toepser-Ziegert (eds), *NS-Presseanweisungen der Vorkriegszeit*, p. 875.

177 "how to fly our warplanes": Trautloft, *Als Jagdflieger in Spanien*, p. 26.

177 "a happy conclusion": Fröhlich (ed.), *Die Tagebücher von Joseph Goebbels*, Part I, Vol. 3/II, p. 156.

178 pyres made of wooden pews: see, for example, "Priester verbrannt," *Berliner Lokal-Anzeiger*, 6 Aug. 1936.

179 "for all nations": Bohrmann and Toepser-Ziegert (eds), *NS-Presseanweisungen der Vorkriegszeit*, p. 882.

180 1.8 billion gallons were drunk: Theo Gläss (ed.), *Zahlen zur Alkoholfrage*, Berlin, 1938.

181 "there's nothing like being a soldier": *Deutschland-Bericht der Sopade*, July 1936, pp. 830f.

182 "But don't you ever tell me": cited in Jutta Rosenkranz, *Mascha Kaléko: Biografie*, Munich, 2007, p. 60.

182 "It's you I steer toward": Mascha Kaléko, "Für Einen," from *idem, Das lyrische Stenogrammheft*, p. 94.

For Someone

The others are the deep blue sea
But you are the port
Believe me, you can be at peace.
It's you I steer toward.

For all the storms that found me
Leaving my sails short.
The others are the vibrant sea
But you are the port.

You're the lighthouse, the destination
Your sleep is disturbed no more.
The others are just waves in motion
While you are the port.

© Rowohlt Taschenbuch Verlag GmbH, Reinbek bei Hamburg 1978 digital rights © dtv Verlagsgesellschaft, Munich 2015

183 "in the last two years": cited in Gisela Zoch-Westphal, *Aus den sechs Leben der Mascha Kaléko*, Berlin, 1987, p. 69.

184 "the Führer and the state": BAB, NS 10/51.

184 "He's too unmasculine for him": Elke Fröhlich (ed.), *Die Tagebücher von Joseph Goebbels*, Part II, Vol. 1, Munich, 1996, p. 272.

185 "even hatred": Erich Ebermayer, *Eh' ich's vergesse: Erinnerungen an Gerhart Hauptmann, Thomas Mann, Klaus Mann, Gustaf Gründgens, Emil Jannings und Stefan Zweig*, Munich, 2005, p. 184.

186 "puts himself in danger": Zuckmayer, *Geheimreport*, p. 131.

186 "you could rely upon": Thomas Blubacher, *Gustaf Gründgens: Biographie*, Leipzig, 2013, p. 199.

187 "No, of course not": Marcel Reich-Ranicki, *Mein Leben*, Stuttgart, 1999, pp. 125f.

Thursday, 13 August 1936

190 "laid claim to her achievement": Victor Klemperer, *Tagebücher 1935– 1936*, Berlin, 1995, pp. 122f.

191 "not permitted either": cited in Jutta Braun, "Helene Mayer: Eine jüdische Sportlerin in Deutschland," in *Gesichter der Zeitgeschichte: Deutsche Lebensläufe im 20. Jahrhundert*, Munich, 2009, p. 92.

193 respected the IOC's principles: see Rürup, *1936*, p. 57.

193 "in the American South": Bericht des deutschen Nachrichtenbüros, 21 Oct. 1935, BAB, R 43II/729.

194 "last for many years": Bericht des deutschen Nachrichtenbüros, 22 Oct. 1935, BAB, R 43II/729.

195 "the real position is in Germany": George S. Messersmith to Cordell Hull, 15 Nov. 1935, UOD, MSS 109.

196 "(Olympic laughter—snort!)": Alfred Kerr, "Nazi-Olympiade," *Pariser Tageszeitung. quotidien Anti-Hitlerien*, 13 Aug. 1936.

198 "with the cruelty left out": James (ed.), *Chips: The Diaries of Sir Henry Channon*, p. 111.

198 "for a short time": Fröhlich (ed.), *Die Tagebücher von Joseph Goebbels*, Part I, Vol. 3/II, p. 158.

198 "the focus than previously": Bohrmann and Toepser-Ziegert (eds.), *NS-Presseanweisungen der Vorkriegszeit*, p. 886.

200 "Of course not": cited in Dave Anderson, "The Grande Dame of the Olympics," *New York Times*, 3 July 1984.

200 "with the club foot": cited in Richard Witt, *Lifetime of Training for Just Ten Seconds: Olympians in Their Own Words*, London, 2012, p. 101.

203 "slice of her": Ledig-Rowohlt, "Thomas Wolfe in Berlin," p. 72.

204 "pieces by Count Eulenburg": Emil Szittya, *Das Kuriositäten-Kabinett*, Konstanz, 1923, p. 60.

204 "rain begins to fall": Wolfe, *You Can't Go Home Again*, p. 533.

205 "as unmistakable as death": ibid., p. 537.

Friday, 14 August 1936

209 "It's Madame de Berlichingen": "Ein Zeuge tritt ab," *Der Spiegel*, 2 March 1955, p. 13.

211 "blood and liver sausage": Salomon, *Der Fragebogen*, p. 454.

213 chafing dish: on the dishes served in Horcher's, see Heckh, *Eine Fussbank für die Dame: Eine kulinarische Revue*, Stuttgart, 1969.

214 "details about the incident": BAB, R 58/2320.

215 "the toughness we admire": *Die Olympischen Spiele 1936*, Vol. 2, p. 71.

217 "gets Streicher with it": cited in Franco Ruault, *Tödliche Maskeraden: Julius Streicher und die Lösung der Judenfrage*, Frankfurt/Main, 2009, p. 9.

217 "horny Jewish goats": "Hungernde deutsche Mädchen in den Klauen geiler Judenböcke," *Der Stürmer*, No. 35, Aug. 1925.

217 "butcher of Breslau?": "Ritualmord? Wer ist der Kinderschlächter von Breslau?" *Der Stürmer*, No. 28, July 1926.

217 "carved-up Polish girl": "Der Bluthund. Furchtbare Bluttaten jüdischer Mordorganizationen. Das geschächtete Polenmädchen," *Der Stürmer*, No. 39, Sept. 1926.

218 "made me laugh": Fröhlich (ed.), *Die Tagebücher von Joseph Goebbels*, Part I, Vol. 3/I, p. 277.

218 "The Blood Sin": "Die Blutsünde," *Der Stürmer*, No. 35, Aug. 1936.

218 "Jew-free": "Bad Orb ist judenfrei," *Der Stürmer*, No. 34, Aug. 1936.

218 "girls of the white race": "Die Judenpresse," *Der Stürmer*, No. 32, Aug. 1936.

Saturday, 15 August 1936

221   "a test for your nerves": Fröhlich (ed.), *Die Tagebücher von Joseph Goebbels*, Part I, Vol. 3/II, p. 160.

224   "'a woman of impulses, I guess'": *Sydney Morning Herald*, 17 Aug. 1936.

224   "with a cut-throat razor": *B.Z. am Mittag*, 15 Aug. 1936.

225   "for five years": BAB, R 58/2320.

227   "'What should become of this man?'": "... und das Kulturleben der Nichtarier in Deutschland?" *Das 12-Uhr-Blatt*, 15 Aug. 1936.

227   "taken with our operas": Eike Geisel and Henryk M. Broder, *Premiere und Pogrom: Der Jüdische Kulturbund 1933–1941*, Berlin, 1992, p. 254.

228   "not appropriate to its nature": *Das 12-Uhr-Blatt*, 15 Aug. 1936.

228   "territory of the Reich": Prussian Gestapo to Customs Investigations, 15 Aug. 1936, LAB, B Rep. 202 No. 4258.

232   "extravagance of Göring's": James (ed.), *Chips: The Diaries of Sir Henry Channon*, p. 112.

233   "are permitted": Bohrmann and Toepser-Ziegert (eds), *NS-Presseanweisungen der Vorkriegszeit*, p. 895.

Sunday, 16 August 1936

236   "Forestry Sections 12, 13 and 17": BAB, R 58/2320.

238   "one big fool": Wolfe, *You Can't Go Home Again*, pp. 549, 550, 553, 555.

239   "idiot": Werner Jochmann (ed.), *Adolf Hitler: Monologe im Führerhauptquartier 1941–1944. Aufgezeichnet von Heinrich Heim*, Munich, 2000, p. 118.

241   "enjoying himself": James (ed.), *Chips: The Diaries of Sir Henry Channon*, p. 112.

241   in the past twenty days: *Das 12-Uhr-Blatt*, 18 Aug. 1936.

242   "information survived": Werner Finck, *Alter Narr—was nun? Die Geschichte meiner Zeit*, Frankfurt/Main, 1978, p. 63.

242 "up to my neck in it": ibid, p. 65.

242 "I got married": ibid., p. 73.

243 "bring up the rear!": Werner Finck, "Kleine Olympia-Conférence. Schlussakkord," *Berliner Tageblatt*, 16 Aug. 1936.

243 "concise and effective": Fröhlich (ed.), *Die Tagebücher von Joseph Goebbels*, Part I, Vol. 3/II, p. 161.

244 "very last detail": William H. Dodd, *Diplomat auf heissem Boden: Tagebuch des USA-Botschafters William E. Dodd in Berlin 1933–1938*, Berlin, 1964, p. 382.

245 "peace on earth": Mann, *Tagebücher. 1935–1936*, p. 354.

245 "At the Reich Chancellery": Fröhlich (ed.), *Die Tagebücher von Joseph Goebbels*, Part I, Vol. 3/II, p. 161.

246 1.3 million nights: for this and other statistics, see *Amtlicher Bericht 11. Olympiade Berlin*, Vol. 1, p. 420.

246 half a billion reichsmarks (1.25 billion dollars) to Berlin: on Hitler's later claims, see Henry Picker (ed.), *Hitlers Tischgespräche im Führerhauptquartier*, Munich, 1979.

247 "Hitler and the Third Reich": François-Poncet, *Als Botschafter in Berlin*, p. 267.

247 "first on the Jews": Klemperer, *Tagebücher 1935–1936*, pp. 121f.

What became of…?

249 "mutual impotence": Zuckmayer, *Geheimreport*, p. 94.

251 "would have done so": Charlotte Schmidtke to Eberhard Denzel, 12 April 1939, LAB, B Rep. 202 No. 4258.

252 "tremendous, wonderful": "Es war wie in New York: Kult-Regisseur Billy Wilder über das Berlin der zwanziger Jahre," *Spiegel Special*, No. 6/1997, p. 54.

253 "go to Dajou's place again!": Meyerinck, *Meine berühmten Freundinnen*, p. 113.

NOTES

253 "In that year": Mascha Kaléko, "Einem kleinen Emigranten," from *idem, Sämtliche Briefe und Werke in vier Bänden*, ed. Jutta Rosenkranz.

For a Little Émigré
(To Steven)

You whom I loved before he lived
Born of unreason and of love
The light of pale hours and heaven's reward
My little son.

You, my child, fully owned my heart
When you were still nothing, a far-off glimmer
From your father's dark eyes
In that year.

You'd just got your first tooth
When they set ablaze the roof.
The dark man, the bitter medicine
Its name was Berlin.

You learned to get up again having fallen.
Your stroller rolled around the world.
You said thank you, merci and danke
You genius with words.

Time, place and stage were badly chosen
But the plot seems not wrong to me
You're already striving for the stars
A small tree from my dream.

You whom I loved before he lived
You glimmer from those distant eyes
I place this book in your tiny hand
You émigré.

© dtv Verlagsgesellschaft, Munich 2012

254 "any other authors": "Gisela, das Hitlerkind," *Die Zeit*, No. 28/1966.

257 "at the Egyptian embassy": Customs Inspector Scherer to Chief Prosecutor, Regional Court, 24 Jan. 1938, LAB A Rep. 358–02 No. 118497.

260 "waved me off fearfully": Meyerinck, *Meine berühmten Freundinnen*, p. 112.

262 "loved Germany so very much": Brysac, *Mildred Harnack und die Rote Kapelle*, p. 17.

263 "send me a telegram": Schaap, *Triumph*, p. 211.

266 "investigative custody": Amtsgericht Berlin, Sitzung vom 11.1.1937, LAB, A Rep. 358–02 No. 18117.

266 "in the mountains and left": Ledig-Rowohlt, "Thomas Wolfe in Berlin," p. 75.

267 " 'Love to both of you. Tom' ": ibid., p. 76.

268 "There was no reason for it!": Wolfe, *You Can't Go Home Again*, p. 598.

269 " 'All I ever said was: Cheers!' ": Salomon, *Der Fragebogen*, p. 281.

Archives and Bibliography

Archives and Collections

Archiv der Humboldt-Universität Berlin
    Sektionsbuch 1936
Archives de la Préfecture de police Paris
    Bestand 77 W: Renseignements Généraux
Bundesarchiv Berlin (BAB)
    NS 10/51
    R 43II/729
    R 58/2320
    R 58/2322
    R 58/2324
    R 8076/236
Entschädigungsbehörde des Landes Berlin
    Reg.-No. 276422
Harvard University, Houghton Library (HLB)
    The William B. Wisdom Collection of Thomas Wolfe
Landesarchiv Berlin (LAB)
    A Pr.Br.Rep. 030–02–05 No. 20
    A Pr.Br.Rep. 030–03 No. 670, 1050
    A Pr.Br.Rep. 030–06 No. 204
    A Pr.Br.Rep. 031 No. 114, 116
    A Pr.Br.Rep. 031–02 No. 80

A Rep. 109 No. 6058

A Rep. 341–04 No. 44538

A Rep. 341–05 No. 3771

A Rep. 342–02 Nos 25875, 29423, 57128, 60171

A Rep. 342–05 No. 3005

A Rep. 358–02 Nos 341/1, 341/2, 18117, 20353, 98420, 118497, 118498, 118512, 118513, 124848, 124849, 124850

B Rep. 202 Nos 4257, 4258, 4434–4441, 6337

B Rep. 207 No. 0456

B Rep. 207–01 No. 1291

B Rep. 358–02 No. 98118

P Rep. 125 No. 110

P Rep. 355 No. 421

Österreichisches Staatsarchiv, Archiv der Republik (ÖSTA/ADR)

Neues Politisches Archiv, Politische Berichte Berlin, No. 172–183/1936.

Politisches Archiv des Auswärtigen Amtes

    R 98726 bis 98744

University of Delaware (UOD)

    MSS 109: George S. Messersmith papers

Wisconsin Historical Society, Library Archives Division

    Louis P. Lochner Papers

    Sigrid Schultz Papers

Bibliography

"Alle Welt ist begeistert: Die Boykott-Bewegung gegen Hitlers Olympiade 1936 in Berlin scheiterte," in *Der Spiegel*, No. 5/1980, pp. 116–29.

Amtlicher Bericht 11. Olympiade Berlin 1936, 2 vols., Berlin, 1937.

Anderson, Dave, "The Grande Dame of the Olympics," *New York Times*, 3 July 1984.

"Bad Orb ist judenfrei," *Der Stürmer*, No. 34, Aug. 1936.

Baedeker, Karl (ed.), *Berlin und Potsdam*, Leipzig, 1936.

Biagioni, Egino, *Herb Flemming: A Jazz Pioneer around the World*, Alphen, 1977.

Blubacher, Thomas, *Gustaf Gründgens: Biographie*, Leipzig, 2013.

Bohrmann, Hans, and Gabriele Toepser-Ziegert (eds.), *NS-Presseanweisungen der Vorkriegszeit: Edition und Dokumentation*, Vol. 4/1936, Munich, 1993.

"Borchmeyer im Endlauf," *Olympia-Zeitung*, 4 Aug. 1936.

Brandt, Willy, *Erinnerungen*, Frankfurt/Main, 1989.

Braun, Jutta, "Helene Mayer: Eine jüdische Sportlerin in Deutschland," in *Gesichter der Zeitgeschichte: Deutsche Lebensläufe im 20. Jahrhundert*, Munich, 2009, pp. 85–102.

Brysac, Shareen Blair, *Mildred Harnack und die Rote Kapelle: Die Geschichte einer ungewöhnlichen Frau und einer Widerstandsbewegung*, Berlin, 2003.

Delmer, Sefton, *Die Deutschen und ich*, Hamburg, 1963.

"Der Bluthund. Furchtbare Bluttaten jüdischer Mordorganizationen. Das geschächtete Polenmädchen," *Der Stürmer*, No. 39, Sept. 1926.

Deutschland-Bericht der Sopade, Third Series, Prague, 1936.

"Die Blutsünde," *Der Stürmer*, No. 35, Aug. 1936.

"Die Judenpresse," *Der Stürmer*, No. 32, Aug. 1936.

Die Olympischen Spiele 1936, Vol. 2, Berlin, 1936.

Documents on British Foreign Policy 1919–1939, Second Series, Vol. 17, London, 1979.

Dodd, Martha, *Meine Jahre in Deutschland 1933 bis 1937: Nice to meet you, Mr. Hitler!*, Frankfurt/Main, 2005.

Dodd, William E., *Diplomat auf heissem Boden: Tagebuch des USA-Botschafters William E. Dodd in Berlin 1933–1938*, Berlin, 1964.

Donald, David Herbert, *Look Homeward: A Life of Thomas Wolfe*, Boston, 1987.

Ebermayer, Erich, *Eh) ich's ve"gesse: Erinnerungen an Gerhart Hauptmann, Thomas Mann, Klaus Mann, Gustaf Gründgens, Emil Jannings und Stefan Zweig*, Munich, 2005.

"Ein Zeuge tritt ab," *Der Spiegel*, 2 March 1955, pp. 10–19.

Ernst, Walter, "Die Entwicklung des Institutes für gerichtliche Medizin und Kriminalistik der Universität Berlin," Diss., Berlin, 1941.

"Es war wie in New York: Kult-Regisseur Billy Wilder über das Berlin der zwanziger Jahre," *Spiegel Special*, No. 6/1997, pp. 48–55.

Fest, Joachim C., *Das Gesicht des Dritten Reiches: Profile einer totalitären Herrschaft*, Munich, 1988.

"Festlicher Abend in der Staatsoper," *Berliner Lokal-Anzeiger*, 7 Aug. 1936.

Finck, Werner, *Alter Narr—was nun? Die Geschichte meiner Zeit*, Frankfurt/Main, 1978.

Finck, Werner, "Kleine Olympia-Conférence. Schlussakkord," *Berliner Tageblatt*, 16 Aug. 1936.

"Foto-Wettbewerb," *Elegante Welt*, No. 15/1936, p. 64.

François-Poncet, André, *Als Botschafter in Berlin 1931–1938*, Mainz, 1949.

François-Poncet, André, *Tagebuch eines Gefangenen: Erinnerungen eines Jahrhundertzeugen*, Berlin, 2015.

Fröhlich, Elke (ed.), *Die Tagebücher von Joseph Goebbels*, Part I, Vol. 2/II, Munich, 2004.

Fröhlich, Elke (ed.), *Die Tagebücher von Joseph Goebbels*, Part I, Vol. 2/III, Munich, 2004.

Fröhlich, Elke (ed.), *Die Tagebücher von Joseph Goebbels*, Part I, Vol. 3/I, Munich, 2005.

Fröhlich, Elke (ed.), *Die Tagebücher von Joseph Goebbels*, Part I, Vol. 3/II, Munich, 2001.

Fröhlich, Elke (ed.), *Die Tagebücher von Joseph Goebbels*, Part II, Vol. 1, Munich, 1996.

Fromm, Bella, *Als Hitler mir die Hand küsste*, Berlin, 1993.

Gay, Peter, *Meine deutsche Frage: Jugend in Berlin 1933–1939*, Munich, 1999.

Geisel, Eike, and Henryk M. Broder, *Premiere und Pogrom: Der Jüdische Kulturbund 1933–1941*, Berlin, 1992.

"Gisela, das Hitlerkind," *Die Zeit*, No. 28/1966.

Gläss, Theo (ed.), *Zahlen zur Alkoholfrage*, Berlin, 1938.

Heckh, Karl, *Eine Fussbank für die Dame: Eine kulinarische Revue*, Stuttgart, 1969.

"Herr Hitler kissed by excited woman," *Sydney Morning Herald*, 17 Aug. 1936.

"Herrliche Welt des Scheins. Die Scala im Olympia-Monat," *Berliner Lokal-Anzeiger*, 6 Aug. 1936.

Hübner, Emanuel, *Das Olympische Dorf von 1936: Planung, Bau und Nutzungsgeschichte*, Paderborn, 2015.

"Hungernde deutsche Mädchen in den Klauen geiler Judenböcke," *Der Stürmer*, No. 35, Aug. 1925.

James, Robert Rhodes (ed.), *Chips: The Diaries of Sir Henry Channon*, London, 1993.

"Jesses Märchen," *Der Spiegel*, No. 1/2015, p. 105.

Jochmann, Werner (ed.), *Adolf Hitler: Monologe im Führerhauptquartier 1941–1944. Aufgezeichnet von Heinrich Heim*, Munich, 2000.

Kaléko, Mascha, *Das lyrische Stenogrammheft*, Reinbek bei Hamburg, 1993.

Kaléko, Mascha, *Verse für Zeitgenossen*, Reinbek bei Hamburg, 1992.

Kennedy, Richard S., and Paschal Reeves (eds.), *The Notebooks of Thomas Wolfe*, 2 vols., Chapel Hill, 1970.

Kerr, Alfred, "Nazi-Olympiade," *Pariser Tageszeitung. quotidien Anti-Hitlerien*, 13 Aug. 1936.

Kessler, Harry Graf, *Das Tagebuch: Vierter Band 1906–1914*, Stuttgart, 2005.

Klemperer, Victor, *Tagebücher 1935–1936*, Berlin, 1995.

Kopp, Roland, *Wolfgang Fürstner (1896–1936): Der erste Kommandant des Olympischen Dorfes von 1936*, Frankfurt/Main, 2009.

Krüger, Arnd, *Theodor Lewald: Sportführer im Dritten Reich*, Berlin, 1975.

Ledig-Rowohlt, Heinrich Maria, "Thomas Wolfe in Berlin," in *Der Monat. Eine internationale Zeitschrift für Politik und geistiges Leben*, Oct. 1948, pp. 69–77.

Long, Kai-Heinrich, *Luz Long—eine Sportlerkarriere im Dritten Reich: Sein Leben in Dokumenten und Bildern*, Hildesheim, 2015.

MacDonogh, Giles, "Otto Horcher: Caterer to the Third Reich," *Gastronomica*, Vol. 7, No. 1 (Winter 2007), pp. 31–38.

Mann, Thomas, *Tagebücher. 1935–1936*, ed. by Peter de Mendelssohn, Frankfurt/Main, 1978.

Meyerinck, Hubert von, *Meine berühmten Freundinnen: Erinnerungen*, Düsseldorf, 1967.

Morsch, Günter (ed.), *Sachsenhausen: Das Konzentrationslager bei der Reichshauptstadt*, Berlin, 2014.

Nowell, Elizabeth (ed.), *The Letters of Thomas Wolfe*, New York, 1956.

"Olympiasiegerin Tilly Fleischer grüsst die Leser der Nachtausgabe," *Berliner illustrierte Nachtausgabe*, 2 Aug. 1936.

Ossietzky, Carl von, "Gontard," *Die Weltbühne*, 16 Dec. 1930.

Picker, Henry (ed.), *Hitlers Tischgespräche im Führerhauptquartier*, Munich, 1979.

Pientka, Patricia, *Das Zwangslager für Sinti und Roma in Berlin-Marzahn: Alltag, Verfolgung und Deportation*, Berlin, 2013.

Polster, Bernd (ed.), *Swing Heil: Jazz im Nationalsozialismus*, Berlin, 1989.

"Priester verbrannt," *Berliner Lokal-Anzeiger*, 6 Aug. 1936.

Reich-Ranicki, Marcel, *Mein Leben*, Stuttgart, 1999.

Riefenstahl, Leni, *Memoiren*, Munich, 1987.

Rock, Christa Maria, "Unser Ziel ist klar," *Das Deutsche Podium*, 25 April 1941.

Rogers, Steven B., "'She Looked Like One of the Valkyries': Who Was Thomas Wolfe's German Girlfriend?" *Thomas Wolfe Review*, Vol. 21/1997, pp. 8–20.

Roos, Daniel, *Julius Streicher und Der Stürmer 1923–1945*, Paderborn, 2014.

Rosenberg, Alfred, *Die Tagebücher von 1934 bis 1944*, ed. by Jürgen Matthäus and Frank Bajohr, Frankfurt/Main, 2015.

Rosenkranz, Jutta, *Mascha Kaléko: Biografie*, Munich, 2007.

Ruault, Franco, *Tödliche Maskeraden: Julius Streicher und die "Lösung der Judenfrage,"* Frankfurt/Main, 2009.

Rürup, Reinhard (ed.), *1936: Die Olympischen Spiele und der Nationalsozialismus*, Berlin, 1996.

Salomon, Ernst von, *Der Fragebogen*, Reinbek bei Hamburg, 2003.

Schaap, Jeremy, *Triumph: The Untold Story of Jesse Owens and Hitler's Olympics*, Boston, 2007.

Schäfer, Hans Dieter, *Das gespaltene Bewusstsein: Vom Dritten Reich bis zu den langen Fünfziger Jahren*, Göttingen, 2009.

Schirach, Baldur von, *Ich glaubte an Hitler*, Hamburg, 1967.

Schmidt, Paul, *Statist auf diplomatischer Bühne 1923–45: Erlebnisse des Chefdolmetschers im Auswärtigen Amt mit den Staatsmännern Europas*, Bonn, 1953.

Schuh, Willi (ed.), *Richard Strauss—Stefan Zweig: Briefwechsel*, Frankfurt/ Main, 1957.

"Schwarze Kunst Basketball," *Der Angriff*, 8 Aug. 1936.

"Sherbini will verkaufen," *Berliner Herold*, 20 Jan. 1935.

Smith, Arthur L., "Kurt Luedecke: The Man Who Knew Hitler," *German Studies Review*, Oct. 2003, pp. 597–606.

Speer, Albert, *Erinnerungen*, Berlin, 2007.

Stauffer, Teddy, *Es war und ist ein herrliches Leben*, Berlin, 1968.

Stokes, Lawrence D., "Thomas Wolfe's German Girlfriend: Further Thoughts on Thea Voelcker," *Thomas Wolfe Review*, Vol. 29/2005, pp. 5–20.

Stokes, Lawrence D., "Thomas Wolfe's Other German Girlfriend: Who Was Lisa Hasait?" *Thomas Wolfe Review*, Vol. 30/2006, pp. 103–17.

"Sven Hedin besucht ein Arbeitsdienstlager," *Berliner Lokal-Anzeiger*, 7 Aug. 1936.

Szittya, Emil, *Das Kuriositäten-Kabinett*, Konstanz, 1923.

Tillenburg, H. P., "Klirrender Stahl im Kuppelsaal: Wir besuchen die olympischen Amazonen," *Olympia-Zeitung*, 7 Aug. 1936.

Trautloft, Hannes, *Als Jagdflieger in Spanien: Aus dem Tagebuch eines deutschen Legionärs*, Berlin, 1940.

Trenner, Franz (ed.), *Richard Strauss: Chronik zu Leben und Werk*, Vienna, 2003.

Treue, Wilhelm, "Hitlers Denkschrift zum Vierjahresplan 1936," *Vierteljahreshefte für Zeitgeschichte*, 3 (1955), Vol. 2, pp. 184–210.

Trimborn, Jürgen, *Riefenstahl: Eine deutsche Karriere*, Berlin, 2002.

"Tumult im Luxusrestaurant," *Berliner Herold*, 11 Nov. 1934.

"... und das Kulturleben der Nichtarier in Deutschland?" *Das 12-Uhr-Blatt*, 15 Aug. 1936.

"Unterrichtung über Rassengesetze," *Nationalsozialistische Parteikorrespondenz*, 7 Aug. 1936.

"Wife of Californian surprised at stir she caused," *Milwaukee Sentinel*, 3 Nov. 1936.

Winter, Horst, *Dreh dich noch einmal um: Erinnerungen des Kapellmeisters der Hoch- und Deutschmeister*, Vienna, 1989.

"Wir gratulieren, Herr Goebbels!" *Die Rote Fahne*, 18 Dec. 1931.

"Wir sprachen Thomas Wolfe," *Berliner Tageblatt*, 5 Aug. 1936.

Witt, Richard, *Lifetime of Training for Just Ten Seconds: Olympians in Their Own Words*, London, 2012.

Wolfe, Thomas, "Brooklyn, Europa und ich," *Die Dame, Illustrierte Mode-Zeitschrift*, Vol. 3/1939, pp. 39–42.

Wolfe, Thomas: *You Can't Go Home Again*, New York, 2011.

Wolffram, Knud, *Tanzdielen und Vergnügungspaläste: Berliner Nachtleben in den dreissiger und vierziger Jahren*, Berlin, 2001.

Zellermayer, Ilse, *Drei Tenöre und ein Sopran: Mein Leben für die Oper*, Berlin, 2000.

Zellermayer, Ilse, *Prinzessinnensuite: Mein Jahrhundert im Hotel*, Berlin, 2010.

Zoch-Westphal, Gisela, *Aus den sechs Leben der Mascha Kaléko*, Berlin, 1987.

Zuckmayer, Carl, *Geheimreport*, Munich, 2007.

Illustrations

bpk—Bildagentur für Kunst, Kultur und Geschichte, Berlin: 116, 206 (Hans Hubmann), 132 (adoc-photo), 146 (Kunstbibliothek, SMB/Walter Obschonka), 234 (United Archives/Erich Andres)

Emanuel Hübner, Münster: viii

Private collection: 220

Ullstein Bild, Berlin: 34, 102, 174 (Lothar Ruebelt), 52, 84, 160, 188 (ullstein bild), 66 (Heinz Perckhammer), 248 (AP)

Die Dame. Illustrierte Mode-Zeitschrift, no. 16, 1936, p. 38: 20 (Humboldt University Library, Berlin, Historical Collections, AZ 81377)

Index

INDEX

Berlin Locations